Advance Praise

"Cindy Goldrich expands her mission of providing parents the proper tools for supporting their ADHD children. The important pillars of education, emotional regulation (for both the kids and the parents!), and respectful communication are solidly planted in the pages, paving a collaborative path for navigating the complexities of ADHD. The actionable strategies are clearly articulated. You will feel like she is in the room with you conversing in an authentic and empathic voice."

—**Roberto Olivardia, PhD,** clinical psychologist and lecturer, Department of Psychiatry, Harvard Medical School

"Goldrich's *8 Keys to Parenting Kids & Teens with ADHD* is an approachable, clear, and compassionate guide that will improve the lives of both kids and their parents as parents navigate the challenges and rewards of raising complex kids. She urges parents to see their child in their amazing uniqueness, while providing specific and clear strategies parents can implement across multiple ages for the challenges faced. Grounded in a clear and concise understanding of ADHD, this book is a framework for empathetic and effective parenting—as well as a much happier and healthier family life. Brava!"

—**Melissa Orlov,** founder of adhdmarriage.com and author of *The ADHD Effect on Marriage*

"Cindy Goldrich's *8 Keys to Parenting Kids & Teens with ADHD* feels like having a trusted coach with you—someone who can guide you in raising a child with ADHD. This new edition blends compassion with practical tools you can start using immediately, providing hope, clarity, and strategies that work."

—**Tamara Rosier, PhD,** founder of the ADHD Center of West Michigan and author of *Your Brain's Not Broken* and *You, Me, and Our ADHD Family*

"This second edition is loaded with important concepts, useful strategies, and a ton of heart to help with the day-to-day of parenting a child with ADHD. Not only will it help you navigate the all-too-common landmines, but more importantly it will keep you focused on what matters most: maintaining a positive relationship with your child."

—**Ari Tuckman, PsyD, MBA,** author of *The ADHD Productivity Manual*

8 Keys to Mental Health Series
Babette Rothschild, Series Editor

The 8 Keys series of books provides consumers with brief, inexpensive, and high-quality self-help books on a variety of topics in mental health. Each volume is written by an expert in the field, someone who is capable of presenting evidence-based information in a concise and clear way. These books stand out by offering consumers cutting-edge, relevant theory in easily digestible portions, written in an accessible style. The tone is respectful of the reader and the messages are immediately applicable. Filled with exercises and practical strategies, these books empower readers to help themselves.

8 KEYS TO PARENTING KIDS & TEENS WITH ADHD

8 KEYS TO PARENTING KIDS & TEENS WITH ADHD

SUPPORTING YOUR CHILD'S EXECUTIVE FUNCTION

Cindy Goldrich

EdM, ADHD-CCSP

Norton Professional Books

An Imprint of W. W. Norton & Company
Independent Publishers Since 1923

Copyright © 2026, 2015 by Cindy Goldrich
Foreword copyright © 2026 by Babette Rothschild

All rights reserved
Printed in the United States of America

For information about permission to reproduce selections from this book, write to Permissions, W. W. Norton & Company, Inc., 500 Fifth Avenue, New York, NY 10110

For information about special discounts for bulk purchases, please contact W. W. Norton Special Sales at specialsales@wwnorton.com or 800-233-4830

Manufacturing by Versa Press
Book design by Daniel Lagin
Production manager: Gwen Cullen

Library of Congress Control Number: 2025945472

ISBN: 978-1-324-08341-2 (Paperback)

W. W. Norton & Company, Inc., 500 Fifth Avenue, New York, NY 10110
www.wwnorton.com

W. W. Norton & Company Ltd., 15 Carlisle Street, London W1D 3BS

Authorized EU representative: EAS, Mustamäe tee 50, 10621 Tallinn, Estonia

1 2 3 4 5 6 7 8 9 0

This book is born from a place of love, compassion, and hope. I dedicate this to the countless parents, students, and professionals I have had the privilege of knowing, learning from, and supporting. Your stories, struggles, and triumphs have shaped and deepened my understanding far beyond what any research or training could offer. You are the heart of this work.

My greatest gratitude and love go to my children, Carly and Benji, who continue to inspire me with their wisdom, resilience, and kindness. Watching them step into their own lives and begin families of their own fills me with joy and pride beyond words. Thank you for reminding me daily of the enduring power of connection, growth, and unconditional love.

Contents

Foreword

I t is almost impossible to ignore the impact of attention deficit hyperactivity disorder (ADHD). In recent years, discussions of ADHD, its symptoms, and its treatment have become increasingly common in the news, in the shows we watch, and across social media. In fact, one might even suspect that the media is blowing this out of proportion. However, a close look at the facts shows that, indeed, the diagnosis of ADHD is on the rise, and the overall number of children impacted is huge. The U.S. Centers for Disease Control and Prevention (CDC), using data from 2022, estimates that more than 11% of American children—about 7 million—qualify for this diagnosis (CDC, 2024). In 2022, the number of American children who had received an ADHD diagnosis increased by 1 million compared to 2016, with boys diagnosed at about twice the rate of girls. Moreover, it is recognized that a significant portion of these children will carry their symptoms into adulthood, leading to challenges in school and at home.

What are parents to do? Currently, the treatment of choice is pharmaceuticals, with over 50% of children with ADHD receiving medication (CDC, 2024). Although prescription drugs have been shown to be helpful, these children also need support as they learn and strengthen the skills they'll use across their lifetime. By picking up this book, you've taken a valuable step to helping your child build these skills. This 2nd edition of *8 Keys to Parenting a Child with ADHD* is not only timely, but is also a major contribution to the existing literature. Filled with the most updated knowledge, this book offers parents a wealth of information to make informed decisions about meeting their child's needs, with a plethora of strategies, tools, and skills that will supplement drug treatments.

As the parent of a child with ADHD, you face a myriad of challenges. Like all parents, you want the best for your child, but helping and guiding a young person with ADHD is not an easy task. There can be times of frustration and despair, although with the proper support and guidance, there can also be enjoyment, triumph, and success—in the short term and throughout your child's life. Cindy Goldrich helps you chart a path to that success, breaking ADHD down into the executive function challenges it can include, while providing practical advice on how to help your child approach them. Executive function describes a set of necessary cognitive skills that help us regulate our own behavior, including our ability to make and achieve goals, exercise self-control, delay gratification, and so on. Children with ADHD and other executive function challenges develop these skills more slowly and may struggle to apply them without additional support. The strategies herein are designed to effectively strengthen executive function with these struggles in mind. Not surprisingly, features of executive function like impulse control and delayed gratification have repeatedly been shown to be essential skills for success in life.

Among a wealth of wisdom in this resource, Goldrich's overarching mantra is *parent the child you have*. It is this wisdom that sets her apart as an expert in the field. She recognizes that ADHD is not comprised of a single set of difficulties, and that every child is unique. There is no one-size-fits-all for Goldrich or in this book. Goldrich will help you recognize the unique needs of your particular child and then support and guide you in adapting your parenting style to your child's needs. That is why she is so perfect to author this book. She has decades of experience aiding parents in helping their ADHD children, and she knows how to be supportive through these challenges. You will feel that she, indeed, has your back.

Goldrich will also help you connect with resources that can offer support beyond the 8 Keys. At the end of the book, you'll find recommended books and websites for parents and kids, as well as additional information on accommodations, treatment, and more strategies for use at home. I also encourage you to seek out other resources online. Recently, media executives and child educators have realized that they can use the broad platforms of television and the internet (particularly YouTube) to help children better develop executive function. The following is my favorite example:

In May 2013, *Sesame Street*, a production of the Sesame Workshop (formerly the Children's Television Workshop), released an amazingly clever, informative, and entertaining parody music video that helps kids (and adults—participants in my professional trainings *love* it!) increase their executive function through exercising greater self-control. The video is a faithful and clever parody of Icona Pop's 2012 hit song and music video "I Love It" and features Cookie Monster struggling with a decision to postpone eating a chocolate chip cookie despite his characteristic intense craving. With song and dance, Cookie Monster and his fellow Muppet dancers and singers illustrate skills including self regulation, self-control, delayed gratification, mindfulness, and self-soothing. To find this video on YouTube, type "Me Want It (But Me Wait)" in the search box.

Among other features, Goldrich will help you strengthen your own executive function so you can better manage your parenting challenges. But in addition to that, improving your executive function will in turn empower you to more effectively bolster your child's functioning. It's a kind of pay-it-forward scenario: Goldrich uses her own executive function to fortify yours, and you use yours to help develop and strengthen your child's. It is with this kind of positive approach that Goldrich will help you to spin gold from what may look like straw, access silver linings, and help your children blossom even when it appears they are stuck in mud.

—Babette Rothschild, MSW, LCSW

REFERENCES

U.S. Centers for Disease Control and Prevention. (2024, November 19). *Data and Statistics on ADHD*. https://www.cdc.gov/adhd/data/index.html

Introduction to the First Edition

They don't mean to frustrate you. They don't want to make life difficult and challenging for you or for themselves.

Just as some children have trouble learning to read, kids with ADHD often have trouble managing their attention, time, and materials. Many also have trouble tolerating frustration, being flexible, and solving their problems effectively. Just as decoding words is a learned skill, your child may need extra support learning and developing these other skills as well.

Rewards and punishments can't teach skills—but you can. It may take incredible patience, learning, understanding, investigation, and perseverance on your part, but it's worth it!

Whether we are aware of it or not, we all hold beliefs about how we ought to parent our children—until, of course, our instincts or logic fail to yield the results we expected or desired. Often, by the time parents seek my guidance, they have experimented with various parenting strategies and received different advice (welcome or not) from several individuals. One challenge we face as parents is determining when to encourage our kids and when to step back. When should we offer support, and when should we allow our children to navigate things on their own, even if it means facing failure or disappointment?

Some children, given our guidance and a variety of appropriate opportunities, will generally perform as we would expect, as long as we provide a safe, nurturing environment. However, for some kids, all the love and logic we can muster doesn't seem to be enough to help them cooperate and succeed.

Why? Is it that we aren't doing it "right"? Before we begin pointing fingers and instilling guilt, I ask you to consider the nature of the child you are parenting.

Every person is born with unique chemistry, physique, and temperament—and no operator's manual! Often, we come to realize that we might have a particularly challenging child only after we are already struggling. If you have a child who struggles due to an inability to regulate attention, impulsivity, or activity level, chances are you are familiar with the world of ADHD.

Our journey together begins with an overview of what ADHD is beyond the characteristics most often mentioned: impulsivity, hyperactivity, and inattentiveness. So much of what we now understand about ADHD, we have learned during the past decade or so. In fact, by the time you finish reading the first chapter, you will realize that the term "attention deficit hyperactivity disorder" really does not come close to explaining what parents and professionals truly experience with their children.

As you become more educated about and aware of how ADHD truly affects all aspects of your child's life, you will notice a shift in the way you view and interact with them. This will enable you to help build their confidence, resilience, and life skills. You will become increasingly aware of how you need to adjust your parenting style to meet your child's needs. You might need to reframe your thoughts about your child and their actions. You may change how you communicate and respond to your child, and you may also have to adjust how you organize your home and daily life.

This parenting style is what I call *parent the child you have*, and it influences all my work as a Parent Coach. Family members, friends, and even well-meaning teachers and professionals may offer advice and strategies aimed at helping you "fix" or "teach" your child. You should listen to your inner voice and adapt your parenting to meet the needs of your unique child. For some, this may involve applying stricter control; for others, it could mean providing more guidance and support; and for yet others, it might require reducing certain obligations or short-term expectations. These are some of the challenges I can help you navigate and overcome.

For many of you, there is so much chaos, stress, arguing, and waffling that it's exhausting. Many parents wonder if their child misbehaves as a way of seeking attention. Research and experience have shown us that this is generally not the case. In fact, without effective parenting skills, many parents become trained by their children's challenging behavior—don't ask about homework, don't ask them to do chores, don't ask them to stop playing on the computer—or risk confrontation, endless frustration, or constant disappointment.

As we explore in greater detail in the chapters ahead, children often rely on behavior rather than skills to solve problems they perceive. For instance, a child who desires candy in a store might throw a tantrum (the behavior) until their parent gives in, instead of having a rational discussion or negotiating for what they want (using appropriate communication skills) or simply coping with not getting what they want in that moment (utilizing the child's ability to tolerate frustration). When children, or even adults, depend on behavior rather than skills to address their problems, negative and destructive behavioral patterns can develop.

When parents choose to ignore disruptive behavior in an attempt to teach their children not to act this way, it generally does little to encourage more positive behaviors. Instead, it can lead to more severely challenging behaviors in the future.

My goal is to empower you to take charge of your parenting role and protect the health and well-being of all family members. I want to help you feel confident in your decision making regarding how you parent your challenging kid. I also help you reduce the stress and doubt you have been experiencing.

I will emphasize the ways in which parents can regain order and control. Many people are uncomfortable using the word "control" in relation to parenting, as they don't want to be seen as "overly strict." However, some parents must learn to recognize the value of being leaders and guides to their children, as this gives them a sense of safety, security, and confidence.

As your coach, I encourage you to develop your investigative muscles. I ask that you remain curious, not judgmental, and strive to uncover the true motivations behind your child's challenging behaviors. As parents, we must understand what motivates our kids, what fears they may have, their genuine talents, and the various areas of their lives that require support. Only then can we cultivate tools and strategies that allow us to guide them, intervene in their lives, and inspire them as they grow. We will focus on enhancing and strengthening effective interpersonal skills for both you and your child as a means to improve conflict resolution.

I challenge you to take ownership of the decisions you make as a parent. You will gain confidence to act on the rules and guidelines you establish for your child based on well-founded principles and awareness. Your parenting style will be proactive, not reactive (i.e., based on your child's actions). We lay a foundation for your own acceptance and trust in yourself, as well as mutual trust between you and your child. As I mentioned at the beginning, you will learn to *parent the child you have.*

I offer a range of parenting perspectives and techniques that I have found can dramatically improve family relationships and happiness. Some of the ideas resonate more loudly and feel more comfortable for you than others, but I encourage you to give them each a try.

The statistics pointing to the hazards of undiagnosed and untreated ADHD are daunting, and they are real. The rate of divorce, incarceration, drug abuse, underemployment, and debt is much greater among individuals with ADHD than it is in the general population. However, as you will see, the potential for a uniquely magnificent life is also a real and reachable goal. As parents, your job is to look at your child's ADHD not as a curse or character flaw but as a challenge and difficulty that must be managed and an opportunity that must be explored.

I believe that each child is genuinely creative, resourceful, and complete. Their path may not be smooth but the obstacles are not insurmountable. This takes time. You need to disregard the opinions and advice of well-meaning people who lack experience or real knowledge of the disorder. Even today, unfortunately, not everyone is informed about the impact of ADHD or the support available for individuals with ADHD. I encourage you to refer to the resources in the appendices for additional support and information.

All children need to understand the boundaries of what they can and cannot do, but this is especially true for kids with ADHD due to the additional challenges they encounter. Children with ADHD often don't follow the same rules as other kids—whether for better or worse. They may push your buttons more than typical children. It's not just your imagination. Their strong independence, determination, and tendency to question expectations will ultimately benefit them in life.

As parents, you need tools to help your child operate. You have been blessed with a creative, dynamic, independent thinker. This child may challenge you to question your own motives and expectations more than you anticipated. The good news—and your incentive to truly intervene—is that the brain is dynamic and continues to grow, even into adulthood. While it may take a while to see the fruits of your labor, the seeds you plant now in teaching your child tools and strategies will take root. One day, when you least expect it, you will see your child doing something you taught them long ago that they resisted doing until now.

Making lasting changes requires hard work and consistency on your part. If you are open to it, this can be a tremendous opportunity for your personal growth as well. The rewards are worth the effort. You will experience greater happiness, reduced stress, more time, and enhanced warmth and connection with your family. With *parent the child you have* as your guiding principle, you will be prepared to help your child thrive.

The content of this book is based on "Calm and Connected: Parenting Children and Teens With ADHD and Executive Function Challenges." This is a seven-session workshop that I developed and have facilitated with thousands of parents over the years. The principles presented here apply to parenting children of all ages—until they have "launched" and become independent. While some changes you implement are immediate, others take time as old patterns are broken, trust is built, and new skills are acquired.

I encourage you to give yourself a few days' break between reading each chapter. Many of the principles and activities I ask you to consider may take some time to consider and implement.

At the end of each chapter, I include "Guiding Thoughts." These are quotes or statements that summarize or represent the lessons from the chapter. Consider writing down these thoughts and placing them somewhere visible, and set aside time each day to reread each statement. By focusing on just a few key ideas, you may find it easier to remember and apply the lessons from this book.

I also recommend some activities for you to do by yourself, with your parenting partner, or possibly with your child. These will assist you in implementing the changes you wish to make.

GUIDING THOUGHT

Parent the child you have.

The Wonderfulness of Me[*]
by Robert Tudisco

If you took all of the things that were special about me,
you could put them all together and call it AD/HD.
No better, no worse, just different that's me,
I'm really not crazy, please try and see.

Like a talented wizard in a world full of "Muggles,"
it's no wonder all you see is frustration and struggles.
As I daydream and drift, you think no one's there,
but nothing could be further from the truth, believe me, I swear.

I see your impatience as my mind starts to wander,
but you don't know the depth of the thoughts that I ponder.
For creative thinkers, get lost in deep thought,
which leads to the illusion that they cannot be taught.

I know trying to reach me can give you the blues,
but I wish for just once, you could walk in my shoes.
To see things through my eyes, you would be amazed,
at the speed and sheer volume my thoughts seem to blaze.

---

[*] Robert M. Tudisco, used with permission. Robert M. Tudisco is a disability attorney, author, and an adult diagnosed with ADHD.

I'm not lazy or stupid, if only you knew,
how truly difficult it is to limit myself and think like you do.
But, I can see things that you'll never see,
it's like second nature, because I am me.

With lightning fast reflexes, I can switch gears,
to be firm and inflexible is the worst of my fears.
I'm calm in a crisis and know just what to do,
for I'm in great company, Mozart, Edison, and Churchill to name
    just a few.

So show me some patience, as I'm patient with you.
Just a little tolerance, it's long overdue.
Please try and understand me, along with my AD/HD,
it's a very big part of the wonderfulness of me.

Introduction to
the Second Edition

A DECADE OF PROGRESS—
REFLECTIONS AND UPDATES

Wow! When my publishers informed me it was time for an updated edition of *8 Keys to Parenting Children with ADHD*, I could hardly believe it had been a decade since the first edition was published. So much has changed in my life, and there have been countless changes in parenting and ADHD as well.

On a personal note, I'm now a grandmother—or Gigi, as I'm called! Both of my children are launched and thriving, and I've discovered that parenting doesn't end when your kids are in their 20s. In fact, sometimes it feels like they're the ones parenting me!

On the professional front, my practice has expanded to include a stellar team of ADHD coaches and two professional programs. I now train others to become ADHD Parent Coaches and ADHD Teacher Trainers, equipping them to provide parents and school staff with the tools and strategies needed to help students manage the impact ADHD has on learning, motivation, and behavior (see the resources section for information about professional training). In fact, I recently coauthored a book with my daughter, who, for a decade and counting, has been an amazing elementary special education teacher. The book is titled *ADHD, Executive Function & Behavioral Challenges in the Classroom: Managing the Impact on Learning, Motivation, and Stress.*

In my work, I've become even more passionate about the challenges and opportunities facing parents and teachers. I've also grown more engaged in advocating for legislative changes to support our education system. I feel strongly that our society will be better off when parents and educators are empowered to understand the social and emotional impact of ADHD and executive function challenges on learning, motivation, behavior, and the entire family system. That's why I've taken my work to Capitol Hill, meeting with congressional and senatorial staff to lobby for better ADHD services and increased support for educators and students. I'm especially committed to pushing for ADHD training for all teachers. If you're interested, I've shared my thoughts and suggestions in a blog post titled "Train All Teachers About ADHD Challenges," which you can find on my website.

Note to parents: I know how frustrating it can be when you feel your child isn't receiving the services they need and deserve. But remember, most teachers are just as passionate as you are about helping your child succeed. Unfortunately, extraordinary teachers are leaving the profession in record numbers due to stress and a lack of resources. I've had the privilege of working with dedicated teachers nationwide who truly want more knowledge and support to help your children. As you work with them, approach these conversations with patience and compassion.

In this updated edition of *8 Keys to Parenting Children with ADHD*, I've included new insights and resources. I've expanded the chapter on executive function and added more guidance on having important conversations with your children, particularly when addressing differing concerns and perspectives. I've also shared my thoughts on helping your child transition into post–high school life.

One of the most gratifying outcomes of writing this book has been hearing how much it has touched so many families. I hope you, too, find the support and guidance you need in this new edition. Remember, *you are never alone on this journey.* And there's no such thing as a perfect parent—we all learn as we go. You can be a terrific parent even if you're not a perfect one. Showing up, listening, and caring matter far more than getting everything right.

8 KEYS TO PARENTING KIDS & TEENS WITH ADHD

KEY 1

GET EDUCATED

How ADHD and Executive Function Challenges Impact Learning, Motivation, Behavior, and the Family System

Start from wherever you are with whatever you've got.

—JOHN ROHN

Parenting is HARD. Parenting a complex child is even harder! That's why this first key is all about education. The more you understand your child's unique needs and the ways ADHD and executive function (EF) impact their behavior and learning, the better equipped you'll be to guide and support them. As you gain knowledge, you'll also find clarity in how to respond to your child's struggles and how to support their growth in meaningful ways. (If you would like additional guidance and support, coaching can help. See Appendix A on coaching for more details.)

Throughout my work with parents, I often hear recurring questions, such as:

- How do I know if I am enabling or supporting my child each time I try to help?
- What boundaries should I set that are appropriately restrictive while encouraging growth, independence, accountability, and responsibility?
- What kind of consequences can I impose that will build skills and not just be punitive?

Now is a great time to take a moment and commit to recognizing that whatever has brought you to this place is just where you are now. I often hear parents express guilt, concern, and confusion regarding how they have been parenting their kids. Know this: *Poor parenting cannot and does not cause ADHD; it is a neurodevelopmental disorder.* ADHD is real! Some people still believe that ADHD is caused by factors like poor parenting, sugar, or food additives. However, research has consistently shown that these claims are not supported by scientific evidence (Centers for Disease Control and Prevention, 2023; National Institute of Mental Health, n.d.). Harvard psychiatrist George Bush states that "ADHD is a neurobiological, neurodevelopmental disorder that is present from birth and manifests in different ways across the lifespan. While trauma or parenting can modify symptom presentation and coping, neither one plays a causative role in ADHD" (personal correspondence, October 21, 2014). In fact, imaging studies show differences in the structure and activity between the brains of people with and without ADHD. In people with ADHD, there is a consistent pattern of below-normal activity in the neurotransmission of the chemicals dopamine and norepinephrine in the brain's prefrontal cortex (the front part of the brain). This underactivity impacts critical functions like attention, impulse control, and emotional regulation. Additionally, the *reward and motivation* centers in the brain are understimulated due to lower levels of dopamine. The prefrontal cortex itself is thinner and matures more slowly in individuals with ADHD. It's important to note that this does *not* imply any deficit in intelligence or ability to succeed. With the right support and strategies, kids with ADHD can thrive.

Note: Have you noticed that typical behavior modification techniques—such as sticker charts or if/then reward systems—don't work very well for kids with ADHD? This difference in brain activity helps explain why. When the reward and motivation centers are understimulated, these external motivators may not carry the same weight for kids with ADHD as they might for their neurotypical peers. For now, simply notice this pattern and reflect on what you've observed in your own child. Later in the book, we discuss the impact of reward programs in greater detail and explore how to create effective motivation plans tailored to your child's unique needs.

Thankfully, there is a growing awareness that ADHD is a real and impactful condition. However, understanding it doesn't always mean knowing how to handle the atypical behaviors we often see in kids with ADHD. Love, logic, and intuition—though essential—are not always enough to help parents navigate the complex and challenging behaviors they face every day.

Understanding ADHD's impact goes beyond the daily challenges your child might face. Untreated ADHD can have serious, long-term consequences: not only for the individual but for society as a whole. Studies show that untreated ADHD increases the risk of accidental injuries, substance use disorders, mental health challenges, and struggles in school and work environments. Tragically, untreated ADHD is also a contributing factor in the school-to-prison pipeline—a cycle where children with unrecognized or unsupported ADHD may face disciplinary measures that exclude them from educational opportunities, leading to disengagement and interactions with the justice system.

This reality highlights the critical importance of getting educated about ADHD and advocating for the support your child needs. By understanding their challenges, you can help reduce the risk of these outcomes, setting the stage for a brighter, more successful future. Early intervention, combined with informed and compassionate approaches, can make all the difference. Beyond these personal and family challenges, the societal implications of untreated ADHD are profound.

Unfortunately, most teachers—and even many therapists, pediatricians, and psychiatrists—have not been formally trained in the academic, social, and emotional impact ADHD has on individuals throughout the lifespan. While these professionals care deeply about their students and patients and may have valuable experience, experience alone is not the same as specialized knowledge. ADHD is a nuanced condition that requires understanding its complexities, including how it affects EF skills, behavior, and motivation.

As a parent, you are your child's most important advocate. Building a support team that includes knowledgeable experts is essential for helping your child thrive. One of my passions is providing ADHD teacher training to schools, which helps educators better understand how ADHD affects children in the classroom and equips them with practical tools for student success. However, most teachers receive little to no formal training on ADHD and are often unprepared to effectively manage its challenges. This gap in knowledge means that many children with ADHD struggle unnecessarily, even though public schools are legally required under the Individuals With Disabilities Education Act (IDEA) to provide appropriate services—a guarantee not extended to private or nontraditional schools.

Appendix B offers further insights into the significance of training teachers, therapists, and other related professionals and the resources available to assist them in enhancing their understanding and effectiveness when working with children who have ADHD. I have also addressed this topic on my blog ("Train All Teachers About ADHD Challenges" and "Advocate for ADHD Teacher Training," both accessible at www.ptscoaching.com).

WHAT IS ADHD?

When most people think about ADHD, they associate it with three main traits: *impulsivity, hyperactivity,* and *inattentiveness.* However, science and research have helped us understand that these traits are really just the "tip of the iceberg," says Chris Zeigler Dendy (2003). There is much more that lies beneath the surface and impacts every aspect of a person's life.

Let's start with some clarification: Until 1987, what we now call ADHD was referred to as attention deficit disorder (ADD). Many still use this term, especially when distinguishing whether someone has the "hyperactivity" component. However, this distinction is technically outdated. Sadly, before 1968, the disorder was even more poorly understood and was labeled as "minimal brain dysfunction" or "minimal brain disorder." Thankfully, our understanding of ADHD has come a long way. As you will see shortly, I believe the current name is still far off what would be most descriptive!

Currently, the fifth edition of the *Diagnostic and Statistical Manual of Mental Disorders* (*DSM-5*; American Psychiatric Association, 2013) categorizes ADHD into three "presentations," reflecting the different ways ADHD can manifest:
- ADHD—hyperactive/impulsive
- ADHD—inattentive
- ADHD—combined hyperactive/impulsive and inattentive

Interestingly, a person's presentation can change over time. For example, we often see a reduction in hyperactivity as children grow older, though challenges with impulsivity and attention may persist.

WHAT DOES IT FEEL LIKE TO HAVE ADHD?

Think of your child's brain as a city with streets and avenues carrying traffic. These streets represent neuron pathways, and the traffic includes all the information, sensory inputs, impulses, feelings, and instructions the brain must process. For some children, the traffic lights aren't in sync. Neurotransmitters, the chemicals that help brain cells communicate, sometimes don't function as they should. It's as if the traffic signals regulating the brain's flow are malfunctioning. Imagine it's Friday afternoon rush hour in your city, and the traffic lights go out—what happens? Gridlock, traffic jams, frustration, and chaos. This is what's happening inside your child's head.

You can also think of your child's brain like their bedroom. All the clothes and belongings are there, but who knows where? Clothes might be under the bed, buried in piles, hanging out of drawers, or stuffed into the closet. Similarly, when your child needs to access information in their brain, it's there—it just may take some time to find it.

This internal chaos explains why some children may appear so controlling. They don't feel in control of their internal thoughts and actions, so they try to control their environment instead. This lack of internal order also contributes to their difficulty with transitions, new situations, and sudden changes.

Many children—and some adults—seek stimulation to keep the "traffic cop" in their brain awake, even if that stimulation comes from negative behavior. Have you noticed how your child might suddenly start bugging a sibling or creating havoc out of nowhere? Now, imagine how hard it is for some children to sit still in class when they're bored, and their brain feels chaotic. This constant effort to stay alert in nonstimulating environments is why many children with ADHD come home from school mentally exhausted. It also explains why projects often get abandoned after completing the "fun" or interesting parts.

THE VALUE OF A THOROUGH DIAGNOSIS

Can't we just go to Dr. Google and figure out if it's ADHD? While it might be tempting to rely on quick online checklists or observations from someone who only sees your child in one setting, diagnosing ADHD is much more nuanced than that. Maybe your child struggles in a particular class because the subject doesn't interest them or feels especially difficult. Or perhaps they're distracted because it's the only class where they get to chat with their best friend. ADHD symptoms must be observed in multiple settings, and a thorough evaluation goes far beyond surface-level observations.

It's important to seek a diagnosis if you notice your child consistently struggling with attention, behavior, or managing daily tasks in ways that seem different from those of their peers or developmental stage. I firmly believe that parents should trust their instincts: If something feels off, it's worth investigating.

A formal diagnosis is invaluable in unlocking the right support for your child. It can guide treatment options, including appropriate medication if needed, ensure access to school services, and even make therapies more accessible through insurance coverage.

When ADHD is diagnosed early, your child has the best chance for positive outcomes. Early intervention allows them to learn strategies for managing their symptoms before challenges escalate, setting them up for success in school, relationships, and life.

Appendix C includes valuable information on who can diagnose ADHD, what a comprehensive evaluation entails, and practical tips for accessing testing.

OVERDIAGNOSED, UNDERDIAGNOSED, AND MISDIAGNOSED

When I speak to parents and professional groups, one of the most common questions I'm asked is "Do you think ADHD is overdiagnosed?"

My answer is always the same: Yes, ADHD is overdiagnosed. But it is also underdiagnosed—and often misdiagnosed. While the criteria for diagnosing ADHD are well established, the reality is that the process of diagnosing ADHD is not consistent across professionals or settings. Some people report their concerns to a professional and leave the office with a diagnosis after only a brief conversation, without the comprehensive evaluation steps I outlined earlier. This can lead to overdiagnosis, where ADHD is labeled without sufficient evidence or investigation.

At the same time, there are many cases where ADHD is overlooked entirely. Girls, for example, often present with inattentive symptoms rather than hyperactivity, which may cause their struggles to go unnoticed in the classroom. Children from underserved communities face significant barriers to accessing trained professionals, leaving many without a diagnosis or proper support. Misdiagnosis is another challenge, as ADHD symptoms can overlap with those of anxiety, trauma, or learning disabilities, leading to confusion and incorrect labels. These discrepancies highlight the importance of seeking knowledgeable professionals and ensuring every child receives a thoughtful, accurate diagnosis.

CHANGING TIMES, CHANGING EXPECTATIONS

Adding to these challenges is the changing landscape of education and childhood development. Kindergarten classrooms, for example, no longer look like they did years ago when play centers and hands-on exploration were central to the day. Instead, today's classrooms often resemble structured mini-first-grade environments, emphasizing academics rather than the developmental benefits of play.

Play is vital in developing self-regulation and social–emotional skills. It helps children learn to inhibit impulsive behavior, collaborate with others, and engage in verbal problem solving as they negotiate roles and rules. However, by reducing opportunities for play and pushing young children beyond their developmental readiness, we may be mistaking behaviors that stem from natural immaturity for ADHD or exacerbating challenges for children who already struggle with attention and self-regulation.

Technology has further transformed the classroom and home environments. Screens, while offering some benefits, have become a pervasive force in children's lives, fundamentally changing how they learn, interact, and engage with the world. Classrooms and homework assignments often rely on screens, which can become sources of distraction, reducing kids' ability to focus for longer periods. The constant stimulation of digital devices, with their instant gratification and endless notifications, may also contribute to shorter attention spans and an increased desire for immediate rewards. For children with ADHD, who already struggle with attention regulation and impulse control, these dynamics can create additional hurdles.

It's also important to recognize that times are not just changing academically but socially as well. The rise of social media and the internet has introduced pressures and influences that are sometimes outside of parents' detection and control. These factors can amplify the challenges of ADHD, making it even harder for children to cope, thrive, and perform as they otherwise might.

While I won't focus heavily on screen time and the influence of social media in this book, I encourage you to be mindful of how technology impacts your child's learning, motivation, and behavior. Appendix D provides more information and ideas for managing screens so you can decide what works best for your family.

THE GENETIC BASIS OF ADHD

ADHD has a strong genetic basis and is, therefore, largely hereditary (estimates are about 80%; Thapar et al., 2013). As I mentioned previously, it's common for parents to recognize their own childhood struggles in their child's experiences. For some, this realization brings comfort and a sense of connection. "My daughter is just like I was," they might say. "School was so hard, and I felt helpless. I don't want her to suffer like I did." For others, the reaction is different. They might feel that because they "survived" strict parenting and tough love, their child should be able to as well. "I did what was expected because I had no choice," one parent might say. "Why can't my Jonny? I think you are being too soft on him, which is why he behaves as he does."

NEURODIVERSITY AND SEEING THE WHOLE CHILD

Before diving into the symptoms and traits of ADHD, I want to emphasize something important: ADHD is just one part of who your child is. Right now, you may be struggling tremendously, and those struggles are very real. However, never lose sight of your child's strengths, unique qualities, and untapped potential.

The concept of neurodiversity helps us reframe how we think about ADHD and other neurodevelopmental conditions. *Neurodiversity* describes the vast differences in brain function and behavior within the human population. It recognizes that variations in thinking, learning, and behavior are natural and contribute to the rich diversity of people. ADHD is often considered a neurodivergent condition because it involves differences in how individuals think, process information, and interact with the world. While these differences can create challenges, they also bring unique strengths—like creativity, resilience, and innovative thinking—that deserve to be recognized and nurtured.

When we embrace this perspective, we shift from focusing solely on what's "wrong" to seeing the whole child and their full potential. I also encourage the use of "person-first" language, which helps us remember to see the child before the diagnosis. Instead of saying "an ADHD child," say "a child with ADHD." This subtle change reminds us that ADHD is just one aspect of your child's identity—it does not define who they are.

We explore some of the more challenging traits of ADHD in this chapter, but I'd like you to keep this in mind: ADHD also comes with unique strengths and possibilities. Many successful people have not only managed their ADHD but thrived because of the gifts it brings—whether it's creativity, resilience, or an entrepreneurial spirit. So, hang in there while I discuss some of the difficulties you may be seeing right now. We end this chapter on a more positive note, and in the chapters that follow, I guide you on how to help your child embrace their unique wiring and truly thrive.

ADHD IN GIRLS AND WOMEN

ADHD often presents differently in girls and women, which can lead to underdiagnosis and delayed intervention. I have worked with so many women who regret the struggles they went through since their behavior was assumed to be due to anxiety or depression. ADHD was not considered. While boys are more likely to exhibit hyperactive and impulsive behaviors, girls tend to display more inattentive symptoms, such as daydreaming or trouble focusing. These behaviors are less disruptive and, therefore, less likely to be noticed in classroom settings or other structured environments.

Also, girls and women with ADHD are more likely to internalize their struggles, leading to higher rates of anxiety and depression. They often develop coping strategies that mask their symptoms, further delaying a proper diagnosis. Unfortunately, when ADHD in girls and women goes undiagnosed and untreated, it can result in the same negative consequences seen in boys, such as academic underachievement, low self-esteem, and behavioral challenges.

It's also important to note that these patterns are not exclusive to girls. Boys and men with the inattentive presentation of ADHD may experience similar challenges. Recognizing these differences is crucial in providing appropriate support and intervention for all children with ADHD.

INATTENTIVE ADHD: THE EMOTIONAL SIDE

For children with inattentive ADHD, the world can often feel overwhelming and hard to navigate. These children may appear introverted or shy, not because they lack interest in others but because their brains are constantly working to catch up, process information, or focus on what's being asked of them. They might feel like they're drifting through conversations or class discussions, unsure how to jump in or express themselves. This internal struggle can lead to frustration, self-doubt, and even loneliness as they wonder why keeping up seems easier for everyone else.

As a parent, it can be tough to see your child retreat into themselves, especially if you're naturally more outgoing or don't share the inattentive presentation of ADHD. You might worry about their social interactions, wondering if they're missing out on friendships or important childhood experiences. It's important to remember that their quieter demeanor doesn't mean they don't care about connecting with others—it just means they may need more support to find their voice and navigate social situations. With understanding, encouragement, and the right tools, these children can build confidence and meaningful relationships in their own unique way.

ADHD's CONNECTION TO COGNITIVE DISENGAGEMENT SYNDROME

There's another condition closely related to ADHD that researchers are still exploring. It's called cognitive disengagement syndrome (CDS), previously known as "sluggish cognitive tempo." This is not currently part of the *DSM*.

People with CDS often appear drowsy, low energy, or easily fatigued. They might daydream excessively, seem easily confused, or move at a slower pace than others. While CDS overlaps with the inattentive presentation of ADHD in about half of the cases, many experts believe it may be a separate condition. Although CDS is not yet recognized in the *DSM*, it represents an important area of research that helps us better understand kids who don't fit the traditional ADHD profile.

IS IT AN ATTENTION DEFICIT?

As I mentioned earlier in this chapter, the term "attention deficit" doesn't really capture what ADHD is all about. It's not that people with ADHD can't pay attention. Rather, they struggle with *attention regulation*. They can pay attention—but not always when they need to, for as long as they need to, or on what they need to.

This difficulty stems from below-normal activity in the brain's neurotransmission of dopamine and norepinephrine. This explains why someone with ADHD might be deeply focused on a game for hours but be unable to stay tuned into their math homework for more than 5 minutes. When they're highly interested or internally motivated, they may even experience *hyperfocus*, becoming so absorbed that they block out everything else. On the flip side, when something feels boring or unengaging, they may struggle to focus at all, resisting even their best efforts.

To better understand what this feels like, imagine watching your favorite TV show while hearing the volume from five other channels at the same time. You're trying to follow the plot, but snippets of dialogue, music, and flashing images from other channels keep pulling your focus. It's not that you're not paying attention; it's that your attention is being pulled in multiple directions. This "multifocus" challenge is what many people with ADHD experience, making it hard to stay focused on one task or conversation.

This struggle to regulate attention makes focusing on a task difficult and also makes *transitions*—shifting focus from one activity to another—particularly challenging. For example, your child might resist stopping a game to start their homework, not just because they prefer the game but because transitioning requires shifting their entire focus. I discuss transitioning further when I cover attention regulation later in the chapter.

Impulsivity

> *By the time I think about what I'm gonna do . . . I already did it!*
>
> —DENNIS THE MENACE

Interrupting, blurting out, grabbing things, throwing things. . . . These poor kids; they don't always mean to misbehave, it's part of their neurobiology. Their brains often seem to operate by the motto, "Ready, fire . . . aim." Due to lower levels of dopamine, which provide natural reinforcement for the brain, many people with ADHD also engage in risky behaviors to seek high stimulation.

Helping kids manage their impulsivity is one of the greatest challenges parents and professionals face. While impulsivity is part of the diagnosis, it's not fair to "punish the disability." It's important to help kids learn to anticipate situations that may trigger their impulsivity and develop strategies to navigate them. At the same time, children with ADHD need guidance to take responsibility for their actions in ways that build self-awareness and self-regulation.

One possible support for managing impulsivity is appropriate medication, which can help regulate some of the brain's natural deficits. However, regardless of that choice, there are steps you can take to help your child become more aware and curb some of their natural impulsivity.

Strategies for Managing Impulsivity

The biggest challenge is helping kids catch themselves in the moment—just before they act. Here are some ways to help them develop both awareness and skills for self-control:

- *Teach interrupting phrases*: Give your child simple, respectful phrases (such as "May I add . . .") to help them know how and when they can join a conversation. Practice this during family conversations, like at mealtime or in the car, so they can get used to interrupting appropriately.

- *Create a private signal*: Agree on a discreet signal to remind your child to "Wait, think, and then go." This can be helpful during playdates, social gatherings, or public outings.

- *Set clear expectations*: Especially for younger children, discuss the rules and expectations for games, gatherings, or outings beforehand. Planning together can help them anticipate challenging moments and think through their actions.

- *Collaborate with teachers*: Work with your child's teacher to use consistent strategies and language at school and home. This consistency reinforces the tools your child is learning to use.

- *Build self-awareness*: Help your child recognize their thoughts and choose not to act on them. For example, your child might learn to say, "I'm really bored waiting, but I can do it a little longer without getting in trouble," or "I'm angry that he has the ball, but I can ask for it or wait my turn."

By preparing for situations that might overwhelm your child, equipping them with practical strategies, and fostering accountability without blame, you can help them navigate their impulsivity with greater confidence and success.

Hyperactivity

When I think of children with ADHD, I often picture Tigger from *Winnie the Pooh*: boundless energy, constant motion, and an enthusiasm that can sometimes overwhelm everyone around them. For kids with ADHD, it can feel like there's an internal motor that never stops, often revving up even more during moments of boredom or stress. While this energy can be challenging to manage, it's also part of what makes these kids so vibrant and dynamic.

Hyperactive children are often identified earlier by teachers and parents because their behavior tends to stand out in group settings. However, it's important to distinguish between a naturally active child and one whose hyperactivity is part of ADHD. A good clinical assessment can help clarify this difference, providing insight into how to best support your child's unique needs.

Sense of Time

Does your child (or perhaps someone else in your family!) spend way too long in the bathroom? Or do you know someone who's always late—and always surprised by it? Or maybe they're rushing you to leave, and you're thinking, "But we have 5 more minutes!" These behaviors aren't just quirks; they reflect a genuine challenge in how people with ADHD perceive and manage time.

Research shows that the ability to measure the passage of time is often weaker in people with ADHD compared to their neurotypical peers. This difficulty doesn't improve with ADHD stimulant medication (Barkley, 1997). It's not just about inattention to the moment but also inattention to the future. Edward Hallowell describes this as "time is now and not now" in his book *Driven to Distraction* (Hallowell & Ratey, 1995). For a child with ADHD, that quiz on Friday feels far away when it's only Monday—why worry about it now? If tomorrow isn't the due date, today isn't the "do date."

People with ADHD live so much in the moment that they often act without considering past experiences or future consequences. That paper due on Friday? That's "not now," so why worry about it? Aunt Susan is coming over tonight, and you want them to clean up? "Not now," so what's the rush? Soon and later feel abstract, and only the present moment seems real. As a result, warnings about what will happen later often don't resonate.

EXECUTIVE FUNCTION DEFICITS

Over the past few years, there has been a growing focus in parenting and education on EF skills. These self-regulating abilities are essential for accomplishing nearly everything we do, from planning a project to managing emotions. You can think of EF skills as a group of specialized managers in the brain, each responsible for a specific task, like organization, time management, or impulse control. And who's in charge of these managers? You are the Chief Executive Officer (CEO), making sure each manager is well trained, supported, and equipped to do their job effectively.

EF skills reside in the prefrontal cortex, the brain's front region, and they start developing in infancy. This is the same region of the brain I discussed earlier when introducing ADHD. While most children fully develop these skills by the time they are 25–30 years old, for kids with ADHD, the process is slower—about 3–5 years behind their peers. This means a child with ADHD might function more like a 9-year-old when they are 12, or a 16-year-old when they are 20. This delay often leaves parents feeling as though their child is "younger" than their actual age.

It's a bit like seeing a very tall kindergartener. Because they look older, we naturally expect them to act more maturely than their years. Similarly, children with ADHD are often highly intelligent, and we mistakenly assume their EF skills are just as advanced as their intellectual abilities. The reality is that intelligence and EF skills are entirely separate. Let me say this very clearly: This delay has nothing to do with intelligence or your child's potential for success. But it might explain why your incredibly bright child struggles to pack their backpack at the end of the day while their peers seem to do it with ease! Recognizing this distinction can help you better understand your child and adjust your expectations accordingly.

As you'll discover, several experts now refer to ADHD as an EF disorder. It's almost impossible to have ADHD without experiencing significant EF deficits. Some argue that renaming ADHD to reflect these deficits—perhaps something like "executive function disorder"—would be more accurate, though it's important to note that not everyone with EF challenges has ADHD.

Before diving into the descriptions of the eight EF skills, I want to leave you with an important analogy. Think about how we approach a child with dyslexia. If they struggle with reading, we don't say, "We taught you that already—you should know it by now!" Instead, we provide ongoing support, recognizing that they may continue to need help even years down the road. It's the same with EF skills. If your child struggles, they don't need repeated expectations—they need

FIGURE 1.1:
Executive Function Skills Chart

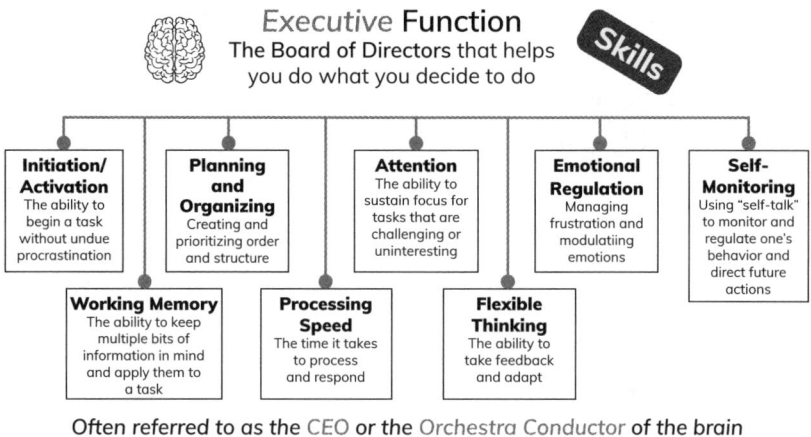

Executive **Function**
The Board of Directors that helps
you do what you decide to do

Skills

Initiation/ Activation	Planning and Organizing	Attention	Emotional Regulation	Self- Monitoring
The ability to begin a task without undue procrastination	Creating and prioritizing order and structure	The ability to sustain focus for tasks that are challenging or uninteresting	Managing frustration and modulatiing emotions	Using "self-talk" to monitor and regulate one's behavior and direct future actions

Working Memory	Processing Speed	Flexible Thinking
The ability to keep multiple bits of information in mind and apply them to a task	The time it takes to process and respond	The ability to take feedback and adapt

Often referred to as the CEO or the Orchestra Conductor of the brain

© Cindy Goldrich

your patience, understanding, and support. They need guidance, strategies, and tools to help them succeed.

Throughout this book, you will learn how to support your child's EF development. This will involve adjusting your perspective, understanding their unique needs, and creating a home environment where they can thrive. For now, let's start by exploring what these skills are and how they impact your child's daily life.

INITIATION/ACTIVATION

Does your child struggle to get started on tasks? They may know exactly what to do, but taking that first step can feel insurmountable—almost like their "engine" just won't start. I always remind parents that *ADHD isn't a problem of knowing what to do; it's a problem of doing what they know!* And remember what we said about time: "Time is NOW and NOT NOW." For many kids with ADHD, urgency doesn't register until the "fire is at the door," making it hard for them to prioritize or act proactively.

Most people benefit from having a *structure*, a *strategy*, and a *routine* to help them initiate tasks. For example, when I prepare to write each day, I start by clearing off my desk. Then, I set a timer for 10 minutes to check emails, knowing that without it, I might go down a rabbit hole and lose track of time. When the timer goes off, it signals my brain that it's time to start writing. Creating similar systems can help your child too.

Tip: Gently help your child recognize this challenge without criticism. Begin with a neutral, nonjudgmental observation: "I notice you're [playing with your blocks/looking at your math book/ just hanging out]." This opens the door for connection and collaboration as you guide them into action. Here are some strategies that may help:

- *Be the momentum starter*: Sometimes, your presence at the beginning of a task can help them gather the momentum they need. Sit with them as they organize their materials or brainstorm the first part of an assignment together.

- *Create a starting ritual*: Simple routines can signal "It's time to begin." This might include setting up their workspace, doing five jumping jacks, or using a timer to transition into action mode.
- *Use a timer to signal readiness*: Work together to set a timer at an agreed-upon start time. This external cue can serve as a gentle nudge, shifting them from "not now" to "now."
- *Frame the task as finite*: Knowing an activity will end makes starting feel less overwhelming. For instance, explain that homework will take 15 minutes or chores will be done in 20 minutes.

By supporting your child in overcoming initiation challenges, you're not just helping them complete tasks—you're building their confidence and equipping them with strategies they'll carry into the future.

WORKING MEMORY

Working memory is often referred to as the brain's "mental work-space" or "search engine." It's where we temporarily store, retain, and manipulate information needed to complete tasks, make decisions, or engage in conversations. For example, when someone gives you directions to their house or you memorize a phone number to dial, you're relying on your working memory.

However, research shows that *up to 80%–85% of individuals with ADHD experience working memory impairments*, and their working memory often functions below typical levels. This can create significant challenges in various aspects of learning and daily life, including reading comprehension, following multistep instructions, and solving math problems.

Imagine this common scenario: You ask your child, "Can you go upstairs, grab your backpack, shoes, and tennis racket, and on the way back down, get my water bottle and turn off the light?" For many parents, the outcome is frustrating—your child may return with only one or two items or forget the task entirely. It's easy to assume they aren't listening or don't care but what if the real issue is a working memory deficit? When we shift our mindset from frustration to problem solving, we can start to implement strategies that support their unique challenges.

Working memory is essential for:
- Holding and concentrating on thoughts in the moment.
- Manipulating information, such as sequencing steps or solving problems.
- Managing both receptive and expressive communication (e.g., following instructions or sharing ideas clearly).
- Retaining and integrating details for tasks like reading comprehension or solving math problems.

For children with ADHD, working memory deficits can impact how they:
- Process and recall multistep instructions.
- Organize information for assignments or projects.
- Remember characters, plots, or details in stories.
- Complete calculations or other sequential tasks.

HELPING YOUR CHILD NAVIGATE WORKING MEMORY CHALLENGES

Recognizing that your child may have a weaker working memory reframes the situation from blame to empathy. Instead of thinking, "Why can't they just listen?" you might ask, "How can I help them remember this more effectively?"

It's also important to recognize that working memory is sensitive to anxiety, stress, and pressure, which can further impair its effectiveness. This is why you might find yourself relying on lists when feeling overwhelmed and why your child might need extra support in high-pressure situations.

Here are a few strategies to help your child:

- *Break tasks into smaller steps*: Instead of asking for multiple things at once, give one instruction at a time.
- *Create visual aids*: Use charts, sticky notes, or checklists to help them keep track of what needs to be done.
- *Encourage note-taking*: Teach your child to jot down basic notes or keywords for tasks requiring memory, like reading comprehension or multistep math problems.
- *Use repetition*: Have them repeat back instructions to ensure they've retained the information.
- *Incorporate mnemonic devices*: Create simple acronyms or phrases to help them remember sequences or concepts.

By implementing supportive tools and building awareness of your child's needs, you can help your child navigate the challenges of working memory deficits, paving the way for more successful and less stressful learning experiences.

PLANNING AND ORGANIZING

Planning requires anticipating future events and creating a strategy to meet a goal. For children with ADHD, planning is especially challenging because it depends on accurately understanding time: how long things take, when they need to happen, and how to sequence tasks. While intelligence and planning are unrelated, a child's natural abilities can sometimes mask how much support they need in this area. A bright, articulate child may still struggle to prioritize homework or packing their backpack efficiently over playing a game.

Effective organizing, on the other hand, involves applying structure or systems to materials and information. It's not just about tidying up but creating a method that allows for easy access and use later—whether that's organizing a desk, breaking down a project, or prioritizing tasks on a to-do list.

Remember, people with ADHD often live in the present moment, making it hard for them to grasp the steps required for future success. For example:

- *The reward system*: The ADHD brain is driven by interest and urgency. "Later" doesn't register as a compelling reason to act now.
- *Time blindness*: As discussed in the "Sense of Time" section, time feels abstract. A book report due in 2 weeks might as well be a year away—until the deadline is staring them in the face.
- *Working memory*: Planning requires juggling multiple pieces of information, like deciding what materials are needed, how long each task will take, and what steps need to happen first. For children with ADHD, this cognitive load can feel overwhelming.

You can help your child externalize time and break big goals into manageable steps. Here are some practical ways to support them:

- *Make tasks concrete*: Use calendars, checklists, and visual aids to map out what needs to be done and when. For example, if a project is due in 2 weeks, work backward to identify daily or weekly tasks.
- *Teach prioritization*: Help your child distinguish between "must do" and "nice to do" tasks. This skill is essential for balancing homework, extracurricular activities, and downtime.
- *Model planning*: Show your child how you organize your own time. For instance, if you're preparing for a family trip, walk them through your process of making lists, packing, and organizing the schedule.
- *Break it down*: Long-term projects or multistep tasks can feel overwhelming. Help your child divide them into smaller, achievable steps

with clear deadlines. For example, "Today, let's choose the book for your report. Tomorrow, we'll outline the first chapter."

• *Incorporate routines*: Consistent daily habits, like packing their back-pack the night before or reviewing tomorrow's schedule at dinner, can build foundational planning skills.

Planning and organizing skills don't develop overnight, and your child will need guidance and practice. Just as a coach helps an athlete develop skills through repetition and encouragement, you will need to guide your child toward greater independence. Start with close supervision and gradually step back as they become more confident in their abilities.

PROCESSING SPEED

Processing speed is the pace at which a person takes in information, thinks it through, and responds. For children with ADHD, processing speed is often slower than their peers, which can make it harder to complete tasks, answer questions, and keep up with classroom demands. Importantly, *processing speed has no relationship to intelligence*. A highly intelligent child can still have a slower processing speed—it simply means their brain needs more time to process and respond.

One of the best ways to support your child is by reinforcing that *speed does not equal intelligence*. This distinction is critical for both parents and children to understand. Unfortunately, children often equate speed with being "smart." In a classroom, the student who quickly raises their hand and gives the correct answer is often seen as the smartest. Meanwhile, a child with slower processing speed may still be thoughtfully formulating their response but misses the chance to participate. Over time, this can lead to feelings of inadequacy, even in a highly capable child.

For children with ADHD, processing speed challenges often go hand in hand with weaker working memory and difficulties regulating alertness. ADHD brains are wired to respond to interest and urgency, so tasks that don't feel engaging or time pressured can seem nearly impossible to tackle. Add anxiety, stress, or pressure to the mix, and it can further slow down their ability to process and perform.

For example, imagine you're rushing through the store and you ask your child, "Do you want the red one or the green one?" They hesitate, so you repeat yourself quickly—but instead of helping, this added pressure makes it even harder for them to decide. The stress clouds their ability to process the information and respond, leaving both of you frustrated.

In school, slower processing speed can make timed tests, quick transitions, and multistep assignments especially challenging. Children with ADHD might start to disengage when they can't keep up—not because they don't care or don't understand, but because it feels overwhelming.

Helping your child navigate slower processing speed starts with recognizing and respecting their unique pace. Here are some strategies to help:

- *Slow down*: Rushing or adding pressure often backfires. Instead, allow extra time for transitions and responses. Patience can make a world of difference.
- *Simplify expectations*: While your child may show interest in many activities, focusing on just one or two can help them achieve greater success and confidence.
- *Offer breaks*: For longer activities, build in short breaks to let your child reset and recharge. Movement, snacks, or music can stimulate their brain and help them refocus.

Remind your child that needing more time doesn't mean they're less capable—it simply means their brain works differently. Celebrate their deep thinking, creativity, and persistence, and help them see the value in their unique way of processing the world.

With your support, your child can learn to manage their pace, advocate for their needs, and approach tasks with confidence.

ATTENTION

Children with ADHD often face significant challenges in regulating their attention. While they can focus—and sometimes intensely—it's not always when they need to, for as long as they need to, or on the right task. External distractions, like background noise and internal distractions, like their own thoughts, constantly pull them away from the task at hand.

At the same time, ADHD often swings to the opposite extreme: hyperfocus. When deeply absorbed in one thought or activity, people with ADHD can lose track of time and their surroundings entirely. Both distractibility and hyperfocus can make transitions particularly difficult, as shifting focus requires effort and energy they may not readily have.

Helping your child regulate their attention starts with understanding these unique challenges and providing tools to navigate them.

The Power of Fidgeting

For children—and many adults—with ADHD, movement and fidgeting aren't just habits; they're tools for improving focus. Activities like chewing gum, doodling, or quietly manipulating a stress ball can stimulate the brain and boost levels of dopamine and norepinephrine, much like ADHD medications. The key is teaching your child to use these tools appropriately.

Help your child see fidgets as tools, not toys. A fidget should stay in the background, quietly supporting their ability to focus on the primary task—whether it's doing homework, listening, or sitting through dinner. Explain that they should use fidgets in a way that doesn't distract others or call attention to themselves. For example, no loud noises, throwing, or banging. If the fidget becomes the focus (e.g., it's being spun or played with noisily), it stops being helpful and becomes a distraction.

Sometimes, staying physically still makes it even harder for a child with ADHD to focus. Movement—like sitting on a wobble cushion, standing while working, or even walking around—can help them stay engaged. Similarly, music can act as a helpful background tool. It doesn't have to be classical; the key is finding something engaging enough to help them focus but not so exciting that it becomes a distraction. Encourage your child to experiment with playlists to discover what works best for them.

Body Doubling

Many children with ADHD benefit from having someone nearby while they work. This is known as "body doubling," and your presence acts as a grounding force, helping your child stay anchored and on track. Even teens may appreciate this support during homework or projects. Think about your favorite coffee shop, where many people work independently on their laptops. Body doubling can be just as effective at home.

Fidgets and movement-based tools aren't just for school—they can help during long car rides, family events, or any situation where sitting still is a challenge. Try different options, such as a stress ball, spinner ring, or even a piece of fabric, to see what works best for your child.

Other Tips for Attention Regulation

- *Chunk time*: Break large tasks into smaller, manageable parts with clear breaks in between. Use visual schedules or timers to signal work and rest periods.
- *Interactive learning*: Make learning active and fun. Play catch while reviewing vocabulary or use flashcards for a matching game.
- *Mindfulness*: Simple exercises like deep breathing or short meditations can help your child practice staying present and calm.

• *Limit multitasking*: Encourage your child to focus on one task at a time to avoid overwhelm.

If your child struggles to use fidgets or other activities appropriately, don't worry—it's a learning process! In Key 5, we explore ways to collaborate with your child to create shared solutions that reduce frustration and help everyone feel more supported.

Transitions: Stopping, Shifting, and Starting
Transitions involve three distinct steps:
1. Stopping the current activity.
2. Shifting focus and movement to the next activity.
3. Starting the new activity.

As parents, we often focus on the final step: getting our child to start the next task. We see and feel the pressure of time and the need to keep things moving. But for children with ADHD, the real struggle often lies in stopping the first activity.

People with ADHD are often deeply immersed in the present moment, and stopping can feel jarring. Maybe it's their favorite activity, and they don't want to stop, or perhaps they worry that if they don't finish now, they'll have to revisit the task later, which adds to their stress.

We explore specific strategies for managing transitions in Key 6. For now, remember that helping your child manage attention and transitions is about more than just completing tasks—it's about empowering them with skills they can carry into adulthood.

FLEXIBILITY

Flexible thinking requires shifting gears and finding new ways to solve problems. For people who struggle with flexible thinking, coping with change can feel overwhelming. They might get stuck and not even understand why. You might notice that they:

- Have trouble accepting other people's ideas.
- Argue the same point over and over.
- Get frustrated when even small things go wrong.
- Repeat the same mistakes continuously.
- Struggle to follow new schedules.
- Get anxious (or angry) when plans change.
- Struggle with unfamiliar or more complicated tasks.

I know it can be challenging—and often frustrating—when your child (or even your spouse, friend, or coworker) seems so inflexible. But remember, they're not doing this to frustrate you. It's just part of how they're wired. One of the best ways to help is to provide as much advance notice of changes as possible. And offering empathy and acknowledging how tough change can be for them can go a long way too.

EMOTIONAL REGULATION

When we think about ADHD, impulsivity, distractibility, and hyperactivity often come to mind. Yet, for many children and their families, emotional regulation presents the greatest challenges. In fact, Russell Barkley (2012), a leading researcher in ADHD, suggests that "deficits in emotional self-regulation" might be a more accurate name for ADHD. Emotional regulation is the ability to manage and respond to emotions in ways that are socially appropriate and proportional to the situation. Interestingly, medical papers dating back to 1798 have always included emotion in the conceptualization of ADHD. This continued until the 1968 edition of the *DSM-II*. However, since then, emotional dysregulation has been excluded from the clinical conceptualization of the condition.

People with emotional dysregulation may have a hard time:

- Inhibiting their initial reaction or response.
- Managing their anger and other intense emotions.
- Being patient and tolerating frustration.
- Shifting their focus away from an upsetting event or toward something more positive.
- Calming down or regaining composure after an emotional outburst.

This is why your child may seem to "lose it" over something minor, give up easily when frustrated, or struggle to persist through challenges. These difficulties impact not only their learning but also their friendships and family dynamics.

THE SOCIAL IMPACT OF EMOTIONAL DYSREGULATION

Barkley (2012) notes that the biggest predictor of social rejection among children and adults with ADHD isn't their hyperactivity or distractibility—it's their difficulty regulating frustration, impatience, and anger. Emotional impulsivity, like overreacting or quickly melting down, can make it hard for children to navigate social interactions successfully.

Children who struggle with emotional regulation may have difficulty taking turns, respecting boundaries, or managing outbursts during conflicts with friends or family. These challenges can lead to feelings of rejection or isolation, further impacting their self-esteem.

Understanding that ADHD is a neurologically based challenge in emotional regulation—not a deliberate choice—can help you approach your child with empathy and patience.

Emotional regulation is a skill that develops over time with support and practice. Your role as a parent is to guide your child in understanding their emotions and building strategies to manage them. This takes empathy, patience, and intentionality.

In Key 5, Teach Collaboration, we explore specific ways to collaborate with your child. You learn how to identify triggers, set realistic goals, and foster collaborative problem solving. For now, focus on modeling your own emotional regulation and creating a home environment that promotes calm and understanding.

Teaching emotional regulation isn't about perfection—it's about progress. These skills grow with time, practice, and the right tools. Most importantly, remind yourself and your child that emotional challenges do not reflect who they are but an opportunity to learn and grow together.

SELF-MONITORING

Self-monitoring is the ability to notice your actions, assess their effectiveness, and make real-time adjustments to stay on track. For children with ADHD, this skill is often underdeveloped, impacting everything from completing tasks to navigating social interactions. Improving your child's self-talk—the internal dialogue we use to plan, problem solve, and reflect on our actions—is essential for strengthening their EF skills.

One way to encourage self-monitoring and self-talk is to "live your life out loud." Narrate your thought process—the steps you take, why you make certain decisions, and how you adjust when things don't go as planned. This helps your child understand that tasks often require forethought, flexibility, and problem solving.

For example, imagine you're preparing dinner for 6 p.m. Around 4 p.m., you might say aloud:

"We're having dinner at 6, and I know it'll take about an hour to prepare. So I'll need to start cooking around 4:45. That gives me time to check if we have all the ingredients. If not, I'll adjust what I'm cooking."

Beyond modeling, actively engage your child in activities that naturally build self-monitoring and EF skills. Use everyday tasks as opportunities to ask questions that encourage them to think critically and plan. For example, when packing for a trip, guide them through the process:

- "How will you know what to wear? Think about the weather, the activities, and how much space you have for packing."
- "What size suitcase will you need? Who will carry it? Are we flying or driving?"
- Have them lay out the items they want to bring and then work together to decide the best way to pack.

Other great activities for developing EF skills include planning a meal, gardening, building with blocks, organizing a playroom, and even imaginary play. These hands-on experiences help children discover tools and strategies to manage tasks effectively, reinforcing their ability to become the CEO of their own brain.

Encourage your child to develop positive self-talk alongside these skills. When they say, "I'm bad at math," help them reframe it to something more growth oriented: "Math feels hard for me right now, but I'm working on it." This small shift empowers your child to see challenges as opportunities for growth rather than signs of failure.

For more support on encouraging a "growth mindset," check out my talk, "Skills for Success," at https://bit.ly/ptsskillsforsuccess.

Developing self-monitoring and self-talk takes time, practice, and support. In Key 5, Teach Collaboration, we explore collaborative strategies to address these challenges and build these critical skills together. For now, focus on modeling, narrating your process, and celebrating progress—no matter how small.

COEXISTING CONDITIONS

Approximately 64% of children with ADHD have at least one coexisting condition, according to the Centers for Disease Control and Prevention (2020).

The presence of these coexisting conditions can complicate both the diagnosis and treatment of ADHD, making it essential to understand and address your child's unique needs. A comprehensive evaluation by a health care professional is critical to ensure your child receives the most effective interventions. Managing these challenges is not just about alleviating symptoms—it's about supporting your child in reaching their full potential.

Below are some of the most common coexisting conditions.

Learning Disabilities

About 20% of children with ADHD have a diagnosable learning disability, often in the areas of reading, written expression, or math (DuPaul et al., 2013). This overlap highlights the importance I referenced during the discussion about getting a comprehensive educational evaluation alongside an ADHD assessment to understand your child's learning profile fully.

When you consider the steps involved in writing, for example, you'll see why it is such a challenging process for many children with ADHD. Writing involves numerous EF skills, such as organizing thoughts, holding ideas in working memory, applying grammar and spelling rules, and focusing on the task at hand. Any deficits in these areas can make writing assignments overwhelming and frustrating.

Many children with ADHD also struggle with poor handwriting, which can stem from challenges beyond physical coordination.

While occupational therapy may help address handwriting difficulties, teaching your child proper typing skills can be a game-changer. When I speak to parents and educators, I often ask, "At what grade does your school typically teach typing—meaning proper 10-finger typing using the QWERTY method?" Sadly, I frequently hear that typing instruction is either not offered at all or introduced too late, often in middle school.

Most occupational therapists I've spoken with agree that typing is best taught around second or third grade when children's motor skills are sufficiently developed, but their handwriting struggles have not yet caused significant frustration. Some schools say they teach typing earlier, but when you dig deeper, you may discover that students are only offered typing practice after completing other desk work. Unfortunately, children with slower processing speeds or other challenges are often the ones who take longer to finish their work and miss out on these opportunities—the very kids who would benefit the most from developing strong typing skills. If your school does not offer formal typing instruction by third grade, I strongly encourage you to teach your child privately.

Dyslexia and ADHD: A Common Overlap

It is not unusual for individuals with ADHD to also struggle with reading skill development. In fact, approximately 25%–40% of people diagnosed with ADHD also have dyslexia (Shaywitz & Shaywitz, 2008). This significant overlap highlights the importance of understanding and addressing both conditions to support your child's success.

Dyslexia is a brain-based language disorder that affects areas of the brain responsible for detecting and processing speech sounds and their corresponding letters. Early speech and language delays, such as difficulties with expressive or receptive language, delayed speech development, or trouble with social communication, are common precursors to dyslexia. In fact, approximately 15% of children with

ADHD experience speech and language difficulties, compared with just 3% of children without ADHD. These early challenges can provide valuable clues for identifying and addressing dyslexia.

While many children seem to pick up reading naturally with minimal effort, most need guided practice to develop into confident readers. For children with dyslexia, this process requires even more intentional, structured instruction to help them learn the connections between letters, letter groups, and their sounds, and translate those connections into fluent reading of words and sentences.

Unfortunately, not all schools teach reading in ways that reflect the best evidence-based practices. Many of you may have heard of the podcast series *Sold a Story*, which explores why so many children across the country struggle to read and the widespread use of ineffective teaching methods. I wrote about this issue and how parents can advocate for better reading instruction in my blog post, "Is Reading Being Taught Effectively in Your School District?" You can find it on my website, ptscoaching.com.

By understanding the connection between ADHD and dyslexia, and by advocating for evidence-based reading practices, you can help ensure that your child has the tools they need to succeed academically and develop a lifelong love of learning. If your child's learning disabilities significantly impact their education, they may qualify for formalized accommodations, modifications, or support services through an Individualized Education Plan (IEP) or a 504 plan. These resources can help ensure your child receives the support they need to thrive academically. See Appendix E for information on IEP and 504 plans and Appendix F for some common accommodations and modifications.

Difficulty Falling Asleep and/or Waking Up

Twenty-five to 50% of children with ADHD experience difficulties with sleep habits (Reuters, 2009). There are numerous reasons for this beyond the possible side effects of stimulant medications.

For some children, a bombardment of thoughts as they lie in bed can make falling asleep seem impossible. Additionally, their circadian rhythm (the roughly 24-hour cycle that regulates sleep) may be unusual. You might notice that your child behaves like a bear in winter when you attempt to wake them. There are alarm clocks specifically designed for very deep sleepers (e.g., Clocky, Sonic Bomb, Ramos). Keep in mind that part of the challenge may relate to the motivation to begin the day. In Key 5, you will learn tools to explore that in greater detail.

Melatonin is a hormone naturally produced by the body that regulates sleep–wake cycles. Exposure to artificial light from devices like computers, tablets, and smartphones before bedtime can suppress melatonin production, making it harder to fall asleep. A study published in *Applied Ergonomics* found that 2 hours of exposure to a bright tablet screen at night reduced melatonin levels by about 22%.

To promote better sleep, try the following:

- *Limit screen time before bed*: Aim to reduce the use of electronic devices at least 1 hour before bedtime. Support for dealing with this issue will be addressed in Key 5, Teach Collaboration, and in Appendix D.
- *Consider blue light–blocking glasses*: These glasses can help reduce the impact of blue light on sleep by filtering out the blue wavelengths emitted by screens.
- *Consult your child's doctor*: Discuss whether melatonin supplements might be appropriate to help your child fall asleep.

Substance Abuse

Between 5% and 40% of people with ADHD struggle with substance abuse, including drugs and alcohol (Wilens & Morrison, 2011). This wide range reflects the critical difference between those who have been effectively treated and learned to manage their ADHD and those who have not received adequate support. Untreated ADHD is often linked to higher rates of *substance* use, as individuals may turn to substances as a way to self-medicate. Research suggests that successfully treating ADHD during childhood significantly reduces the risk of substance abuse later in life, highlighting the importance of early intervention and ongoing support.

Autism Spectrum Disorder (ASD)

About 14% of children with ADHD are also diagnosed with ASD, compared with 2.78% of children in the general population (Centers for Disease Control and Prevention, 2020). While ADHD and ASD are distinct conditions, they often share overlapping challenges, such as difficulties with social communication, impulsivity, and EF.

Sensory and Auditory Processing Challenges

While not formally recognized in the *DSM-5*, sensory processing disorder (SPD) and auditory processing disorder (APD) often co-occur with ADHD, creating additional hurdles in learning, communication, and daily life.

SPD involves difficulties responding to sensory input, such as sounds, textures, or lights. For children with SPD, sensory experiences may feel overwhelming or insufficient, leading to distraction, emotional outbursts, or constant movement. Occupational therapy with a sensory integration approach can help children develop strategies for processing sensory input more effectively.

APD affects the brain's ability to interpret sounds, even with normal hearing. Children with APD may struggle to follow verbal instructions or distinguish speech from background noise, which can impact language development and classroom performance. Speech and language therapy, as well as visual aids and written instructions, can help support auditory processing skills.

Depression

Approximately 18% of children with ADHD also have depression, compared with only 1% of children without ADHD (Centers for Disease Control and Prevention, 2022). It is important to recognize that depression can sometimes manifest as irritability, anger, or aggression. While the challenges of undiagnosed or untreated ADHD can contribute to depression, research suggests there may also be a biological link between the two conditions. Psychiatrists generally recommend treating depression first, as this can make it easier to manage ADHD symptoms.

Oppositional Defiant Disorder

Oppositional defiant disorder (ODD) occurs in approximately 25% of children with an inattentive presentation of ADHD and up to 50% of those with a combined presentation (Barkley, 2013). Children with ODD often display angry, violent, and disruptive behaviors toward parents, caregivers, and other authority figures. These behaviors may include chronic aggression, frequent outbursts, arguing, ignoring requests, and intentionally engaging in annoying actions. For many parents, these behaviors create the greatest stress and discord in family dynamics, surpassing even the academic struggles and challenges with time management, organization, and inattentiveness.

Many people, including Barkley, believe that ODD is actually a *potential* (rather than a coexisting condition) as a result of the condition of ADHD, especially for those with either hyperactivity/impulsivity or combined presentations. People with ADHD, especially those with impulsivity, are often very quick to express their emotions. When you look closely at the diagnostic criteria of the *DSM-5* for ODD, you will see that the need for *emotional self-regulation* is mentioned in seven of the eight symptoms. It is believed that this contributes to ODD behaviors.

A special note to parents: Your children need to view you as capable, calm, and assertive. They must trust that you can set and hold boundaries consistently, even when another adult isn't present. By remaining steady in both your communication and your discipline, you help them feel secure—even when they struggle with your limits.

Anxiety

Up to 39% of children with ADHD also have an anxiety disorder (American Psychiatric Association, 2013). Anxiety can present as excessive worry, avoidance of new or challenging situations, or difficulty initiating tasks. For children with ADHD, anxiety can compound difficulties with focus and EF, creating a cycle of stress and underperformance.

Obsessive-compulsive disorder (OCD), which coexists with ADHD in 8%–25% of cases, is often classified as an anxiety disorder (American Psychiatric Association, 2013). The intrusive thoughts and repetitive behaviors associated with OCD can further exacerbate the EF challenges already present in ADHD, making daily tasks and transitions even more difficult.

I find that anxiety often has a significant impact on the challenges faced by children with ADHD. Anxiety can prevent a child from participating, starting tasks, trying new strategies, or thinking clearly. Without effective coping techniques, children experiencing anxiety will often do whatever they can to alleviate that feeling, which may include avoiding or pushing away the object or person they associate with their stress. I believe this is a major contributing factor to the development of ODD.

In the following chapters, I focus on strategies to help reduce the impact of anxiety on your child's behavior and performance.

WHAT ELSE IS PART OF ADHD?

Performance Inconsistency

"If he did it once, why can't he always do it?" I often hear parents and teachers voice this frustration about the inconsistent performance of children with ADHD. It's exasperating when your child repeatedly makes the same errors in judgment or action or fails to do something you know they are fully capable of doing. I often use a helpful phrase to address this challenge: "ADHD is not a problem of knowing what to do, but rather a problem of doing what you know." The difficulty lies in the "when," "where," and "how," not just the "what."

It's important to remember that ADHD is not a challenge of intelligence. In fact, many people with ADHD have above-average intelligence, with a significant number being considered "twice exceptional" (intellectually gifted individuals who also have a disability). While your child may sometimes appear lazy or unmotivated, often, as we explore later, there's much more going on beneath the surface. Neuropsychologist Samuel Goldstein has observed that a significant portion of children's performance on cognitive tests—including IQ tests—is not about how much they know, but how effectively they can demonstrate that knowledge, a skill deeply influenced by executive function (S. Goldstein, personal communication, 2013).

So much depends on the strategies and support systems in place. Think of EF skills and the other challenges children face as being like stars in the brain's universe. When children struggle to perform as they know they can, I like to say, "It's as if all the stars in the universe aren't lined up properly."

Sensitivity to the Physical Environment

I often find that children with ADHD are particularly bothered by the tag on their shirt, the seam of their sock, and so on. They may also be highly sensitive and prefer wearing their hoodie even when the weather doesn't require it. My suggestion is to believe that their concern is real for *them*, just as we each experience temperature differently. Attempting to convince a child that the seam on their sock is "not a big deal" and that they should simply adapt sends the message that their feelings are not understood or taken seriously.

WHAT MESSAGES DOES THE WORLD GIVE KIDS WHO HAVE ADHD?

Very often, the unspoken messages that kids receive can be the most damaging to their confidence and self-esteem. I have often heard school personnel say that "all children are treated equally" and that "no child is made to feel uncomfortable because of any learning differences or ADHD." Unfortunately, while that may be their intention, my practice is filled with parents and kids who have had quite a different experience.

For example, when David's new friend found out he was in Resource Room, his friend said, "But I thought you were smart"— mistakenly assuming that anyone needing support could not be intelligent. After staying up all night to study for a math test only to fail it, Sam was told by his teacher that he just needed to "try harder." When Sarah worked hard to organize the game in a way that helped her manage her anxiety, her friend told her that she was being "too controlling and bossy." After asking the basketball coach to explain, yet again, the play the team was being asked to practice, Michael was told he was "too much trouble" and needed to "pay better attention."

Without self-awareness, effective coping strategies, and sometimes sheer determination, these moments can chip away at a child's sense of self-worth. That's why empathetic adults—teachers, coaches, or parents—are so crucial. These moments of misunderstanding can also serve as opportunities for advocacy and education. Helping others understand that intelligence and ADHD are not mutually exclusive can build awareness and create a more inclusive environment for your child.

SIBLING RELATIONSHIPS

Having a child with ADHD can significantly impact family dynamics, especially the relationships between siblings. You may find that much of your time and energy goes into supporting or managing your child with ADHD—whether it's helping with homework, attending doctor's appointments, redirecting behavior, or addressing disciplinary issues. This can sometimes leave the other children in the family feeling overlooked. Compounding the situation, a child with ADHD may unintentionally overwhelm, annoy, or embarrass their siblings, both at home and during social events or gatherings.

At the same time, siblings often develop unique strengths from these experiences, such as patience, empathy, and problem-solving skills. Acknowledging and celebrating these qualities can help your other children feel valued and appreciated.

When possible, take the time to help your other children understand the challenges their sibling with ADHD faces. Frame the conversation in a way that highlights how everyone has their own unique strengths and struggles. Reinforce the idea that "fair" doesn't mean "equal." For example, you might say, "Just because one person needs glasses doesn't mean everyone does—it's about giving each person what they need to thrive."

Make an effort to find moments to connect individually with each child, showing them that they are valued and appreciated. Be mindful of the potential burdens your child with ADHD may place on their siblings and have open discussions about coping strategies and setting boundaries to ensure everyone in the family feels supported and respected.

Additionally, validate your children's emotions, whether they feel frustrated, jealous, or overwhelmed. Let them know their feelings are normal and encourage them to share openly. Consider holding occasional family meetings or carving out dedicated family time to strengthen bonds and ensure everyone feels heard. With understanding and proactive communication, you can foster a sense of unity and mutual support within your family.

MEDICATION: A TOOL, NOT A CURE

Deciding whether to use medication is one of the most personal and challenging decisions a parent can face. It can feel overwhelming, fraught with worry, and deeply tied to your desire to do what's best for your child. Some parents are firmly against it, while others turn to it after exhausting other options. My role isn't to persuade you but to provide clear, balanced information and support you every step of the way.

And know this: Choosing to use medication does not mean you've failed as a parent, nor does it mean you're taking the "easy way out." Medication can help regulate brain function, but as the saying goes, "pills don't teach skills." While it can be a valuable tool, it's not a replacement for teaching strategies, fostering emotional resilience, or building the skills your child needs to thrive.

Think of medication like wearing glasses. Glasses don't teach someone how to read but they make the words clearer so they can focus on learning. Similarly, ADHD medication helps regulate brain function, making it easier for your child to focus, manage emotions, and engage meaningfully with the world. It doesn't replace the hard work of teaching skills or providing emotional support but it can make your child more available to learn, grow, and connect. Refer to Appendix G for details on managing this complex decision.

BENEFITS OF MEDICATION

Proper ADHD medication can help in many ways, including:

Cognitive and Emotional Benefits

- Improving focus and attention regulation (American Academy of Pediatrics, 2019)
- Enhancing working memory and processing speed (National Institute of Mental Health, n.d.)
- Supporting emotional regulation and stability (Cleveland Clinic, n.d.; Neuroscience News, n.d.)

Behavioral and Social Benefits

- Reducing hyperactivity and impulsivity (NYU Langone Health, n.d.)
- Lowering irritability and obsessive tendencies (Cleveland Clinic, n.d.; Neuroscience News, n.d.; NYU Langone Health, n.d.)
- Reducing disruptive, aggressive, or noncompliant behavior (Cleveland Clinic, n.d.; Neuroscience News, n.d.; NYU Langone Health, n.d.)
- Increasing acceptance by peers (ADDitude Magazine, n.d.; NYU Langone Health, n.d.)

Functional Life Improvements

- Improving academic and workplace performance (ADDitude Magazine, n.d.; National Institutes of Health, n.d.)
- Enhancing driving skills and reducing accidents (National Institutes of Health, n.d.)
- Supporting consistent routines (ADHD Awareness Month, n.d.)
- Reducing family conflict (ADHD Awareness Month, n.d.)

Medication is a tool to help your child access these benefits, but it works best as part of a broader plan that includes skill-building strategies, supportive relationships, and a nurturing environment.

WHEN TO TALK TO YOUR CHILD ABOUT ADHD AND MEDICATION

Parents often wonder when and how to discuss ADHD and medication with their children. Keep in mind that by the time they reach about 10 or 11 years old, most children have likely heard ADHD mentioned at school, on TV, or in movies—often in less than positive ways. Additionally, children with access to the internet may come across an overwhelming amount of information—some factual and supportive—but some misleading or potentially detrimental.

As with other sensitive and important topics, educating your child about ADHD is often best coming from loving parents who can provide a supportive perspective and be available to answer questions and concerns. Start by asking your child what they already know and be prepared to offer a balanced, encouraging picture that empowers them to navigate their challenges. Later sections and chapters in this book provide further guidance to help you achieve this goal.

If your child is being tested for ADHD and is aware that not all children undergo such testing, they may feel concerned or upset. Explain that testing is a way to understand why certain challenges— such as learning, sitting still, or paying attention—may feel harder for them, and that the goal is to find ways to help. Use specific examples to support your explanation, and strive to remain nonjudgmental and compassionate.

If your child is taking medication, help them understand why. This not only aids in their acceptance but also allows them to give valuable feedback to you and their prescribing doctor about how the medication makes them feel. As they grow older, encourage them to communicate openly about their experiences and any misconceptions they may hear from peers or the media. Highlight their strengths and remind them that ADHD is just one part of their complex, amazing self.

Framing ADHD as just one aspect of who your child is—no more defining than being left-handed or having a passion for art—can help normalize the condition. When introducing medication, use simple, positive language to explain its purpose. For example:

> "This medicine helps your brain work its best. It's like wearing glasses—it doesn't change who you are, but it makes things clearer so you can focus and feel calmer. That's why we still practice strategies to manage challenges—because 'pills don't teach skills.'"

By involving your child in these discussions and decisions, you can help them feel empowered, confident, and ready to take an active role in their treatment journey.

YOUR PERSPECTIVE—AND WHY DOES IT MATTER?

By now, you may be feeling overwhelmed or saddened by the challenges your child is facing. Many parents in my workshops express regret or even guilt about how they've spoken to or interacted with their child in the past. I've heard comments like:

> "I just assumed he was lazy. Now I see he was trying hard but couldn't keep all the thoughts in his head at once."

> "I focused so much on his messy room that I didn't realize the stress it was causing all of us."

> "My dad pushed me hard, so I thought that's what I needed to do. But it's not working, and we fight all the time. I see now that my approach isn't helping."

> "I was putting all the pressure on my son to change, not realizing how much of the struggle came from what, how, and when we were expecting him to do things. I see we need to make changes, too."

Your perspective as a parent is the most critical factor in your efforts to support your child. These school years can be incredibly tough for a child with ADHD. Family members, teachers, and peers may, intentionally or not, send messages that your child isn't "good enough." External forces often dictate how many successful experiences your child has each day.

It's essential to maintain a "disability perspective." No one likes to think of their child as having a disability but acknowledging and accepting that ADHD is a real and impactful challenge is key. This doesn't mean lowering your expectations; it means believing the diagnosis, recognizing the obstacles, and adjusting your approach as needed to meet your child where they are.

As difficult as it is for you to watch, imagine what it feels like for your child not to be in full control of their actions, thoughts, or attention. They are not lazy—they often struggle with fear, avoidance, or skill deficits. Even when they want to focus, their brains may simply refuse to cooperate.

This daily negativity can weigh heavily on their sense of optimism and capability. As parents, we must counterbalance these messages by helping our children discover their strengths, passions, and interests— those things that light them up and drive them. These are the keys to helping them not only survive but thrive, especially in school, where they often have little choice about what they must focus on.

Your job is to stack the deck in their favor, ensuring they experience as many positive moments as possible. Strengthening your child means not only building their skills but also adjusting your expectations and environment to reduce unnecessary stress. Together, these efforts can help your child grow into their best self, feeling supported, capable, and understood.

PARENTING WITH CONNECTION AND COMPASSION

I once had a father tell me that his father was very strict. He recalled spending hours on school assignments, driven by wanting to please his father and fearing the consequences if he didn't. He managed to "get through," but at what emotional cost? While he succeeded in completing the work, he later realized that "getting through" didn't mean he was learning in a way that truly inspired him or aligned with his passions. The pressure to perform left him feeling disconnected—not just from his schoolwork but also from his father. As he reflected, he resented the lack of understanding and compassion he had received as a child and lamented the relationship he never got to have.

As I discussed in the introduction, each parent must find peace with their upbringing and learn to "parent the child they have." Recognizing and understanding your child's struggles—not just academically but emotionally—allows you to foster connection, compassion, and growth that supports who they are, not who we expect them to be. By reframing how we interpret behavior and expectations, we can create an environment where children feel seen, understood, and empowered to thrive.

WHAT IF YOU HAVE ADHD TOO?

Parenting is challenging under any circumstances, but when you're also managing ADHD yourself, it adds an extra layer of complexity. Staying organized, following routines, and managing emotional reactions can feel overwhelming, especially when helping your child navigate similar struggles.

The first step is recognizing how your own ADHD may be influencing your parenting. This awareness can deepen your empathy for your child while allowing you to develop strategies to support both of you. Getting proper support for your ADHD—whether through medication, coaching, or therapy—can make a significant difference. It's important to know that taking care of yourself isn't selfish; it's one of the most effective ways to support your family. Appendix H offers valuable insights and strategies to support you in parenting when you have ADHD.

IT'S ALL IN HOW YOU FRAME IT

Some of the world's most successful people credit ADHD as a key factor in their accomplishments. David Neeleman, founder of Jet-Blue Airlines, has said he "would never have been able to do this" without ADHD, noting how his unique perspective fueled his innovative approach to business. Musician will.i.am of the Black Eyed Peas, channels his ADHD-fueled creativity into excelling as a singer, producer, and entrepreneur. Journalist Lisa Ling has spoken about how her ADHD drives her relentless curiosity and passion for storytelling, enabling her to become a renowned journalist and broadcaster. Entrepreneur Sir Richard Branson has often attributed his adventurous spirit and ability to think outside the box to his ADHD. These individuals remind us that ADHD is not a limitation—it's a difference that can become a superpower when understood and harnessed.

As parents, your perspective can help your child see ADHD as just one part of who they are—not a flaw or deficit. In fact, the very traits that may frustrate you now could become their greatest strengths.

Here's a fresh way to reframe common ADHD traits:

- Hyperactive → full of energy
- Strong willed → tenacious, persistent, determined
- Daydreamer → creative, imaginative
- Daredevil → risk taker, adventurous
- Aggressive → assertive
- Slow processor → deep thinker
- Questions authority → independent thinker

- Lazy → laid back, relaxed
- Argumentative → persuasive
- Manipulative → great delegator
- Bossy → signs of leadership
- Distractible → curious, out-of-the-box thinker
- Poor sense of time → lives in the moment
- Hyperfocus → super productive, detail oriented

When you view your child through this lens, it becomes easier to see their potential. As I mentioned earlier, undiagnosed and untreated ADHD is disproportionately linked to challenges like undereducation, underemployment, and other negative outcomes. Yet, ADHD is also disproportionately common among successful entrepreneurs. This stark contrast underscores the critical importance of early intervention and ongoing support.

Ned Hallowell, author of *Driven to Distraction* (Hallowell & Ratey, 1995), describes people with ADHD as having "magnificent brains," comparing their brains to Ferraris with bicycle brakes. The challenge is to strengthen those brakes—and that's where your knowledge, support, and guidance make all the difference. Remind your child often of the power and beauty of their "magnificent brains."

YOU NEED A BLACK BELT IN PARENTING

As you know, parenting a child with ADHD is no ordinary challenge. Basic rules, structures, and reasoning that work for most children often fail to produce the desired results. To complicate matters, if you're unsure how best to respond to your child's erratic, frustrating, or challenging behaviors, you might inadvertently worsen the very behaviors you're trying to address.

When you find yourself holding back on your expectations because you're worried about how your child might react, it's important to know that you could unintentionally be teaching them that their emotions can be used to influence others. They might start to realize that throwing a tantrum or showing frustration gets people to back off—a habit that can be hard to unlearn.

During the National CHADD Conference in 2010, Russell Barkley (2010) said that

> The arguing, defiance, refusal is a learned behavior—not genetic, not biological. It arises out of a pattern of behavior we have understood for 40 years. The way parents manage the emotional gambits of the child may make the emotions of the child better or worse and may teach the kid that emotions are a tool to use on others.

In fact, research supports this. A study found that children whose parents avoided disciplinary actions out of fear of the child's response exhibited increased symptoms of ODD in the following year (Burke et al., 2008).

Parenting your child may require more effort and intentionality than most children need. That's why I say you need a *black belt in parenting*! Your child needs to lean on your strength, feel secure in your presence, and know you are a steady anchor amid their chaos, stress, and anxiety.

To do this, you must cultivate calm, consistency, and predictability in your parenting. There will be moments when your child seems to hate you, expressing frustration or anger. In those times, remember that beneath it all, they know you love them and are doing what you believe is necessary to be the parent they need. Embrace our mantra: *Parent the child you have.*

Over the next seven chapters, we methodically build a framework for strong, supportive, and empathic parenting. By understanding the motivations behind your child's behavior, you'll be better equipped to guide them in adapting to their environment with both compassion and effectiveness.

So, before diving into the next chapter, take a few days to observe your child with curiosity rather than judgment. For example, if your child doesn't come down when you call them for dinner, ask yourself:

- Are they hyperfocused on their activity?
- Do they intend to come but get distracted?
- Are they unaware how much time has passed since saying, "I'll be down in a minute"?
- Are they avoiding coming for a reason they're unable or afraid to share?

With knowledge, intention, and persistence, you'll develop the tools and confidence needed to support your child's growth and well-being. By embracing the philosophy of *parent the child you have*, you'll gain the confidence, skills, and strategies to trust your instincts and adapt to your child's unique needs. This is where your journey begins.

GUIDING THOUGHTS

- Maintain a disability perspective—acknowledge their challenges while you remember to embrace your child's strengths.
- Fair does not always mean equal—it means giving each child what they need to thrive.
- ADHD is not a lack of intelligence; it's a difference in how the brain works.
- Stay in the present and let your dreams for your child evolve as they do.
- Live your life out loud—share your process, not just the result.
- ADHD is not a problem of knowing what to do. It is a problem of doing what you know.
- ADHD is just one part of who your child is—it does not define them.
- *Parent the child you have.*

HOMEWORK

1. *Be an observer of yourself and your child*: Take note of your interactions—what you like and don't like. Observe how much unstructured time you spend together and what happens during that time. Notice behaviors that may align with the ADHD traits discussed in this chapter. The key here is to simply observe without judgment or worry about making changes—just notice.

2. *Write a letter to your child*: This letter is for your eyes only and will not be shared with your child. It's an opportunity to express unspoken thoughts and feelings. Start with what makes you angry or frustrated, then write about what makes you sad. Next, reflect on any fears or regrets you may have regarding your child. Finally, focus on the love and positive feelings you have—the special moments or qualities that make you feel good. Pour everything into this letter, including the frustrations and joys. Once you're ready, rip it up and let it go. Use this exercise to forgive yourself and your child and begin your new path forward.

3. *Start a binder for your child's records (if you haven't already)*: Use this binder to maintain a comprehensive history of important documents and information about your child. While it's hard to predict what you'll need in the future, keep in mind that organizations like the College Board (which governs the SAT, LSAT, MCAT, and ACT) require historical documentation for accommodation requests. This could be necessary even if your school has approved accommodations all along.

4. Suggested binder sections:

   – Doctors and professionals consulted (include contact information)

   – Professional evaluations

   – Medications (name, dosage, duration of use, and impact)

   – Report cards and progress reports

- Standardized testing results

- School communications

- IEP and/or 504 plans

- Yearly observations (milestones, concerns, and successes)

Always keep original copies for your records. What feels clear now may fade over time, and having organized documentation makes a world of difference.

5. *Post the Guiding Thoughts where you can see them daily*: Read them each day and reflect on how they align with your weekly goals and intentions. You may also choose to add your own "guiding thought" to keep yourself focused and inspired.

6. *Join my PTS Coaching newsletter*: https://bit.ly/newsletterpts and Facebook page: https://www.facebook.com/ptscoaching

KEY 2

CREATE CALM
Why It Matters More
Than You Think!

Leadership is a matter of having people look at you and gain confidence,
seeing how you react. If you're in control, they're in control.

—TOM LANDRY, HEAD COACH, DALLAS COWBOYS (1960–1988)

Do you ever find yourself, or perhaps your partner, saying things like "If you would just calm down . . ." or, "I find myself yelling and getting so frustrated"? If you're like many parents I know, you may start the day promising, at least to yourself, that this time you'll stay calm. It's so common to feel this way, especially when life feels chaotic, or your child's behaviors seem unmanageable. But somehow, life happens, and before you know it, the calm you promised yourself is out the window.

In the last chapter, I asked you to take a few days to simply observe how the broader description of ADHD and EF skills development is impacting various aspects of your child's life and your interactions together. In this chapter, we explore why calm matters so much and, more importantly, practical ways you can start creating it—even when it feels impossible.

WHAT ROLE DOES "CONTROL" PLAY IN PARENTING?

As much as many children might disagree, most parents are not interested in just being in charge or giving orders. Sure, it's nice to have things "our way" sometimes, but the parents I work with genuinely want to live in a happy, peaceful coexistence with their children: one filled with laughter and joy, along with respect, learning, and a bit of hard work.

Yet, pretty early on, many parents find themselves in a position where they have to give orders, set limits, and control much of the activity and decision making in the household. Why? Because creating a safe, structured environment where learning can happen and daily essentials get done requires some level of parental guidance and authority.

Some children are like *clay*: flexible and adaptable. You can guide them with gentle, loving hands, and they'll mostly follow along. They may complain or resist occasionally, but they eventually do what's asked.

Other children are more like *cactus flowers*: beautiful and sweet on the inside, but not very flexible and sometimes prickly. These strong-willed children aren't easily guided and often resist being rushed or pushed. They open up on their own terms and timelines. For these children, what feels like a reasonable request—eat your dinner, clean your room, do your homework—can feel like an unwelcome challenge, if not an outright battle.

Parenting requires finding the balance between "control" and "controlling." Without this balance, households often become filled with fighting, chaos, and stress. It's exhausting—for both you and your child.

Control in parenting isn't about micromanaging or overpowering your child. Instead, it's about thoughtfully deciding when to take charge and when to let go of the reins. We explore the "when" and the "how" of this balance later in the book. But for now, let's look more closely at the impact control—or the lack of it—has on our children's lives.

THE IMPACT OF EF ON LEARNING AND PERFORMING

Take a moment to imagine what these challenges might feel like for your child every day. It's like having a chaotic mix of colors swirling together in their brain—beautiful but overwhelming all at once. These traits impact more than just their ability to focus or follow through; they influence their emotions, relationships, and even how they see themselves. ADHD affects each child differently. As the saying goes, "If you've met one person with ADHD, you've met one person with ADHD." Every child's experience is unique, but certain traits tend to create the greatest challenges for many children with ADHD. Remembering this can help you approach your child with greater understanding and patience as we continue building strategies together.

Now, look at the graphic (Figure 2.1). For some students, even this third-grade math problem can feel overwhelming. Imagine the teacher reading the problem aloud to the class. First, *attention*—can your child tune out all distractions and focus solely on the problem? Second, *working memory*—can they hold the details in their mind and connect them to what they already know about solving math word problems? Then comes *planning and organizing*—do they know which steps to take first? As for *flexibility*, perhaps they're thinking, "Why do I have to show all the steps? I can figure this out in my head!"

Now consider *processing speed*. Some children might start comparing the problem to their own life experiences: "She has to be at school at 8:30. I have to be at school at 7:30. That's not fair." Or, "I didn't even get to eat breakfast today—I'm starving." Other students

FIGURE 2.1:
Impact on Executive Function Skills

The impact of *executive functions* on learning & performing

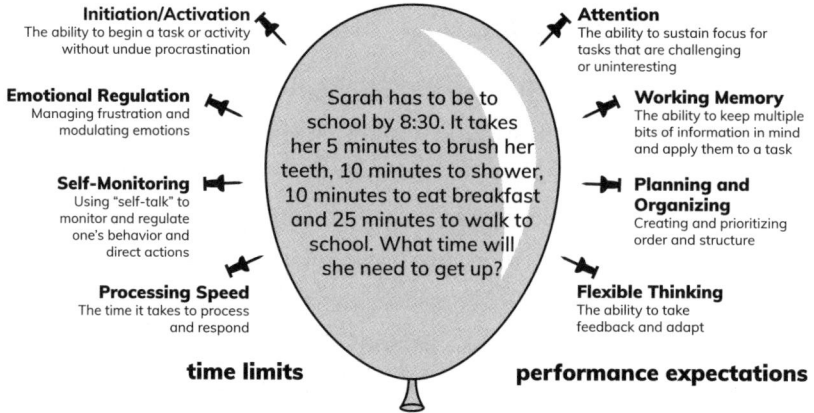

Initiation/Activation
The ability to begin a task or activity without undue procrastination

Emotional Regulation
Managing frustration and modulating emotions

Self-Monitoring
Using "self-talk" to monitor and regulate one's behavior and direct actions

Processing Speed
The time it takes to process and respond

Attention
The ability to sustain focus for tasks that are challenging or uninteresting

Working Memory
The ability to keep multiple bits of information in mind and apply them to a task

Planning and Organizing
Creating and prioritizing order and structure

Flexible Thinking
The ability to take feedback and adapt

Sarah has to be to school by 8:30. It takes her 5 minutes to brush her teeth, 10 minutes to shower, 10 minutes to eat breakfast and 25 minutes to walk to school. What time will she need to get up?

time limits

performance expectations

© Cindy Goldrich

may need to slow everything down and process the problem at their own pace, replaying the details in their head. While many classmates have already started working, some students are still piecing together the information in their minds, struggling to catch up.

For *self-monitoring*, are they aware that their peers have already taken out paper and pencils to begin? And *emotional regulation*—perhaps they're getting agitated, thinking, "I hate math problems!" Then, the teacher adds, "You have 5 minutes, and this is a pop quiz that counts toward your grade." The pressure intensifies.

UNDERSTANDING THE PRESSURE ON EFS

Imagine the balloon representing the mental space your child needs to compute the answer to a math problem, keep track of a homework assignment, or decide how to respond in a social situation. Every effort to use an EF increases the pressure inside the balloon. When children face time limits, performance demands, or unexpected challenges, their mental resources can be quickly overwhelmed, leading to frustration, avoidance, or shutdown.

Why does this happen? When stress intensifies, the brain's *amygdala*, which governs emotional reactions, takes over. The brain shifts into *survival mode*, prioritizing immediate safety over logical thinking. What happens in survival mode? The familiar responses of *fight, flight,* or *freeze* kick in. Increasingly, experts are also recognizing another response: *fawn/fib*. This occurs when someone seeks to escape harm in the short term by appeasing or pleasing the person they perceive as a threat to keep them happy.

During this survival response, the *prefrontal cortex*—the part of the brain responsible for EFS like planning, organizing, and regulating emotions—disengages to prioritize rapid, instinctive reactions. This is why your child might feel like they "just can't think straight" during moments of heightened stress. Without access to the thinking brain, learning, problem solving, and decision making become nearly impossible.

USING THE EMOTION THERMOMETER

One way to support your child in managing stress is by creating an *emotion thermometer* (Figure 2.2). This visual tool helps children identify and label their emotions as they escalate. Work with your child to create the thermometer during a calm moment, using examples from their daily life to describe how they feel, think, and act at each level—from calm and relaxed at the bottom to frustrated, angry, or overwhelmed at the top.

How to Use the Emotion Thermometer

1. *Teach during calm moments*: Explain that emotions, like the weather, change throughout the day, and the thermometer helps track these changes.

FIGURE 2.2:
Emotion Thermometer

Emotion thermometer

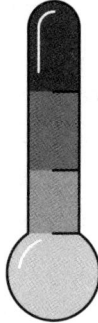

how you **feel**	how you **act**	result
Furious Enraged Boiling mad	Swear / curse / yell Become physical Shut down	Can't reason Anger others Risk punishment
Angry	Raise voice Say angry things	Not able to listen Trouble thinking
Upset Annoyed Frustrated	Calmly express feelings Act annoyed or upset	Can still listen Willing to compromise and reach solution
Calm	Happy Content	Productive Able to work with others

Without calm there is no learning!

© Cindy Goldrich

2. *Practice identifying feelings*: Ask your child, "Where do you think you are on the thermometer right now?"

3. *Plan calming strategies*: Help them match their "temperature" to appropriate coping tools. For instance, if they're "a little frustrated," they might try deep breathing, but if they're "about to burst," a break and use of their "Calm Kit" (details to come later in this chapter) might work better.

The emotion thermometer is a flexible tool you can revisit regularly. It's not only helpful at home but can also be a supportive resource for teachers or caregivers.

STRESS AS THE GATEKEEPER
TO LEARNING

What happens when you try to motivate your child in these moments? Maybe you offer a reward or consequence—what we often call the carrot or the stick: "If you do this, then this will happen, but if you do that, then this will happen." While well intended, this approach can add stress and pressure, potentially pushing some children further into survival mode. I think of stress as the gatekeeper to learning. Even mild stress increases cortisol levels in the prefrontal cortex, impairing EF for most people. While it might seem that adding a little pressure could motivate and improve performance, this is rarely the case for children with ADHD. Think of the balloon as representing the cognitive space they have to use in their brains at that moment. Our goal is always to keep that balloon inflated and resilient.

We explore the impact of rewards and consequences more deeply later in the book, but for now, consider how these interactions might feel for your child in the moment.

It's not just academics that can overwhelm your child. They may also feel similarly overwhelmed during sports, social activities, or even routine tasks like cleaning their room or getting ready for bed. The cumulative effect of navigating these challenges throughout the day can leave them exhausted, dysregulated, and prone to emotional outbursts.

As Russell Barkley (2012) explains, this phenomenon can be likened to having a "limited fuel tank" for self-regulation. For children with ADHD, that tank depletes more rapidly because of inherent deficits in *emotional regulation* and other EFS. Sleep, nutrition, and exercise also play a critical role in replenishing this fuel tank, determining how much energy your child has available to manage daily challenges.

The more your child is in situations requiring EFS that are weak for the task, the more their self-regulation resources are depleted. After a day of school, your child may not only be tired but also dysregulated and much more prone to their ADHD symptoms. Imagine your child's body as a fuel tank, with their face being the fuel gauge. If that tank is running on empty and they're taxed further without an opportunity to refuel, even minor requests can lead to conflict.

THE POWER OF CALM

When children lose their cool or don't do what we feel they need to be doing—or, worse, if they are doing things we feel they shouldn't be doing—what feelings does this conjure up in most parents? Frustration, impatience, fear, anxiety, even anger? These emotions often stem from a deep desire to help our children succeed, avoid harm, or simply make it through the day without chaos. But what do our children very often need most from us at these times? Someone who is calm, in control, safe to be with, and accepting of who they are and what they are experiencing.

This is not easy—especially when you feel a clock ticking due to work needing to be done, medication wearing off, other people's needs pulling at you, or your own emotional regulation being stretched thin. Yet, it's crucial to remember that our emotional reactions can set the tone for the entire interaction.

Consider this:

- Your wise lectures
- Your pleading and bribing
- Your reassurance
- Your words of wisdom
- Your threats of pending doom

None of these can be properly heard or processed by your child when they are already overwhelmed or dysregulated. While these reactions may feel natural or even justified at the moment, they rarely achieve the desired outcome.

Without calm, no learning can take place, and no problems can be solved. This simple truth underscores how transformative your own emotional regulation can be—not just for navigating tough moments but for building the foundation of a new home where learning and growth are possible.

With each *key*, starting here, I am going to introduce an element to our new home. Just as with any home, we must begin with a solid foundation. For us, that foundation is *CALM* (Figure 2.3).

BUILDING OUR NEW HOME

There are three ingredients to the foundation of our Calm home.

1. Be the Change You Want to See in Your Child: Be CALM

Being calm is a tremendous challenge for many parents—or perhaps for your partner or co-parent. Instead of focusing first on shaping and changing your child's behavior, you need to focus instead on shaping and changing your own. You must resolve to model self-control and self-regulation. And yes, I know all of this is very hard.

Give yourself some grace. This is a family system—your child's reaction impacts yours, just as yours impacts theirs. There will be times when you lose your calm. That's called being human. The goal isn't perfection; it's progress. Calm doesn't mean silent or disengaged—it means responding from a thoughtful, mindful, and measured place. Others may trigger feelings in us or push our buttons, but how we respond is our choice. We own our feelings and our reactions to them.

For each person, how we achieve calm may look different. However, here are a few strategies that many people find helpful:

- *Slow down and take a breath*: A real, calming breath. Slow, deep, controlled breathing can change your brain's chemistry and lower your blood pressure. Yoga is an excellent way to practice this kind of breathing. In just 1 minute, you can experience a difference.

FIGURE 2.3:
House: Calm

Building our home

calm

© Cindy Goldrich

- *Count to 10 slowly and rhythmically in your head*: This is not the same as saying to your child, "I'm counting to 10, and then you'd better . . . " This counting is for you—to slow yourself down and give yourself time to calm.
- *Lower and soften your voice*: When speaking softly, expressing extreme emotion becomes much more difficult. A soft tone can shift the entire mood.
- *Notice your body language*: Try sitting down or putting your hands at your sides. This will help you appear less agitated or threatening.
- *Politely, without judgment, remove yourself from your child if needed*: Be clear that you're not rejecting or avoiding your child but taking time to compose yourself. Discuss this strategy during a calm moment, so your child understands it's a way to model calming techniques—not a sign of anger or withdrawal.

Also, remember that *without calm, no learning can take place.* Calm doesn't mean staying quiet but being deliberate in how you respond:

mindful, thoughtful, and measured. Beyond physical strategies, the language you use when correcting or encouraging your child is just as important. We focus much more on communication in Key 4, but for now, try to notice the tone and words you use. You catch more flies with honey than vinegar—and you'll get more from your child when they can safely hear what you're saying. Replace *shame, blame,* and *criticism* with *tolerance, empathy,* and *support.* For example, instead of saying, "Why can't you ever get your homework done on time?" try "I see that you're struggling to finish your homework. What can we do to make this easier for you?"

Once you begin to change your own behavior, control your anxiety, and become the calm, steady presence your child can count on, you'll see this shift ripple throughout your home. Calm starts with you, but it doesn't stop there. Modeling self-regulation sets the stage for your child to develop those same skills over time.

Remember: Without calm, no learning can take place, and no problems can be solved. Post a sign in a visible place in your home with a reminder: "Your Calm Is Your Power." If you find staying calm particularly challenging because you have ADHD yourself, turn to Appendix H for additional insights and strategies tailored to your needs.

2. Parent the Child You Have!

This philosophy will help you keep perspective as you react and respond to your child.

- *Let go of expectations tied to a timeline*: Remember, your child may be up to 30% developmentally delayed in some areas. This doesn't mean they won't reach their potential—it just might take more time than their peers.
- *Let your dreams for your child evolve as they evolve*: Your child will surprise and delight you as they grow in ways you might not yet imagine.
- *Slow things down and reduce certain expectations, at least for now*: Doors

don't always close forever if your child doesn't do everything now. Let go of the myth that they'll miss out on major opportunities if they don't start certain things right away. History is full of late bloomers: Chef Julia Child didn't learn to cook until her 40s, Grandma Moses began painting at 75 and became one of the most famous American painters, and Col. Harland Sanders used his first Social Security check to launch the Kentucky Fried Chicken franchise at 65. Sometimes, it takes a little extra time for true growth to flourish.

• *Surround yourself with photos of your child that make you smile*: Not the perfect portraits, but the candid shots that capture them living life, being happy, and embracing who they are.

• *Let go of opinions and judgments from others*: Many people won't understand your unique challenges and efforts. For those who do, no explanation is needed. For those who don't, no explanation will ever be enough.

3. Teach Your Child How to Be Calm

There will be times when stress, anxiety, or anger disrupts a calm environment. While some children manage frustration, change, or disappointment relatively well, others may struggle—especially children with ADHD, who often experience delays in emotional regulation. For these children, emotions can escalate from 0 to 100 in the blink of an eye.

Teaching your child why calm matters and how to achieve it can make a world of difference. Choose a relaxed moment—when no immediate problems are pressing—to introduce these strategies. The goal is to help your child understand, value, and take ownership of their emotions and actions. Don't worry if you're not ready to start yet; tools for these conversations will come as we progress through this book.

UNDERSTANDING SLEEP'S ROLE IN CALM

A well-rested brain is a regulated brain. Sleep is essential for growth, stress reduction, learning, and emotional well-being. The American Academy of Pediatrics (AAP) recommends:

- Children ages 3–10 should get 10–12 hours of sleep each night.
- Children ages 11–12 should aim for 10 hours.
- Teenagers need about 9 hours of sleep.

Unfortunately, many teens don't get enough sleep due to homework, extracurricular activities, jobs, and screen time. Adding to the challenge is the natural shift in adolescents' circadian rhythm, which makes it harder for them to fall asleep earlier in the evening. They aren't staying up late just to test your patience—their biological clocks have shifted.

Research shows that when high schools adjust start times to align better with teens' sleep needs, students perform better academically, experience improved mental health, and even become safer drivers!

RECOGNIZING EMOTIONAL CUES

Helping your child identify and respond to their emotions is key to managing stress. Start by gently naming what you notice:

- "You seem tired—do you think that's making things harder right now?"
- "I wonder if you're feeling frustrated because of what happened earlier."

Rather than telling them how they feel, ask with curiosity or offer a neutral observation. This fosters emotional awareness and teaches them to pause and reflect on their state of mind.

You can also help your child recognize the "warning signs" of building stress in their body or thoughts. Does their heart race? Is there tightness in their chest? Identifying these signals early can empower them to take steps to calm down before emotions overwhelm them.

MANAGING TRIGGERS

Certain environments or situations might consistently overwhelm your child. When possible, help them avoid these triggers, or proactively prepare them to navigate challenging settings. For example:

- If visiting Aunt Susan's house to play with cousin Tim usually doesn't go well, it may be better to skip the visit for now and focus on developing coping strategies for future interactions.
- For situations they can't avoid, proactively plan modifications. Discuss taking breaks, choosing a different seat, or preparing an exit strategy ahead of time.

A prearranged signal or code word can be a game-changer. Whether on a playdate or at school, this allows your child to discreetly communicate when they need a moment to reset.

Sometimes, a quick reset at home can make a difference. Sharing a snack, light conversation, or a short game like Connect Four can defuse tension. This isn't about "rewarding" your child for being upset but about helping them regain calm. Once the storm has passed, you can revisit the issue when everyone is in a better frame of mind.

CREATING A CALM KIT

A "Calm Kit" is a practical tool to help your child reset. Younger children might benefit from a physical box filled with comforting items, while older children may prefer a virtual Calm Kit—a list of strategies or apps they can access.

Physical Calm Kit Ideas

- Stickers, crayons, or a small sketch pad
- Bubbles (great for calming breaths)
- Play-Doh or a stress ball
- Laminated cards with fun games like I Spy

Virtual Calm Kit Ideas for Older Children

- A calming playlist
- A meditation app like Calm or Headspace
- Positive affirmations or gratitude lists
- A private journal or notes app for expressing feelings

Creating the kit together is just as valuable as using it. It encourages your child to take ownership of their self-soothing strategies.

THE MIND-BODY CONNECTION

Teach your child to recognize how emotions show up in their body. For example:

- Anger might feel like heat in their chest.
- Anxiety could feel like butterflies in their stomach.

When children recognize these physical cues, they can begin to manage their emotional responses.

Mind–body strategies might include:

- *Naming emotions*: Help them label their feelings (e.g., "I feel nervous") to build emotional awareness.
- *Deep breathing*: To calm your body and mind, practice simple techniques such as inhaling for four counts and exhaling for four counts.
- *Body scanning*: Help them notice where they feel tension and practice releasing it through relaxation exercises.

By introducing these strategies and tools, you're not only helping your child learn to self-regulate but also fostering resilience and independence. It's important to remember that learning to calm down is a skill that takes time, practice, and patience—but it's worth the effort for both you and your child.

FINAL THOUGHTS ON CALM

Over the years, I've heard from countless parents about how the simple shift in their own approach—from justifying yelling to focusing on staying calm—transformed the dynamics of their families. Stress levels dropped, challenges became more manageable, and, most importantly, loving connections grew stronger.

That said, this process may also require you to adjust your expectations—at least for now. You might find you need to increase your tolerance for your child's frustration when they are bored, disappointed, or angry. And sometimes, the best thing you can do isn't solving their problem but simply being present and helping them navigate their feelings.

Remember: Calm is your power. It's the foundation we're building together. Give yourself a few days to digest and practice these concepts before moving on to the next key. Progress doesn't happen overnight—it's built step-by-step. There's no magic you'll find at the end of the book to replace the effort and intention you bring to each moment.

The work starts here. And it starts with calm.

GUIDING THOUGHTS

- Without calm, no learning can take place, and no problems can be solved.
- Stress and pressure can shut some children down instead of motivating them.
- We cannot control others' behavior but we can control our own.

• Modeling calm behavior and managing your own stress are essential to teaching your child how to regulate their emotions and reactions.

HOMEWORK

1. Discuss with your child the value of calming down and why it's important. Choose a calm, stress-free moment for this conversation to avoid it feeling punitive or judgmental. Reflect on the calming strategies from this chapter and begin incorporating them into your daily routine. Collaborate with your child to create a physical or virtual Calm Kit using items or strategies from this chapter that work for them. Practice using the toolkit together during calm times.

2. Create a "Top Five" list of calming strategies for yourself as a personal reminder. Place it somewhere visible—on your desk, bathroom mirror, or phone wallpaper—to reinforce your efforts daily. Remember, forming new habits takes time and repetition, so be patient with yourself!

3. Explore mindfulness or meditation resources in your area or online. For more guidance and ideas, consider reading books like Manuela Mischke-Reeds's (2015) *8 Keys to Practicing Mindfulness* or Susan Kaiser Greenland's (2010) *The Mindful Child*.

KEY 3

STRENGTHENING CONNECTION
A Lifeline for Trust, Growth, and Resilience

Alone we can do so little; together we can do so much.

—HELEN KELLER (1929)

Remember when your children were just cute and cuddly? Sometimes, it's hard to channel those thoughts, especially if you're going through a particularly difficult time. Hopefully, you have several fond photos, memories, and thoughts close enough for you to tap into, even during the most frustrating moments.

Stress or chaos between you and your child may not be a big concern for some of you. For others, it may feel like an ever-present tension: How will the morning go? What will happen when they get home from school? Will the playdate work out? Perhaps your child has a hard time relaxing enough to be available to listen, learn, or adapt to new situations.

In the previous chapter, we explored why calm matters so much (because without calm, no learning can take place!) and practical ways to help you and your child stay or return to calm. Remember, change takes time, practice, and conscious effort. The strategies you're implementing are already laying the foundation for transformation.

Now, let's build on that foundation by focusing on connection. Your relationship with your child is the heart of your home, providing them with the trust, stability, and reassurance they need to navigate life's challenges and thrive. Just as calm is the foundation, connection is the core—a lifeline for your child's growth and resilience (Figure 3.1).

WHAT IS YOUR OBJECTIVE IN BEING A PARENT?

Most parents I work with are genuinely loving, caring people who want the very best for their children. Some have gone to extraordinary lengths to become parents; others have had this greatness thrust upon them. Whatever your path, take a moment to consider your ultimate goals as a parent. What traits do you want your child to develop?

FIGURE 3.1:
House: Connection

Building our home

connection

calm

© Cindy Goldrich

When I ask parents this question, I often hear answers like responsible, independent, resilient, confident, respectful, self-aware, and self-disciplined. I always like to include one more: emotionally connected. Most parents want their children to share a bond of love and warmth with them and their families. But where does happiness fit in? And who is responsible for it? This is a more complex and important question than it may seem.

For instance, imagine your 7-year-old is disappointed that they can't go to the park because there's thunder and lightning. You suggest alternatives, but they're inconsolable, crying and yelling, "It's not fair!" You might wonder: Is it your job to make them happy in this moment, or is it to help them develop the coping skills to manage disappointment? These moments are less about ensuring happiness and more about teaching resilience.

Jonas Salk, the inventor of the polio vaccine, is often quoted in saying "Good parents give their children roots and wings. Roots to know where home is and wings to fly away and exercise what has been taught to them." It's not about shielding them from every disappointment but about equipping them with the tools to navigate challenges. True happiness comes from the pride of accomplishments, not from isolated experiences.

THE IMPORTANCE OF CONNECTION

All children need strong bonds to grow up emotionally healthy. Children with ADHD face unique challenges that sometimes make forming these bonds more difficult but no less essential. As we discussed earlier, the world often sends children with ADHD negative messages: "Stop tapping that pencil," "Why can't you pay attention?" "Get started on your work already!" At school and home, these children often receive more criticism than encouragement. On top of that, they might compare themselves to their peers and feel inadequate, which can compound their feelings of stress and frustration.

Stress exacerbates ADHD symptoms by shutting down the brain's EFS, where impulse control, emotional regulation, and problem solving occur. As we've discussed, when the amygdala takes over, children go into survival mode, making it harder to learn, reason, or connect.

And here's the paradox: Just when children seem the most difficult—aggressive, withdrawn, or defiant—they often need connection the most. All children, even teens, crave connection with their parents, though they may not always show it. You are your child's favorite person—their "favorite toy"! This holds true even during the teenage years when they may seem to push you away. They don't need you to always teach, advise, or correct them. Sometimes, they simply want to feel that you trust them to figure things out while you remain a supportive witness. When they don't feel connected, they may seek your attention in negative ways—often unconsciously—preferring negative interactions to no interaction at all.

The key is to ensure your positive interactions are more animated, engaging, and frequent than any moments of reprimand or correction. Nurturing and building a strong relationship goes beyond simply paying attention—it's about creating a bond that reinforces trust and security. As actor and author Henry Winkler shared during an interview on MSNBC's *Morning Joe* in 2014, "A child knows they are not doing well, you don't need to remind them. All you need to do is keep that child buoyed. Because when you are not doing well, your self-image plummets to your ankles." For children with ADHD, acceptance, encouragement, and positive attention are not luxuries— they are necessities. These elements help them build "armor," fostering a belief in themselves and a hopeful vision of their future.

I once came across a greeting card that perfectly captured this idea. It featured a kitten looking into a mirror, with a lion reflected back. The caption read, "What matters most is how you see yourself." As parents, we have the profound opportunity to shape how our children see themselves, helping them develop a positive internal voice by being their strongest external support.

BUILDING CONNECTION THROUGH ONE-ON-ONE TIME

Deepening your connection with your child takes intentional effort, but it doesn't have to be overwhelming. I suggest setting a realistic and achievable goal: Spend 20 minutes once a week with each of your children for the next 6 weeks. Of course, I hope that this experience will be so meaningful and enjoyable that it becomes a lifelong habit.

This one-on-one time is not just for the child with ADHD—it's for each of your children. It's about building and strengthening individual relationships. And "one-on-one" means one parent with one child, without siblings or other distractions.

Planning One-On-One Time

- *Plan the time with them in advance*: This is a great way to let them know they are important enough to be on your calendar and ensure you're carving out the time.
- *Make it nonproductive time*: Let your child choose the activity, whether it's playing a game, drawing, or just talking. This is an opportunity to take an interest in something they like, even if it's not something you enjoy. Learn about the characters in their favorite video game or let them teach you how to master the next level. Children feel great when they can teach you something for a change.
- *Have extra patience and tolerance*: Do your best to refrain from giving directions or making corrections. Allow them to lead. Focus on the positive and catch them in the act of doing something good.
- *Be fully present*: Set aside distractions, such as phones or chores.

Over time, these moments create a reservoir of positive experiences to draw from during more challenging periods. Connection builds trust, encourages open communication, and reinforces your child's sense of worth.

STRENGTHENING BONDS THROUGH SHARED SIGNALS AND VISUAL CUES

Sometimes words aren't the most effective way to communicate—especially in moments of stress or chaos. A secret family signal can serve as a subtle, private way to build connection and provide reassurance. This might be a hand gesture, a small sign, or even a silly phrase that only your family knows. Think of it as a secret code that says, "I'm here for you" or "We've got this."

Creating this signal can be a fun, collaborative activity. Sit down as a family and brainstorm what your special signal could be. Once you've decided, practice using it in low-stress situations so it becomes second nature when you really need it. Whether it's a discreet hand gesture at the dinner table or a quick tap on the shoulder during a hectic moment, this signal can strengthen your bond and remind your child that they're not alone.

In addition to shared signals, visual reminders can be a powerful way to reinforce connection. A framed photo of a joyful family moment or an image that makes you smile can serve as a daily touchpoint for positivity. Place this photo somewhere prominent—perhaps on the fridge, a bedside table, or your child's desk. To enhance its impact, add a short, affirming phrase like "We've got this" or "Together, we thrive."

Whether through a shared signal or a treasured photo, these practices create a sense of connection and belonging for your child. For children with ADHD, who may struggle with emotional regulation, such reminders can ground them and reinforce their feelings of safety and connection.

THE FORMULA FOR EFFECTIVE PRAISE

Praise is a powerful tool, but for it to truly build your child's self-esteem and motivation, it must be specific, sincere, and focused on effort. Research has shown that in families with a high incidence of noncompliance, there tends to be less active positive recognition and encouragement of good behavior—even when that good behavior exists. As a parent, it's up to you to balance the negative messages your child receives throughout the day, including those they tell themselves.

To visualize this, try the following exercise: Start the day with 10 bracelets or rubber bands on your left wrist. Each time you praise your child, move one to your right wrist. If you correct or reprimand them—even nicely—move one back to your left wrist. At the end of the day, check which wrist has more. It's a simple way to see if your praises outweigh your corrections and remind yourself of the importance of positive reinforcement.

Carol Dweck's (2006) research shows that praising effort rather than intelligence fosters a growth mindset, encouraging children to take risks and persevere. For more support on encouraging a "growth mindset," check out my talk, "Skills for Success," at https://bit.ly/ptsskillsforsuccess.

Here's a simple formula for impactful praise—the three Ns:
1. *Notice* what your child is doing well.
2. *Name* the specific quality or effort you observe.
3. *Nourish* them with warmth and sincerity.

For example:
- Instead of saying, "Good job," try "I see how much effort you put into finishing that puzzle. You're really persistent!"
- Nonverbal feedback, such as a smile or a hug, can also reinforce connection and acknowledgment.

CELEBRATE SMALL MOMENTS

Connection doesn't have to come from grand gestures. Everyday moments—reading a book together, sharing a joke, or cooking a meal—can become cherished memories that deepen your bond.

When your child comes home from school, resist the urge to ask, "How was your day?"—a question that can sometimes feel overwhelming or stressful, much like being asked about work after a long day. Instead, give them space to reconnect casually. Later, consider asking, "What went well today?" This opens the door to positive sharing without adding pressure. For more on this approach, I recommend the book *Stop Asking "How Was Your Day?"* (2021) by Daniel Crawford.

As Trace Adkins (2011) sings in "Just Fishin," a father and daughter go fishing together, and the act is about more than catching fish; it's about creating memories. In the same way, your shared moments create a foundation of trust and connection for your child.

FINAL THOUGHTS

Connection is your child's lifeline to resilience, growth, and joy. It's built in moments big and small, in the way you praise, listen, and spend time together. As Maya Angelou said, "I've learned that people will forget what you said, people will forget what you did, but people will never forget how you made them feel" (Angelou, 1993). Your love and support are the foundation of everything your child will become.

GUIDING THOUGHTS

- Regular time together gives you the best opportunity to teach and guide your child. Connection grows with time and shared moments, allowing you to build deeper, long-term bonds.
- While negative feedback might stop behavior, positive feedback inspires growth.

- Praise with impact: notice, name, and nourish.
- Our children are always watching—let your actions and tone model acceptance and encouragement.
- Deep connection is a family lifeline, fostering resilience, trust, and growth.

HOMEWORK

1. *Plan one-on-one time*: Use the guidelines outlined in this chapter to schedule and enjoy meaningful moments with your child.
2. *Reflect on connection*: After your one-on-one time, jot down one thing you learned about your child and one moment that felt meaningful to you.
3. *Frame a family photo*: Choose a picture that makes you smile and frame it with the saying "Praise every day." Use it as a daily reminder to encourage and support your child.
4. *Track your praises*: Try the bracelet or rubber band exercise from this chapter. Start with 10 bracelets on one wrist and move one to the other wrist each time you praise your child. Move one back if you correct them. Reflect on your balance of praise versus corrections by the end of the day.
5. *Celebrate strengths*: Ask your child to think of 10 words that describe them. Then, ask them to choose the five they are most proud of. Be prepared to tell them three stories of when they demonstrated some positive traits, providing specific examples of when they were at their best.

KEY 4

CULTIVATE GOOD
COMMUNICATION
The Road to Cooperation,
Compliance, and Positive Action

Courage is what it takes to stand up and speak; courage is also what it takes to sit down and listen.

—WINSTON CHURCHILL

Many parents struggle to get their children to listen, comply, or behave respectfully. Do you sometimes feel like you're locked in an endless battle over even the simplest requests? Or maybe you worry that your child isn't working up to their potential, and no matter what you say, it doesn't seem to make a difference.

Have you ever gotten into one of those "yes/no" battles with your child? If you're like most parents, the answer is yes. But here's the truth: these battles rarely end with your child saying, "Okay, you win." I like to think of these moments as a game of choosing teams for baseball. The two captains take turns placing their hands on the bat, working their way up until one of them finally wins. In power struggles with our children, every time we "move up the bat" by escalating the argument, our child does the same. It's exhausting, isn't it?

Here's the key: You don't have to play the game. You can drop the bat. Dropping the bat doesn't mean giving in; it means stepping back, reassessing the situation, and finding a way to redirect the interaction constructively.

To better understand how these dynamics develop, let's start with a story that will feel familiar to many parents. Henry's story reveals not only the challenges of defiance but also how communication, connection, and assumptions play a critical role in building trust and understanding.

YOUR EXPLANATION GUIDES YOUR INTERVENTION

We've all been there—seeing your child playing, watching TV, or on their phone when you assume they should be doing homework. It's 4:30 p.m., and a little voice in your head grows louder: "Shouldn't they be doing their homework?" You've faced this situation before, and that voice tells you to step in. So, you approach your child and ask, "Why aren't you doing your homework?" What assumptions are being made? Common answers I hear from parents include "They're lazy, unmotivated, procrastinating, or defiant." But what are parents feeling in that moment? Often, it's frustration, exhaustion, anger, or even embarrassment, worrying that their child's behavior reflects poorly on them as parents. But beneath those surface emotions lies a deeper worry: If I don't keep pushing, will my child ever succeed? What if they never *launch*?

These feelings and fears, while valid, can lead us to act on assumptions shaped by our own beliefs rather than taking the time to truly understand our child's reality. Before we explore those dynamics further, let me share the story of Henry, a client whose struggles resonate with you.

Henry was a bright tenth-grader whose grades had been steadily declining. His parents contacted me, convinced that he just needed more motivation and organization to get back on track. After all, Henry was capable and had succeeded before—so why wasn't he doing well now?

When I met Henry, he told me about his passion for managing and promoting rap musicians. He wasn't just dreaming—he had done his homework. He researched industry leaders, read trade publications, and studied the business. His eyes lit up as he talked about it.

But his father dismissed Henry's aspirations as unrealistic. A lawyer himself, he envisioned Henry following a traditional path: college, law school, and a stable career. He believed it was his job to help Henry *want* to succeed, using rewards and punishments to push him in the "right" direction.

Though well intentioned, Henry's parents made assumptions about his behavior that didn't align with his reality. They saw his lack of effort in school as laziness or defiance. But for Henry, school wasn't the problem—it was the future his parents were planning for him.

Henry explained it to me simply:

"If I don't do my homework, I won't get good grades. If I don't get good grades, I can't go to college. If I don't go to college, I can't go to law school. And then, I won't have to wear a suit and tie, and I can do what I want—become a rap music manager."

Henry's resistance wasn't about a lack of motivation. It was a protest against a future he didn't want.

Coaching is a partnership that requires a willingness and desire to make changes. At this stage, Henry wasn't interested in coaching. I recognized that the most effective way to support him was to work with his parents. Together, we examined how their assumptions and communication styles contributed to Henry's disconnection and lack of engagement in school.

As they began to acknowledge Henry's passions and show him how skills from school could support his dreams, something shifted. Henry felt seen and heard. With that connection restored, he started to reengage—not because he had to, but because he wanted to.

As parents, our beliefs about our children's behavior shape how we respond—and our responses, in turn, influence their reactions. When we misunderstand or misjudge our child's behavior, we often act on assumptions that don't reflect their reality. These assumptions can create conflict and disconnection, making it harder to foster trust and cooperation.

Henry's story highlights the critical importance of communication— not just any communication, but the kind of deep, intentional sharing that leads to mutual understanding. Without this connection, interactions can easily spiral into a predictable pattern of resistance or non-compliance, which I call the *defiance dance*.

THE DEFIANCE DANCE

The defiance dance (Figure 4.1) describes the exhausting and somewhat predictable interaction you may encounter when your child resists your requests or expectations.

When you make a request of your child (e.g., "Please take out the garbage"), one of two things happens: either your child complies, and the event is over, or they resist, and you start dancing. Resistance can take the form of postponement without an actual plan ("I'll do it later"), outright refusal ("No"), or ignoring you.

When resistance occurs, parents have four options to respond:

1. *Repeat the request*: Continue to repeat yourself in the hopes that your child will eventually comply.
2. *Give up*: Relinquish your request to avoid further conflict.

3. *Threaten consequences*: Issue a warning ("If you don't take out the garbage, no TV tonight").

4. *Assert control*. Follow through with a consequence, such as taking away privileges.

Each of these responses contributes to a back-and-forth dynamic that can feel like an endless "defiance dance." As shown in Figure 4.2, if you give up on your request or assert your control, the dance is over. However, when you keep repeating your request or threaten without following through, it's as if you've become your child's alarm clock, and they keep hitting snooze. They know that at some point—perhaps when your tone changes—it's time to act. And so, the dance continues.

Breaking this cycle requires changing your "dance steps" and rethinking how you approach these interactions. Before we explore

---

FIGURE 4.1:
The Defiance Dance

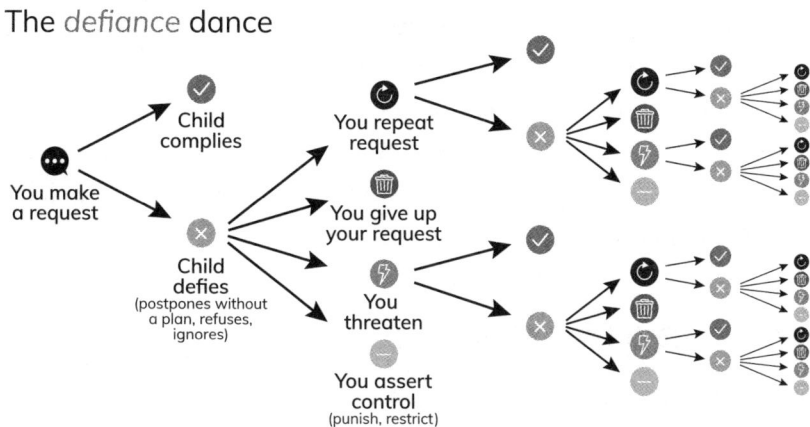

The defiance dance

© Cindy Goldrich

strategies for breaking the defiance cycle, it's important to understand the reasons behind your child's behavior.

UNDERSTANDING RESISTANCE AND NONCOMPLIANCE

Our beliefs about our children's behavior shape how we decide to intervene. While we may view our efforts to influence or motivate as helpful, our children might see them as attempts to control their actions. Even with the best intentions, this dynamic can unintentionally create tension or resistance.

As we explore further in Key 5, Teach Collaboration, it's not always about fixing the child; it's about understanding the parent–child dynamic and fostering opportunities for connection. How we communicate—our tone, timing, and words—can either shut our children down or invite them in.

Breaking the cycle of resistance requires shifting our perspective. Instead of focusing solely on your child's behavior, take a step back and ask yourself: What might be driving this noncompliance? Henry's story underscores the power of intentional and meaningful communication as a pathway to mutual understanding.

Just as calm is the foundation of our parenting and connection is the core of our relationships, communication forms one of the essential walls of our home (Figure 4.2). With the right approach, we can foster trust, encourage growth, and cultivate the cooperation we long to see in our children.

WHY DO KIDS DEFY?

To break the cycle of resistance and noncompliance, we first need to look beneath the surface. Children don't resist simply to upset us; their behavior often reflects deeper struggles. When we focus solely on the behavior, we risk missing the underlying causes—and the opportunity to address them effectively.

Children resist or push back for a variety of reasons. Understanding these reasons can help us respond with empathy and clarity, breaking the cycle of frustration and conflict.

- *Deflecting expectations to protect self-image*: Admitting "I don't understand" or "I feel dumb" is hard. Instead, it's easier to say, "Math is stupid" or "I don't care about how I write." Resistance can serve as a shield to protect one's pride when feeling vulnerable or incapable.
- *Not knowing how to do what is expected*: Children with ADHD or EF challenges may genuinely not know how to start or what to do. A brief distraction can derail them, leaving them feeling overwhelmed and stuck. When they seek help, they may face criticism for "not listening" or "talking too much," which can lead to feelings of shame and avoidance.
- *Hyper-focused*: Sometimes, they truly don't hear you. Children with

FIGURE 4.2:
House: Communication

Building our home

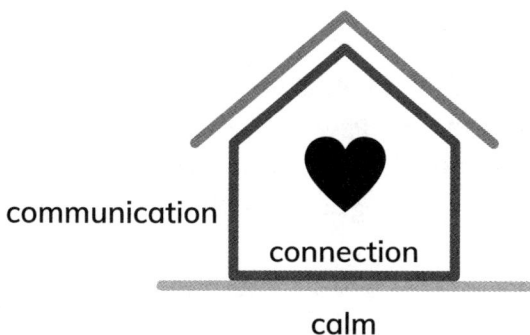

communication

connection

calm

© Cindy Goldrich

ADHD often experience moments of hyper-focus when the outside world fades away. This isn't defiance; it's a byproduct of being deeply engaged in an activity.

- *Asserting independence*: Some children value autonomy more than compliance, even at a cost. Their desire to carve out their own path can be frustrating for parents, but it reflects a natural drive for independence. These children are not stallions to be broken but saplings to be guided and nurtured while still holding them accountable.

- *Unreasonable or unrealistic expectations*: Expectations that do not align with a child's developmental stage or abilities can create frustration and pushback. Even if a child has the intelligence to complete a task, challenges such as working memory deficits, emotional regulation, or slower processing speed can make even simple tasks feel overwhelming. *Parent the child you have*, and set realistic expectations that honor their needs while fostering their growth.

- *Parental inconsistency*: Mixed messages, such as allowing a child to skip a chore one day but scolding them for it the next, erode trust and create confusion. Children thrive in environments with predictable expectations and consistent follow-through.

- *Conflicting expectations between parents*: When parents have different priorities, children can feel caught in the middle, torn between wanting to please both parents and not knowing how to meet opposing expectations. For example, one parent may value sports while the other emphasizes academics, leaving the child feeling overwhelmed and uncertain about whose approval to seek. This emotional tug-of-war can lead to frustration, anxiety, and resistance as the child struggles to navigate conflicting demands without feeling like they're disappointing someone they love.

- *Excessively controlling parenting styles*: Overly rigid rules or expectations, often driven by fear or anxiety, can create unnecessary stress for children. This can lead to battles for independence, especially when their freedoms are far out of step with their peers. While these parents often act out of love, their approach may unintentionally push children to resist harder.

- *Not feeling connected or heard*: Trust and connection are foundational. When a child feels dismissed, unheard, or undervalued, their willingness to comply diminishes. As seen in Henry's story, this disconnection can lead to resistance, even when it comes at the expense of their own success.

These children are not acting out of malice; they are trying to gain control and independence over their lives. Although frustrating, their actions often arise from unmet needs, unexpressed fears, or a desire to be acknowledged and understood.

REFLECTING ON YOUR OWN COMMUNICATION STYLE

Effective communication requires more than just words: It involves timing, tone, and intentionality. To build trust and cooperation, we must let go of shame, blame, and criticism, which often create walls instead of bridges. Replacing these with tolerance, empathy, and support allows us to foster connection and create a safe space where our children feel valued and heard. Here are key areas to consider when reflecting on your communication style:

When Do You Address Issues?

Timing matters. Without calm, there is no learning. Are you addressing an issue when the environment is calm, or when emotions are already heightened? Is your child deeply engaged in something meaningful to them, or are they depleted after a long day at school? Choosing the right moment can make all the difference in how your child receives your message. For example, pausing to reflect before reacting can help prevent unnecessary conflict and defensiveness. Try asking yourself: Is this the right time for my child to truly hear and process what I'm saying?

Many parents feel frustrated, saying, "It's never the right time for my child to listen." This is a common challenge, and part of the solution is helping your child recognize that it's okay to say, "Now isn't a good time," as long as they remain accountable by agreeing to revisit the conversation at a different time. By teaching this skill, you're setting the stage for mutual respect and more productive communication.

Where Do You Communicate?

Are you speaking in a supportive, private space, or are you having sensitive conversations in front of friends or siblings? Children, especially those with ADHD or EF challenges, may feel embarrassed or ashamed when corrected in public. This can shift their focus from the message you're trying to convey to their discomfort at that moment. Instead, aim to communicate in an environment where your child feels safe and supported.

Why Are You Addressing the Issue?

Consider your motivation. Is the issue truly urgent, or is it driven by your own anxiety or frustration? Clarifying your intentions can help you approach the conversation with empathy and purpose rather than reacting out of emotion.

What Are You Trying to Say?

Have you thought through your message, or are you reacting emotionally? If you tend to lecture, be mindful: No matter how wise your words, your child is likely to tune out after the first few sentences. Instead, aim to *be brief, be firm,* and *be gone.* Keep your tone neutral and avoid giving energy to negativity.

Another important strategy is to "connect before you correct." Before jumping into solutions or corrections, take a moment to acknowledge your child's effort, emotions, or intentions. This simple step helps build trust and reduces defensiveness, making it easier for your child to hear your message. For example, you might say, "I see how hard you've been working on your homework—great job getting started! Let's look at the next step together." This approach ensures your child feels supported while gently guiding them toward the behavior or outcome you're looking for.

Some parents worry, "But if I walk away, they just follow me," or "If I leave them, they won't necessarily do what I asked." These are valid concerns, and in Key 5, Teach Collaboration, we explore strategies to address those specific challenges. For now, it can be helpful to acknowledge these struggles with your child and let them know "We're going to work together on what to do during these frustrating situations." This sets the stage for collaboration while maintaining calm and reinforcing your message.

How Are You Delivering Your Message?

Is your tone and body language clear and empathetic, or intimidating? Consider this: "I said no playing with the ball in the house." This can be delivered angrily, pleadingly, or—ideally—with calm conviction and confidence. When your delivery is calm and firm, you model self-control and create an environment where your child feels more open to hearing you.

A Note About Sarcasm

Sarcasm is often justified as humor or a fun way of communicating, but its impact—especially on children—can be harmful. Many children, especially those with ADHD or EF challenges, may take words literally or struggle to understand nuances, leaving them feeling dismissed or belittled.

For example, a parent might say, "Oh, great, another stellar homework report," upon seeing a poor grade. While this may seem like a harmless jab, to the child, it can feel invalidating and even shaming. Sarcasm can erode trust and create emotional distance, shutting down open communication. Instead, aim for clarity and compassion. Replace sarcastic remarks with direct, empathetic communication that fosters trust and respect, building a stronger foundation for connection and growth.

TEACHING BETTER COMMUNICATION SKILLS (IT STARTS WITH US!)

Good communication isn't just about getting your child to listen—it's about creating an atmosphere where everyone feels valued, understood, and safe to express themselves. When children experience being truly heard, they're more likely to trust you, cooperate, and engage in problem solving. Strong communication allows you to uncover the underlying issues driving their behavior, enabling you to address the root causes instead of just the symptoms. By fostering open and respectful dialogue, you lay the foundation for stronger relationships and more effective parenting.

Let's face it: Communication is a skill we all need to work on. Most of us didn't grow up with a formal class on how to communicate effectively—it's something we've learned through trial and error. And yet, here we are, trying to teach our children how to express themselves, listen to others, and handle disagreements. It's no small task, but it's one of the most important skills we can give them.

The good news? This doesn't have to be complicated. Start by choosing a time to have a family discussion about how to improve communication at home. Let your kids know this is about making things better for everyone, not just them. Plan it in advance, and keep it short—no more than 15 minutes. And here's the key: Stick to your word. If you promise it will only take 15 minutes, don't let it drag on.

If necessary, sweeten the deal. Offer a fun dessert afterward, plan it during a special meal, or trade it for something they'd enjoy—like staying up a little later or skipping a chore. The goal is to create a positive, inviting atmosphere that encourages everyone to participate willingly.

This isn't a lecture—it's a conversation. Let them know you're all in this together and that everyone, including you, has things to learn and improve. Once you've set the stage, you can introduce some simple tools and strategies to help everyone feel more heard, respected, and understood.

PRACTICAL STEPS FOR FAMILY COMMUNICATION

Once you've set the stage and gathered everyone, it's time to dive into the discussion. The goal is to explore how your family can communicate more effectively, share ideas, and establish clear expectations for how conversations should proceed.

THE ROLE OF THE LISTENER

Effective communication starts with learning how to truly listen. Often, when children feel unheard, they shut down, resist, or escalate. Of course, listening isn't always easy, especially when emotions are high or when you're juggling multiple responsibilities. But as parents, we set the tone for how communication flows in our home, and active listening is a skill that can transform our interactions with our children. By truly hearing them, we not only address immediate challenges but also build stronger, more trusting relationships over time. Here are three key elements of being an effective listener:

1. Mirroring
Mirroring involves repeating back what you've heard to ensure you've understood correctly. It's not about adding your own interpretation or judgment but rather reflecting their words to confirm their

message. For example, if your child says, "I hate doing math—it's boring," you might respond with "So, you're saying that math feels really boring to you?" This simple step helps your child feel heard and understood. It also allows them a chance to clarify if you've misunderstood.

Why it matters: Mirroring shows your child that their voice is important. It can diffuse defensiveness and create space for more honest, open dialogue.

2. Validating

Validation acknowledges your child's feelings and perspective, even if you don't agree with them. It means affirming "I see you, and your feelings are real." For example, if your child is upset about being asked to clean up, you might say, "I understand why stopping your game feels frustrating." Validation doesn't imply that you approve of the behavior; it indicates that you recognize their emotions as valid.

Why it matters: When children feel their emotions are recognized, they're less likely to resist or feel the need to defend themselves. Validation fosters trust and connection.

3. Empathizing

Empathy goes beyond validation by emotionally connecting with your child's experience. It involves putting yourself in their shoes. For instance, you might say, "It must be really upsetting to stop playing when you're in the middle of something fun." Empathy allows your child to feel that you understand not only their words but also the emotions behind them.

Why it matters: Empathy strengthens your bond with your child. It shows them that you care deeply about their feelings, creating a safe space for them to open up.

FOR THE TOUGHER CONVERSATIONS WHEN THERE'S CONFLICT

There are times when kids are fighting over things or maybe you have a rule or boundary that your children really disagree with. Sometimes these conversations can get heated and it's helpful to structure the conversation so that everyone feels that their voice is being heard.

Explain that these rules are designed to make sure everyone feels heard and respected. For example:

- *Take turns speaking*: This ensures that even the quieter family members have a chance to share their thoughts. You can use a "talking stick" or another fun signal to indicate whose turn it is.
- *Consider using a timer to ensure fairness*: In some families, some people need more time to process their thoughts and may feel rushed to respond, while others keep talking as long as they have the floor. A timer can help create balance, giving everyone an equal opportunity to be heard and ensuring the conversation stays focused.
- *No interruptions*: If anyone has a thought, they can write it down or wait for their turn.
- *Focus on one issue at a time*: Avoid jumping from one topic to another.
- *Ask for clarification when needed*: If someone feels overwhelmed or confused, use a simple hand signal to pause the discussion.

ADDITIONAL COMMUNICATION SKILLS TO KEEP IN MIND

Be Fully Present

Listening isn't just about hearing the words—it's about showing your child they have your full attention. Avoid multitasking while they're speaking. Don't do laundry, browse a magazine, watch TV, or look at your phone. Your visible presence helps create a safe space for your child to express themselves without feeling dismissed or unimportant.

Recognize Emotional Cues

Pay attention to your child's emotional state during conversations. Are they frustrated, overwhelmed, or distracted? If so, pause to acknowledge what they're feeling. A simple statement like "I can see you're upset—do you want to take a break before we talk?" can help them feel validated and give them the space they need to open up when they're ready. Recognizing emotions not only improves communication but also teaches your child how to identify and express their feelings.

Teach When and How to Interrupt

Knowing when to interrupt is just as important as knowing how to do it respectfully. Help your child understand appropriate moments to interrupt, such as during an emergency, when they're feeling overwhelmed, or when they need immediate clarification. Discuss these boundaries as a family to ensure everyone is aligned, emphasizing that interruptions should be purposeful, not impulsive.

Once your child understands when it's appropriate to interrupt, teach them respectful strategies to do so. They can use verbal cues like "Excuse me" or nonverbal signals like raising their hand. Tools like jotting down thoughts on paper for later can also help manage impulsivity. Role-play these scenarios and offer praise when your child uses these strategies effectively. Consider implementing a "do not disturb" signal for focused moments to establish clear boundaries.

If you're the one interrupting, take responsibility for the disruption. Acknowledge the interruption, and before continuing, help the original speaker return to their train of thought. For example, you might say, "I'm sorry for interrupting. You were saying . . . " This demonstrates respect for the speaker and models mindful communication.

Set Communication Boundaries

Healthy communication also means setting boundaries. Let your child know what's acceptable and what's not during conversations. For example, establish that yelling or name-calling won't be part of family discussions. Additionally, agree on times when certain topics are better left for later. For example, a serious conversation about homework might not be ideal right before bedtime or during a rushed morning routine. Clear boundaries make communication more respectful and productive for everyone involved.

Ask Before Offering Advice

Resist the urge to be a problem solver. Sometimes, people simply want to share how they're feeling—they're not looking for advice or solutions. Instead of jumping in with your perspective, ask your child, "Would you like me to help you figure this out, or are you just looking to share?"

In her research on teens and their relationships with their parents, Ellen Galinsky (n.d.) found that teens crave respect and validation. They want adults to listen to them and understand their perspective before offering input. This fosters trust and builds the foundation for healthy communication.

Check for Understanding

Before you share your perspective, explicitly check in with your child to ensure they feel heard. Ask, "Do you feel like I've understood you? Is there anything else you want to share before I respond?" This step reinforces that their voice matters and helps create a balanced, collaborative dynamic.

A FEW FINAL TIPS

Remember, children with ADHD often feed off of other people's energy. When the energy isn't there, they tend to create it. Don't give energy to their excitement by adding more of your own. Sometimes, when they are agitated or yelling at you, it's really because they're upset about a fight they just had with a friend or the disappointment they recently experienced. You don't have to attend every fight you're invited to! Often, the best response is to stay calm and disengage, showing them that not every disagreement has to escalate into a battle.

At the same time, don't always take their behavior or comments personally. Often, it's more about their mood or challenges in the moment than it is about you. Focus on being more excited about the positives than the negatives. Use your praise to highlight their strengths, notice the good stuff they do, and plan quality one-on-one time to reinforce your connection.

As we discussed in Key 3, what you pay attention to grows. This principle applies just as much to communication as it does to connection. When you intentionally focus on the positive qualities in your child— their effort, creativity, or problem-solving skills—it can shift the tone of your conversations and reduce conflict. Noticing and commenting on their positive traits or actions helps build their confidence and fosters a more constructive dynamic between you. By shifting your attention to what's working, you create space for growth and cooperation.

Parenting is a journey, and there will be ups and downs. By prioritizing connection and fostering calm, you're not just addressing today's challenges—you're equipping your child with the tools to navigate their future with confidence and resilience. By staying intentional about your communication and focusing on the relationship you're building, you'll create a foundation of trust, understanding, and cooperation that will serve you both well in the long run.

GUIDING THOUGHTS

- Calm is the foundation of effective communication—without it, connection and learning can't happen.
- Defiance is often a coping technique—look beyond the behavior.

- They won't change their steps until you change yours.
- Notice when, where, why, what, and how you speak.
- Say what you mean and mean what you say.
- Avoid shame, blame, and criticism—replace them with tolerance, empathy, and support.
- You don't need to attend every argument you're invited to.
- Don't always take their behavior personally.
- Be brief, be firm, be gone!
- Connect before you correct.

HOMEWORK

1. *Continue one-on-one time*: Use these moments to build trust and connection.
2. *Observe patterns of behavior*: Notice the recurring, often predictable situations that create stress and frustration between you and your children.
3. *Practice "be brief, be firm, be gone"*: Experiment with clear, concise requests and follow-through.
4. *Make a plan*: Teach your children about communication skills.

KEY 5

TEACH COLLABORATION
The Power of Creating
Shared Solutions

*The beauty of empowering others is that your own power is
not diminished.*

—BARBARA COLOROSO

n this chapter, we explore how to navigate challenges with your
child in ways that not only manage behavior but also build a stronger
relationship and foster their independence for the future. Let's begin
with a brief exercise.

Take a moment to reflect on a recurring behavior pattern you've
noticed in your child. It doesn't have to be the most significant one; just
something you've observed regularly. Perhaps your child resists getting ready for bed or struggles to transition away from screens. Write
down the behaviors you've noticed—yelling, refusing, avoiding—and
try to identify the triggers or expectations your child might be struggling to meet. Who is involved? What's happening around them?
Where and when does this take place?

By considering these factors—the antecedent, precipitant, and
context (the events or conditions that lead to the behavior and the

surrounding environment)—you can start to uncover what drives the behavior. This reflection also helps you understand how the strategies we've discussed can be applied in real-life situations.

Let's take a moment to review where we've been. We began by looking at our children through the lens of neurodiversity, recognizing that their challenges—such as weaker working memory, slower processing speed, difficulty managing emotions, and struggles with time blindness—are very real. These traits can make learning, behavior, and performance especially challenging.

We've seen how our mantra "Without calm, there is no learning," serves as the foundation of our home. We explored the importance of spending regular, stress-free time with our children—time without any specific agenda. Building this bond helps our children feel safe, supported, and prepared to face life's challenges.

We've also discussed the importance of communication and how assumptions about our children's behavior can lead to disconnection and frustration. By learning specific tools for teaching communication skills to the entire family, we've encouraged stronger relationships and tackled challenges through open discussion rather than reactive behavior.

To appreciate why collaboration is so effective, it helps to understand why some traditional parenting strategies often fall short. By examining the assumptions behind these approaches, we can begin to see why they might not lead to the lasting changes we hope for.

TRADITIONAL PARENTING WISDOM

Traditional parenting wisdom often suggests that children misbehave to seek attention, manipulate others, or insist on getting what they want. It assumes that children are primarily motivated by a desire for power and control in their lives. This belief contributes to the mindset that Ross Greene and Stuart Ablon describe as "Kids do well if they want to."

The *battle for control* often begins with a simple request from the parent: something like "Please clean up your toys." As mentioned in the *defiance dance*, if the child doesn't comply, the parent may repeat the request, threaten a consequence, or give in completely.

As Russell Barkley explains, "The arguing, defiance, and refusal is a learned behavior—not genetic, not biological" (Barkley, 2012).

When parents avoid pursuing their expectations or rely too heavily on an authoritarian approach, they inadvertently teach children that emotions—such as yelling, sulking, or refusing—are tools to get others to leave them alone. Over time, this can reinforce the idea that emotional outbursts provide relief from others' demands. It's important to remember that the ability to "manipulate" a person or situation requires skills like forethought, planning, and impulse control—skills that are often underdeveloped or delayed in children with challenging behaviors.

To counter this, many parents turn to a carrot-and-stick approach: "If you do this, then you'll get that; but if you don't, here's the consequence." While this feels logical and actionable, it often fails to address the root causes of behavior. Most parents find that constant punishments and negative consequences do not lead to lasting, positive outcomes.

When we respond this way, we unintentionally "kick the can down the road," delaying the chance to confront challenges directly. Instead of helping our children build the skills to manage their emotions and meet expectations, we risk reinforcing patterns that lead to increased defiance, disconnection, and stress for everyone involved.

WHAT IMPACTS A CHILD'S BEHAVIOR?

To better understand our children's behaviors and address them collaboratively, we need to consider the various factors that influence how they respond to the world around them. While each individual is unique, there are common influences that shape behavior:

- *Social influences*: Peer group dynamics and social pressure.
- *Self-esteem/self-image*: How a child perceives their own abilities and worth.

- *Others' beliefs*: How children interpret others' perceptions of them.
- *Focus on the present*: Many individuals, especially those with ADHD, struggle to consider future consequences and instead focus on immediate gratification or challenges.
- *Learning challenges and neurodiversity*: Cognitive and developmental differences that shape how children process and react to situations.
- *Trauma*: Past experiences can shape emotional responses, such as avoiding activities that feel threatening or overwhelming.
- *Lagging thinking skills*: Deficits in adaptive responses, such as problem solving, emotional regulation, or flexibility (which we explore in greater detail shortly).

These factors don't act in isolation—they interact to create patterns of behavior that we can anticipate and address thoughtfully.

A DIFFERENT VIEW

Research—and our own experiences—lead us to question the belief that "Kids do well if they want to." As discussed in Key 4, children often seek power and control not to dominate others but as a coping strategy for self-protection. When children defy requests, it's rarely an intentional effort to manipulate or misbehave. Parenting styles that rely too heavily on control, bribery, intimidation, or punishment can create resistance rather than cooperation. Inconsistent or unclear rules and expectations often lead to confusion, endless debates, and power struggles, making it difficult for children to engage in meaningful problem solving. When parents lack unity in their approach, it can inadvertently cause anxiety or internal conflict for the child, who may feel torn between trying to please both parents.

KIDS LACK SKILLS—NOT THE WILL

Challenging behaviors are often rooted in a child's lagging skills rather than a lack of motivation or willpower. Sometimes, the "unsolved problem" is their struggle to connect how their present actions might impact future opportunities or relationships. Why might this be?

- Children, especially those with ADHD, often struggle to connect how their present actions might impact future opportunities or relationships. This disconnect makes it harder for them to understand how today's behaviors affect their goals or relationships tomorrow.
- For many, time exists as "now" and "not now," making it harder to feel motivated by future outcomes or delay gratification.
- Children with ADHD often face motivational challenges, struggling to feel driven toward long-term goals or postponed rewards.
- They may struggle with delaying gratification or regulating their emotions due to inflexibility and poor frustration tolerance.
- Children are not always motivated by adult concerns and may not be developmentally prepared to understand the reasoning behind them. For example, an 11-year-old might resist mowing the lawn not out of defiance but because the connection between today's chore and future responsibilities feels too abstract or irrelevant to comprehend. Additionally, their struggles with impulse control and emotional regulation can make such tasks feel overwhelming in the moment.

As parents, we often see the behavior—but not the story behind it. By recognizing these challenges, we can reframe behaviors like refusal, whining, or sulking not as defiance but as opportunities to teach and support growth.

THINKING SKILLS

When we looked at what impacts children's behavior, I mentioned lagging *thinking skills*. Thinking skills are the mental abilities that help individuals adapt to situations, manage frustration, and solve problems effectively. These skills are crucial for regulating emotions, communicating needs, navigating social interactions, and responding flexibly to challenges. They enable children to meet expectations in various settings, such as at home, in school, or in relationships.

Most of the skills needed to behave and perform well fall into these five categories:

1. *Language and communication skills*: The ability to understand others, express thoughts and needs clearly, and communicate emotions effectively.

2. *Attention and working memory skills*: Skills needed to stay focused, follow sequences, keep track of time, and manage multiple thoughts or solutions.

3. *Emotion and self-regulation skills*: The capacity to manage emotions, think before acting, and adjust energy levels appropriately in various situations.

4. *Social thinking skills*: Understanding social cues, engaging positively with others, and recognizing how behavior affects others' feelings and perceptions.

5. *Cognitive flexibility skills*: The ability to adapt to new ideas, see multiple perspectives, and handle changes or uncertainties with ease.

By recognizing these thinking skills as the foundation for behavior, we can start to see challenges in a new way. Rather than focusing solely on the behavior itself, we can shift our perspective to understand the skills that may be lagging—and how this understanding can guide our responses.

THROUGH OUR NEW LENS

Viewing behaviors through this new lens helps us see how lagging thinking skills contribute to social, emotional, and behavioral challenges. Just as children with learning disabilities struggle in areas like reading, writing, or math, research shows that children with behavioral challenges often struggle with flexibility, frustration tolerance, and problem solving.

These skills form the foundation for effective communication, focus, self-control, social understanding, and adaptability. When thinking skills lag, challenging behaviors often emerge, particularly in response to unmet expectations or unsolved problems. For example:

- Cleaning up after dinner.
- Dealing with the seam in a sock.
- Completing homework.

By viewing these struggles as signs of lagging skills instead of defiance, we can shift our approach from managing behaviors to building the skills children need to thrive. This shift also invites us to reexamine common strategies, such as rewards and consequences, and consider their role in supporting—or undermining—our efforts to teach these skills effectively. Let's explore how external incentives can impact motivation and learning.

What Is the Impact of External Incentives on Motivation?

The research is very clear: Rewards and consequences can sometimes be effective.

When Can Rewards Work?

External incentives can help build routines and habits under certain conditions:

- When the task is manageable and within the child's abilities, such as when the work or performance is something they can control (response–able).
- When the reward is provided immediately, as delayed incentives

often lose their impact, especially for children with ADHD or other challenges.

• When stress and pressure are minimal, as excessive pressure can overwhelm a child and reduce the reward's effectiveness.

In these scenarios, incentives can encourage positive behaviors and foster consistency.

When Can Rewards Backfire?

While rewards can be useful in some cases, they can also be detrimental under certain conditions.

Consider the classic *I Love Lucy* episode where Lucy and Ethel are working in a candy factory. Their job is to wrap candies as they move along the conveyor belt. Everything runs smoothly until their boss says, "Okay, let's speed it up." Suddenly, the candies move so quickly that Lucy and Ethel can't keep up. The expectation exceeds their capacity, and chaos ensues.

Rewards can have a similar effect when the demands of a task exceed a child's current abilities. For example:

• When a task requires cognitive skills that are weak or lagging, rewards can add stress and pressure, shutting down thinking and leading to poorer performance.

• When the goal is to teach skills or build relationships, incentives may focus on short-term compliance rather than fostering long-term growth.

• When the child feels misunderstood. For example, offering a reward for completing work faster might leave the child feeling (even if they don't express it) "Do you really think I want to be sitting here all this time while my friends are outside playing? I don't think you understand me very well."

The threat of punishment cannot make the impossible possible. If a child's struggles stem from lagging thinking skills rather than a lack of effort, external incentives can unintentionally lower their self-esteem, making them feel unsupported or misunderstood.

Additionally, rewards can sometimes limit effort. For example, if a child is promised a prize for reading three books, they may lose interest in reading a fourth book once the reward has been earned.

Finally, excessive rewards or pressure can overwhelm a child's cognitive capacity. Remember the image of the balloon with all the pins going in. The more stress we add, the less space children have to think clearly and solve problems effectively.

Whose Behavior Can We Control?

As parents, it's important to recognize that we cannot control other people's behavior—we can only influence their options. Ultimately, the only behavior we have full control over is our own.

Special Note for Parents of Teenagers

This principle is especially important when you are not present to influence your child's behavior directly. For example, when your teenager is at a party or in another setting outside your view, you can only trust that they will make decisions aligned with the values and boundaries you have taught them.

While you can guide them, discuss expectations, and provide strategies, their choices in these moments are ultimately their own. Trust and open communication are essential as you navigate this stage of parenting.

REFRAMING OUR THINKING

We started with the premise that "kids do well if they want to." However, in our hearts, we know that kids want to feel independent, competent, connected, and loved. Sometimes they simply lack the skills they need at the moment.

Just as with a learning disability, a child's challenging behavior is not intentional, goal oriented, manipulative, or attention seeking. As

Ross Greene so poignantly says, "Kids do well if they can" (Greene, 1998, p. 18).

For children to comply and meet expectations:

- Some skills need to be explicitly taught.
- Some problems require guidance and collaboration to solve. For example:
  - How to keep a backpack organized.
  - How to advocate for oneself.
- Some adjustments in parenting style may be necessary to meet a child's unique needs.

Our job as parents is to be a detective. We must explore:

- What is challenging them?
- What are the underlying skills they are lacking?
- What would they do better if they could?

At this point, it's time to build onto our house by adding *collaboration* as a key element (Figure 5.1).

By integrating collaboration into our approach, we reinforce the structure that helps our children thrive.

As we saw in Henry's story, the way we speak to our children and communicate our expectations, concerns, and requests can either shut them down or help build our connection and their trust in us. We need to shift our focus and ask, What is our goal?

- Is it to gain compliance in the moment?
- Or is it to build skills for the long term?

By exploring our real concerns and identifying what's preventing our child from meeting expectations, we can move beyond simply focusing on behavior. Instead, we ask deeper questions:

- What triggered the behavior?
- What skill is the child lacking?
- What is the story behind the behavior?

The answers to these questions guide us in addressing unmet expectations collaboratively and effectively.

THREE OPTIONS FOR ADDRESSING UNMET EXPECTATIONS

In the previous chapter, we discussed the *defiance dance* and how repeating demands or issuing empty threats often leads to power struggles. Let's consider a different approach by exploring *three options* for responding to unmet expectations.

Plan A: Imposing an Adult Solution

Plan A stands for *adult*, where the parent imposes their solution to ensure that expectations are met. This approach is necessary when health or safety is at stake.

For example, if my 5-year-old wants to ride their bike in the street without wearing a helmet, I have no problem saying, "No, you may not

FIGURE 5.1:
House: Collaboration

Building our home

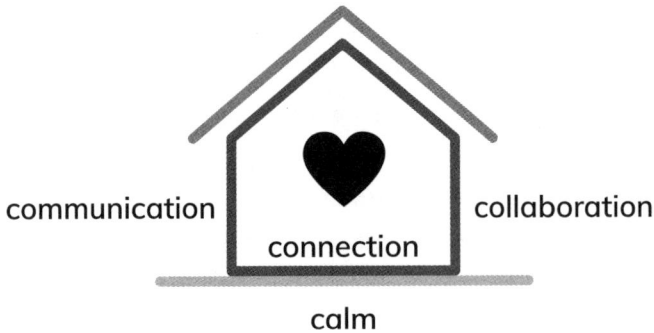

communication   collaboration

connection

calm

© Cindy Goldrich

ride your bike without a helmet." In this situation, it's my responsibility to enforce the rule and prioritize safety.

Plan C: Dropping the Expectation

Plan C stands for *child*, where the parent chooses to let go of their expectation, at least temporarily, and allows the child to lead the solution.

For example, if my 10-year-old wants to go outside to play without wearing a jacket, I might say, "It's cold outside," and drop my expectation that they wear the jacket I suggested. Sometimes, natural consequences—like feeling cold—can be a more effective teacher than imposing our will.

For a teenager, Plan C might come into play if your child refuses to clean their room before hanging out with friends. While you want them to develop responsibility, you might choose to let go of this expectation temporarily and revisit it later when they are more receptive—or even choose to let it go altogether.

Plan B: Collaboration

Plan B stands for *both*, where the parent and the child work together to address the unmet expectation. This approach creates a shared solution that fosters skill building and connection.

The Goals of Plan B

- Reduce meltdowns and defiance.
- Pursue expectations with clear, compassionate communication.
- Provide opportunities to practice lagging *thinking skills*.
- Solve problems in a way that lasts.
- Build trust and connection with your child.
- Encourage open dialogue to understand your child's perspective.
- Reflect on your teaching approach to foster collaboration.

While Plan A and Plan C have their place, Plan B offers a way to teach valuable life skills while fostering trust and connection.

Your belief about why your child struggles will guide how you respond. When you view challenges through the lens of understanding and skill building, it transforms your approach to addressing unmet expectations.

The Beliefs of Plan B

- Kids do well if they can.
- Many challenges stem from lagging thinking skills, not a lack of will.
- Unsolved problems are often predictable patterns of behavior.
- The best way to teach these skills is by using real problems and collaborative conversations, not lectures.
- The best time to solve problems is proactively—when everyone is calm and the issue is not urgent.
- Children build essential life skills by learning to solve problems collaboratively.

By keeping these beliefs in mind, we can address unmet expectations constructively and collaboratively.

WHO'S EXPECTATIONS ARE NOT BEING MET?

Before diving into ways to address unmet expectations collaboratively, it's important to reflect on whose expectations are truly being prioritized. Sometimes, as parents, we invest emotionally in our children's goals, passions, or interests—only to find they don't follow through. For example:

- Your son claims he wants to get in better shape, yet he doesn't exercise.
- Your daughter says she wants to improve at playing guitar but doesn't practice.

While it's wonderful to support and encourage your children, keep in mind:

- They may not have the emotional development to anticipate what's involved in pursuing a goal.
- They may simply be testing out an interest and lose motivation when it's less exciting than expected.

Be cautious about becoming too invested in their personal goals. This can unintentionally create undue pressure and a fear of disappointing you, which may make them hesitant to share their passions in the future. Instead, by stepping back and giving your child the space to explore their interests, you encourage their autonomy and help them develop the skills to manage their own expectations.

THE PROCESS OF CREATING SHARED SOLUTIONS

You've learned about the three options for addressing unmet expectations. Let's take a closer look at Plan B and explore how to use it to create shared solutions. This step-by-step process guides you in addressing challenges collaboratively while teaching critical skills and fostering a stronger connection with your child.

Before we dive into the steps, it's helpful to recognize patterns of thinking that might unintentionally hinder collaboration. One common barrier is relying on *dead-end explanations*. These are labels or generalizations that seem to explain a child's behavior but don't lead to meaningful insight or solutions. Examples include:

- "They just want attention."
- "They're manipulative."
- "They're making bad choices."
- "They have a learning disability."

While these explanations might feel satisfying in the moment, they tend to stop the conversation rather than open it up. Instead of labeling behavior, shift to curiosity: What's really happening? What skills might your child be struggling with? Avoiding these dead ends ensures the collaborative process begins with empathy and focus.

To be truly collaborative, you must approach the situation without a fixed solution or decision in mind. True collaboration requires curiosity, flexibility, and a willingness to explore multiple possibilities. This openness fosters trust and helps your child feel valued in the process.

As you go through the steps, remember: You don't need to tackle every step perfectly all at once—just take it one step at a time, focusing on progress, not perfection. By following this process, you can approach challenges with clarity, empathy, and a focus on long-term growth.

STEP 1: CLARIFY YOUR CONCERN

The first step in Creating Shared Solutions is to fully understand your concern. This means identifying the specific behavior, recognizing its impact, and clarifying why it matters. The more precise and neutral you are, the more effective the conversation will be. Clarify the expectations your child is struggling to meet in a realistic and developmentally appropriate way.

Observe and Describe the Behavior

When you bring up a concern with your child, you want to describe the behavior in a *factual, neutral way*. Avoid assigning blame or making broad generalizations.

Examples
- *Chores*: "I noticed that your laundry hasn't been put away this week."
- *Emotional regulation*: "I noticed you yelled when your sibling borrowed your toy."

- *School expectations*: "I noticed you haven't turned in your last two homework assignments."

Understanding the broader impact of your child's behavior is key to clarifying your core concern. This step helps you uncover the deeper worries or frustrations driving your feelings.

Consider the following:

1. Why Is This a Concern?

Reflect on why this behavior concerns you. Think about its immediate impact and how it might affect your child's emotional or developmental growth.

- *Chores*: Not putting away laundry may create stress when they need clothes.
- *Emotional regulation*: Yelling may make it harder to build positive sibling relationships.
- *School expectations*: Falling behind on homework may reduce their confidence and ability to keep up in class.

2. What Are the Lagging Thinking Skills?

These are deficits in adaptive responses, such as problem solving, emotional regulation, or flexibility (which we referred to in the section above on thinking skills).

3. What Patterns Do You Notice?

- When, where, and with whom do these challenges happen?
- What triggers your child?
- What settings or situations lead to these difficulties?

4. What Is the Impact on Others?

How is this behavior affecting those around your child?

- *Chores*: Clean clothes ending up in the dirty laundry creates extra work.

- *Emotional regulation*: Yelling disrupts the home's calm and upsets siblings.
- *School expectations*. Teachers might not fully understand your child's progress.

5. What Are the Health, Safety, or Well-Being Concerns?

Are there any risks to your child's or others' well-being?
- *Chores*: Items on the floor could create a tripping hazard.
- *Emotional regulation*: Escalating frustration could lead to physical conflict.
- *School expectations*: Stress over incomplete work might affect their emotional health.

Break It Down: What Might Really Be Going On?

Before jumping to conclusions, explore what might be making this expectation hard to meet. *Remember*: Your explanation guides your intervention—so take time to get curious instead of assuming.

Examples
- If mornings are stressful, is it about:
    - Waking up on time?
    - Getting dressed?
    - Remembering to pack everything?
    - Feeling rushed and overwhelmed?
- If homework isn't getting done, is it about:
    - Starting the work?
    - Understanding the directions?
    - Feeling frustrated when things get hard?
    - Managing distractions?
- If your child avoids chores, is it about:

- Forgetting?

- Not wanting to stop what they're doing?

- Not feeling like they get credit for their effort?

Instead of assuming your child is just being difficult, take a step back and ask yourself, "What could be making this hard for them?" This helps you approach the conversation with curiosity rather than frustration and set the stage for a real solution.

- What are your deeper concerns?
  - Understanding the underlying worries and frustrations behind your feelings can unlock the empathy and clarity needed for meaningful conversations with your child. Reflect on why this behavior concerns you now, what about it feels most troubling, and what underlying fears or frustrations it may trigger. Use these prompts to guide your reflection.

- Why does this behavior concern you now?
  - I'm worried that a pattern is developing where my child isn't turning in their homework, which could signal a bigger issue.

- What is the deeper fear or frustration behind that?
  - Falling behind on homework may reduce their confidence and ability to keep up in class.
  - If they don't keep up, they might feel frustrated and start giving up.
  - I'm afraid they will feel inadequate and lose confidence in themselves.

- How might this concern affect your relationship with your child?
  - I worry that ongoing tension about schoolwork could make them feel I'm always critical or unsupportive.

STEP 2: INVITE YOUR CHILD TO PARTICIPATE

Once you have a clear understanding of your concern, the next step is to invite your child into the conversation and foster a sense of teamwork. Preparing for a productive and respectful discussion is crucial to creating shared solutions.

Start by giving your child a heads-up about the conversation. Let them know you'd like to talk about something important so they can mentally prepare. Avoid catching them off guard, as this can create unnecessary tension. If emotions are running high or distractions arise, wait until both of you are calm and ready to engage. If your child says it's not a good time, ask, "When would be better?" It's okay if they say "not now," but they need to choose a time and follow through. Giving them some control over the timing can help them feel more comfortable, but accountability is key.

During the conversation, focus on creating a safe and open atmosphere by conveying empathy, reassurance, and curiosity. This approach encourages your child to share their thoughts and feelings freely, setting the stage for collaboration.

- *Empathy*: Show you're open and ready to understand your child's perspective. While you may not yet know their feelings, demonstrating your willingness to hear them fosters calm and trust.
- *Reassurance*: Let your child know the conversation is not about judgment or punishment. Reassuring them of your intent to understand and support them helps them feel safe.
- *Curiosity*: Invite your child's perspective with open-ended questions to encourage dialogue and understanding.

Start by stating the unmet expectation that you have observed. Use collaborative language to show that you value their input and want to work together to address the issue. For example:

- "I'm not angry. Can you help me understand why?"
- "You're not in trouble. Can you help me understand?"
- "I'm curious—what's going on?"
- "Let's brainstorm how we can resolve this together."
- "What are your thoughts on that?"

Keep the focus on the observable facts.

STEP 3: LISTEN TO YOUR CHILD'S PERSPECTIVE AND CLARIFY THEIR CONCERN

After sharing the challenging behavior, the focus shifts to understanding your child's perspective. Listening actively and reflecting on their concerns is critical for building trust and fostering collaboration. This step is about helping your child feel heard and creating a foundation for meaningful dialogue.

Set a Collaborative Tone

Approach the conversation *with curiosity, not control.* Let your child know they are *not in trouble* and that you want to understand their perspective.

Examples of Openers

- "I noticed that getting homework done has been a challenge. I'm not angry—I just want to understand."
- "I noticed you call me from your room and get upset when I don't come right away. I bet we can figure something out if we talk about it."

Check Your Timing

- Are you calm enough to think and speak?
- Do you have their full attention?

- If it's not a good time, ask, "When would be better?" (They can say "not now," but they must choose a time and follow through.)

Give Them Time to Share

Be patient as your child begins to express their feelings or concerns. They might struggle to articulate their emotions or feel unsure about how to express themselves.

- They may never have reflected on their feelings this way before.
- They may not yet trust that their voice matters or will be truly heard.
- Avoid interrupting—even if there's silence. Silence can be productive, giving them time to process their thoughts.

Encourage Expression in a Way That Works for Them

- Some children *talk it out*.
- Others might prefer *writing or drawing*.

Reflect on What You Hear

Restate your child's perspective to ensure clarity:

- "So you're saying it's hard to focus on homework because you're tired after a long day at school?"
- "It seems like you get upset when you're asked to stop playing in the middle of something exciting."

Ask Open-Ended Questions

Encourage your child to open up by asking thoughtful, open-ended questions:

- "What do you mean when you say . . . ?"
- "What about this makes it so hard? I want to understand."
- "Why do you think this happens sometimes but not other times?"
- "What do you think makes this harder for you?"

Empathy Is Not Agreement

You don't have to agree with your child's concern but you do need to show you understand. Validating their feelings builds trust, even if you see things differently. Instead of debating or correcting, keep the conversation open. If they say, "I hate school," try, "It sounds like school has been really frustrating. Can you tell me more?" This helps them feel heard and encourages them to share rather than shut down.

Watch for "Solutions in Disguise"

- "I don't want to sit next to Sam" → might mean "I'm afraid he'll tease me."
- "I hate math" → could mean "I feel dumb when I don't understand it."

Provide Reassurance

Help your child feel safe and supported during the conversation:

- "You're not in trouble—I just want to understand."
- "This isn't about being right or wrong—I want to figure this out together."
- "I know you must have a good reason for feeling this way."

Acknowledge Their Feelings

Use reflective listening to validate your child's emotions and show them you're fully engaged:

- "It sounds like you're feeling [frustrated/scared] because. . . . Did I get that right?"
- "I hear that you're worried about [insert concern]."
- "What I'm hearing is that you're upset because it feels unfair. Am I close?"
- "It seems like this is really important to you—thank you for sharing."

Try Educated Guessing

If your child struggles to express their thoughts, gently offer potential explanations to guide the conversation:

- "Let me take a guess—are you feeling [frustrated/scared/confused] about . . . ?"
- "Sometimes people feel [overwhelmed/lonely/angry] in situations like this. Do you think that might be part of it?"
- "I wonder if you're worried about what will happen if. . . . Is that close?"

For younger children or those who struggle to express their thoughts directly, consider using playful tools like the Five-Finger Strategy (see Appendix I for full details). This technique uses a simple 1–5 scale to help children share how true a statement feels in a nonconfrontational way.

Stay Focused on Uncovering Concerns

Avoid jumping to solutions too quickly. Gently redirect if the conversation shifts:

- "I hear your idea, but let's make sure we fully understand what's making this hard before we decide what to do."

By actively listening, asking thoughtful questions, and validating your child's feelings, you create an environment where they feel safe sharing. Reassure them that the goal is understanding, not judgment or punishment. This step sets the groundwork for expressing your concerns in Step 4 and working collaboratively toward solutions.

STEP 4: EXPRESS YOUR CONCERNS THOUGHTFULLY

Now that you've listened carefully and reflected on what you've heard, it's time to share your own concerns. Take time to reflect on what you want to share, aiming to foster collaboration and understanding. Approach the conversation with an open mind—stay curious, avoid assumptions, and refrain from judgment. Be open to new ideas and willing to adjust your expectations if they prove too challenging or unrealistic.

Building on what your child has expressed, convey your perspective in a manner that connects to what they've said, reinforcing that this is a collaborative dialogue.

Link Your Concern to What You've Heard

Begin your concern by relating it to your child's perspective. This creates continuity in the conversation and shows that their input matters.

- *Example*: "I hear that you feel frustrated with the amount of homework and how it cuts into your time. I'm also concerned that when homework isn't completed, it might affect your grades, which could limit your options in the future."

Use "I" Statements

Speak from your perspective to avoid blame or defensiveness.

- *Example*: "I'm worried about how this might affect your confidence in school."

Keep It Brief and Clear

This step is about ensuring your concern is understood—not to provide a solution yet.

Remain Open

Encourage your child's reactions and reinforce that this is still a collaborative conversation.

Avoid introducing a solution at this stage. Instead, focus on the impact of the behavior to help your child understand why it's a concern. Your role is to guide your child toward understanding the issue, not to dictate how to fix it. This approach empowers your child to engage in problem solving and fosters a sense of teamwork.

- Focus on the impact of the behavior, not judgment, blame, or your solution.
    - *Resist saying*: "I'm worried that staying up late is making it harder for you to do well in school, so it's important to start getting to bed earlier."

While this statement may seem helpful, it skips the collaborative process and presents the solution outright. Even if going to bed earlier ends up being the solution, guiding your child through the process of identifying the issue and brainstorming together teaches valuable problem-solving skills. By working through the steps collaboratively, you help your child take ownership of the solution and learn how to address challenges independently in the future.

- *Consider developmental readiness*: Think about whether your child is developmentally ready to understand or relate to your concern. For example:
    - Telling an 8-year-old "You need to do your homework so you can get into a good college someday" is unlikely to resonate because the connection to the future feels abstract and distant.
    - Asking a 5-year-old to share toys because "it's important to learn generosity" may not work because they haven't yet developed the ability to grasp such an abstract concept.

Adapt your language to your child's age and understanding.
- Chores
    - *Young child*: "My concern is that when your toys are left on the floor, they might get lost or stepped on, and I want to make sure they stay safe."

   – *Teen*: "My concern is that when your laundry isn't put away, it might get wrinkled or mixed up, making mornings more stressful for you."

- Emotional regulation
   – *Young child*: "My concern is that when you yell, it can hurt feelings and make it harder for others to listen to what you need."
   – *Teen*: "My concern is that when you shout at your sibling, it makes it harder to solve the problem and creates more tension between you two."

- School expectations
   – *Young child*: "My concern is that when homework isn't finished, it can make it harder for you to feel confident in class and keep up with your learning."
   – *Teen*: "My concern is that when assignments aren't turned in, it can make it harder to stay on track in class and might affect your grades."

- *Understanding versus agreement*: Your child does not have to agree with or care about your concern—but you do want them to understand it. Allow and even encourage them to express their perspective. Their input provides valuable insight, even if it differs from your own.
   – "I'm not concerned about not turning in my homework; I think it's a waste of time."
   – "I'm not concerned that my room is messy. I know where my things are."

Even if your child isn't ready to fully understand your concern, clarifying it for yourself will help you approach the conversation with confidence and compassion.

Your goal is to create engagement and conversation.

STEP 5: BRAINSTORM A SOLUTION TOGETHER

Now that both of your concerns are on the table, it's time to brainstorm a solution collaboratively. Frame the process as a partnership. For example, you could say:

- "I wonder if there's a way to resolve the situation that satisfies your concern that [state their concern] and my concern that [state your concern]."

Imagine sitting on the same side of a couch with your child while the problem sits across the room. This visualization helps shift the focus away from the tension between you and your child, reframing the problem as a shared challenge. This approach transforms the conversation from a stressful confrontation into a collaborative effort to find a solution.

1. Let Your Child Take the Lead

Encourage your child to share their ideas first. People naturally favor their own solutions, so giving your child the first opportunity to suggest ideas fosters trust and engagement. This demonstrates that you value their input and are committed to working together.

2. Write Down Every Idea

Capture all ideas, even if they seem unrealistic. Avoid judging or dismissing suggestions at this stage—every idea offers insight into your child's perspective and thought process.

3. Evaluate the Ideas Together

Discuss the proposed ideas to identify a solution that works for both of you. Focus on reaching a win–win agreement that is practical and sustainable. Consider these questions:

1. Does this address both of our concerns?
2. Is it realistic and achievable over time?
3. Will this work in the long run, not just in the moment?
4. Sometimes, a solution seems effective at first but doesn't hold up over time. A plan that relies too much on willpower or is too complicated may not last. Before agreeing, ask yourselves "Is this something we can realistically stick to?" If not, adjust it together.

4. Reflect on Whether the Problem Feels Unsolvable

If you're stuck, take a step back and evaluate whether the issue being discussed is the root problem or merely a symptom of a deeper challenge. Ask questions to uncover the underlying cause and adjust your focus as needed. For example:

1. Is the real issue procrastination in the morning, or is your child not getting enough sleep or feeling too hungry to concentrate?
2. Is the problem a lack of practice in their sport? Are they disengaged because their friends have left the team, or do they feel bullied?

Your beliefs about the problem guide your intervention. Stay curious, ask open-ended questions, and explore the "why" behind the behavior to uncover deeper issues that may need to be addressed.

STEP 6: MAKE AN AGREEMENT AND PLAN TO FOLLOW UP

Once you've brainstormed solutions together, the next step is to formalize your plan by creating a clear agreement. Writing it down helps ensure accountability, mutual understanding, and follow-through. This isn't about contracts or punishments—it's about setting clear expectations so that everyone knows what they agreed to.

Write an agreement together that clarifies each person's role. This process builds accountability, strengthens collaborative efforts, and sets the stage for constructive follow-up discussions.

STEPS TO CREATE AN EFFECTIVE AGREEMENT

1. Write Down the Plan Together
- Define exactly what each person is agreeing to do.
- Be specific to avoid confusion later.

2. Make Sure Everyone Knows Their Role
- *Child's role*: What actions will they take?
- *Parent's role*: How will they support the process without micromanaging?

3. Define How You'll Know the Plan Is Working
- What will success look like?
- How will both of you recognize progress?

4. Check Whether the Plan Is Realistic and Sustainable
A solution that works today might not hold up long term. Before finalizing, ask:
- Is this something we can maintain over time?
- Does it rely too much on willpower or perfect conditions?
- What will we do if it stops working?

5. Set a Time to Check Back In
- Checking in isn't about blame—it's about seeing whether the plan is effective.

- Follow-ups allow you to celebrate progress and make small adjustments if needed.

WHAT TO DO IF THE PLAN ISN'T WORKING

Not every plan works perfectly the first time. If the solution isn't meeting your goals, that doesn't mean it's a failure—it just means you may need to revisit and refine it together. The goal is to stay committed to collaborative problem solving, rather than slipping back into Plan A (imposing an adult solution).

Reassess and Adjust Together

Acknowledge What's Not Working
- Calmly state your observation without blame:
    - "I've noticed we're still having trouble getting out the door on time in the mornings. Let's talk about what might be getting in the way."

Reflect on the Plan
- Ask:
    - "Did one of us misunderstand the expectations?"
    - "Is the plan too difficult to follow consistently?"
    - "Have any new challenges come up since we created it?"

Make Small Tweaks as Needed
- Minor adjustments can make a big difference:
    - If bedtime at 8:30 p.m. isn't helping, try moving it to 8:15 p.m. for a trial period.
    - If following the routine is difficult, consider reminders or small incentives.

Example Agreements

Having a written agreement makes expectations clear and helps ensure follow-through.

Getting Homework Done

- *What is the plan?* → "I will start my homework at 5 p.m. after a 30-minute break."
- *How will we know it's working?* → "If I get my homework done without frustration."
- *What is the parent's role?* → "Give space and trust without hovering."
- *When should we check in?* → "One week."
- *What happens if the plan isn't working?* → "We'll talk about what's getting in the way and adjust."

Handling Frustration With a Sibling

- *What is the plan?* → "When I feel frustrated with my sibling, I will take a deep breath and use words to express my feelings instead of yelling or pushing."
- *How will we know it's working?* → "If I can stay calm and talk it out at least three times this week instead of reacting impulsively."
- *What is the parent's role?* → "Model calm communication and step in to help if needed, without immediately taking sides."
- *When should we check in?* → "After 1 week, we'll talk about how it's going and whether anything needs adjusting."
- *What happens if the plan isn't working?* → "We'll reflect on what's getting in the way—maybe we need a new strategy, like taking a short break before responding."

By structuring the agreement clearly and in writing, both you and your child are committing to mutual accountability in a way that builds trust and shared responsibility.

Remember, the agreement you create today is just a starting point. It's okay to revise it as circumstances change or as deeper concerns emerge.

This process isn't just about solving one issue—it's about showing your child that collaboration works and that they have a voice in shaping solutions.

CELEBRATE YOUR TEAMWORK

Take a moment to celebrate the effort and teamwork you and your child have invested in creating a solution together. Recognize even the small wins—whether it's sticking to a plan for a day, contributing ideas during brainstorming, or simply having an open and honest conversation. Every step forward is a step worth celebrating.

Creating Shared Solutions reinforces the value of collaboration and builds your child's confidence and connection with you. By working together, you are teaching essential life skills such as problem solving, communication, and empathy.

Treat challenges as learning opportunities, not failures. By revisiting and refining the plan collaboratively, you show your child that problem solving is an ongoing process. This reinforces that you are a team working toward a shared goal. Regularly revisiting the plan strengthens your partnership and demonstrates that finding a workable solution is just as important to you as it is to them.

Celebrating your progress doesn't mean the process is complete. Be patient and flexible, knowing that adjustments are a natural part of building trust and creating lasting solutions. Through this process, your child gains a deeper understanding of adaptability, accountability, and constructive problem solving. They learn that challenges can be addressed with resilience and empowerment.

By engaging in this process, you show your child that solutions can evolve over time. This reinforces trust, problem-solving skills, and open communication.

Remember: Anything you can talk out, you don't have to act out.

GETTING STARTED WITH THE PROCESS

Now that you understand how this process works, it's time to put it into practice.

Start by creating a list of the challenges you'd like to address using Plan B. These are the situations where your child struggles to meet expectations or displays maladaptive behaviors. For now, focus on just one issue to begin with.

When choosing your starting point, consider your relationship with your child. If your bond is strong and you can engage in productive conversations, it may help to begin with a challenge that occurs frequently or causes significant frustration. On the other hand, if your relationship is strained or communication is difficult, start with a smaller, more manageable issue—or one your child cares about, like bedtime routines or screen time limits.

Your child might find this process awkward or unfamiliar at first, especially if they aren't used to collaborative discussions or being asked for their input. Acknowledge this openly:

"I know this feels a little different from what we've done before, but I want to make sure we're working together in a way that feels fair and helpful for both of us." By normalizing their discomfort and framing the process as a team effort, you help set a positive tone and encourage participation.

Your initial goal is to help your child see the value of Creating Shared Solutions. This process teaches them that:

- Their concerns will be heard, acknowledged, and addressed.
- They will have a voice in decisions that affect them.

TEACHING THE PROCESS TO YOUR FAMILY

To make this process part of your family's culture, take time to teach everyone how it works. Start by explaining the three plans (A, B,

and C) and how they apply to different situations. Then, outline the
steps for Creating Shared Solutions in simple terms:

1. We listen to and understand each other's concerns.
2. We brainstorm solutions that work for both of us.
3. We write down our plan so everyone is clear on what to do.
4. We check back to see if the solution is working.
5. We adjust the plan if it's not working.

This process benefits everyone in the family, even in situations unrelated to parent–child disagreements. It creates a structured way to
address conflict, build trust, and develop problem-solving skills.

To introduce your family to the process, you might start with a
neutral, low-stakes example. For instance:

Mom says she wants to buy a boat. Dad quickly responds, "No way."

After some back-and-forth, Dad pauses and asks, "Why is having
a boat so important to you?"

Mom reflects and shares, "I love being on the water. It's so peaceful and calming to be surrounded by nature." Then she asks, "What
makes you so against the idea?"

Dad explains, "Boats are expensive and require a lot of mainte-
nance. Plus, when I was growing up, my friend always complained
about being stuck on the family boat every weekend because that's
what his parents wanted to do. I don't want to feel tied to something
like that."

Then, the family can brainstorm ideas together. They might agree
that a good solution would be for the parents to occasionally rent a
boat or perhaps buy a kayak so Mom can enjoy the water without a
big commitment.

This kind of example introduces the idea of collaboration in a safe
and approachable way, showing how understanding each other's perspectives can lead to creative solutions.

MAKE IT A ROUTINE

A regular time creates a safe and predictable opportunity for connection and problem solving, demonstrating to your children that their voice matters and that you're committed to working together as a team.

Consider setting aside specific times for these collaborative conversations, such as during weekly family meetings, Sunday night dinners, monthly dessert dates, or quiet moments before bedtime. These consistent opportunities not only help address ongoing concerns but also create a reliable routine for open communication.

During these times, encourage your child to reflect on any concerns they'd like to discuss—whether it's about your rules, a sibling, or a friend. By having a predictable framework for these conversations, you reinforce the idea that you are partners in solving problems. This process not only fosters trust but also helps your child feel supported, valued, and empowered to share their thoughts and collaborate on solutions.

REVIEWING THE PROCESS— SOME FINAL THOUGHTS

As you begin Creating Shared Solutions with your children, it's important to manage your expectations. Just like with other learning challenges, lagging skills won't improve overnight. Development takes time, and growth often happens gradually. Be patient and recognize that it will take time for everyone—your child and yourself—to trust that this process can work effectively. Remember, the goal is not perfection but progress.

Plan B is one of the most effective ways to teach critical skills and solve problems collaboratively. However, it works best when done *proactively* or *well after* an incident when emotions are calm. Kids and grown-ups alike "do well if they can," so approach the process with patience and tolerance.

TROUBLESHOOTING CHALLENGES

If your child is reluctant to participate or if the Plan B conversation isn't going as planned, pause to consider what might be getting in the way. Ask yourself:

- *Is this a good time to talk?* Are emotions heightened or are there external distractions?
- *Are your fuel tanks full?* Are you both emotionally and physically in a good place to have this conversation?
- *Do they need more time?* Maybe your child needs more time to think about their concerns before discussing them.
- *Is the issue too complex?* Breaking the problem into smaller, more manageable parts may help.
- *Do they trust your sincerity and intention?* If your child doubts your willingness to listen without judgment, they may hesitate to open up.
- *Are you unintentionally using "disguised" Plan A?* Ensure you're not subtly imposing a solution while framing it as collaboration.
- *Have you acknowledged your role?* Taking responsibility for how you might have contributed to the issue can help build trust.
- *Are you using shame, blame, or criticism?* These behaviors can shut down communication quickly.
- *Are you providing sufficient reassurance and empathy?* Show that you understand their perspective and care about their feelings.
- *Are you combining multiple concerns?* Focusing on one issue at a time avoids overwhelming your child or losing clarity. For example:
    - *Avoid*: "Getting ready in the morning takes too long." This combines multiple concerns, such as struggling to get out of bed, choosing clothes, and eating breakfast.
    - *Instead*: "I'm concerned that it's taking you a long time to pick

out clothes in the morning, and that's making you feel rushed." Breaking it into smaller, specific concerns makes it easier to address collaboratively.

WHAT IF THEY STILL RESIST?

If, despite your best efforts, your child continues to resist engaging in the process, it's okay to acknowledge their reluctance. You might say, "I'm willing to have this conversation and work together to come to an agreement. However, if you won't collaborate in good faith, I'll need to make a decision that I believe is best. It's your choice."

This sets a clear boundary while still leaving the door open for collaboration. Remember, the goal of Plan B is to work together, but as the parent, you're ultimately responsible for guiding your child and ensuring their well-being. Sometimes, simply giving them space to reflect and return to the discussion later can make all the difference.

"EMERGENCY" PLAN B

While Plan B works best when done proactively in a calm setting, there will be times when you need to resolve a conflict in the moment. These situations require flexibility and a clear framework to avoid escalation. When tensions run high, it's important to stay calm, recognize the signs of a power struggle, and "drop the bat." In other words, acknowledge that going back and forth in an emotional battle will not lead to a solution. Instead, focus on diffusing the situation and moving forward.

PREPARING FOR EMERGENCIES IN ADVANCE

You can teach your child how to handle these moments before they arise. When things are calm, explain how you'll address conflicts in urgent situations. Set clear expectations, such as:

1. *Calmly plead your case*: "You have one shot—tell me your concern calmly, without arguing or yelling. Help me understand why this is important to you and why you think I should reconsider."
2. *I will listen and consider your perspective*: "I promise to listen carefully and give serious thought to what you're saying."
3. *I will make a decision*: "Once the decision is made, it stands. There will be no further discussion, and we'll move on."

This process teaches your child how to advocate for themselves appropriately, even in emotionally charged moments. It also shows them that their voice matters, while reinforcing your role as the decision-maker.

An Example of Emergency Plan B in Action

Imagine you're picking your child up from a playdate, and they beg to stay longer. You calmly ask them to explain their reasoning. They share that they've been working on a building project for 2 hours and only have a few pieces left to finish.

You consider their perspective and decide based on the circumstances. If time allows, you might agree to stay for an additional 10 minutes. If not, you might explain that it's time to leave and that you'll do your best to help them find a time to complete the project later.

Or perhaps your teenager calls you at 9:45 p.m. asking to stay out past curfew because their friends want to go to a diner. You calmly ask them to explain their reasoning, and they share that they've been working on a stressful group project and want some time to relax and connect with their friends.

You consider their perspective and decide based on the circumstances. If it works, you might agree to extend their curfew by 30 minutes with the expectation that they will text you when they leave and come straight home. If not, you might explain why sticking to the original plan is necessary tonight, but discuss how to plan for similar situations in the future.

No matter the outcome, you've provided your child with the chance to express their perspective and feel heard.

REFLECTING AFTER THE MOMENT

After an emergency situation has been resolved, take time later to reflect on the experience. Ask yourself:
- Was this an isolated event, or is it part of a pattern?
- Do we need to revisit the expectation collaboratively to prevent similar conflicts in the future?

This reflection helps you refine your approach and prepare for future challenges.

START THE PROCESS EARLY

Creating Shared Solutions is a skill that can be introduced even when your children are very young. While younger children might not be able to fully engage in a collaborative conversation, you can still model the language and values behind the process. Explain that you want to hear their concerns, share your own, and solve problems together.

Though it may seem time-consuming at first, this process ultimately reduces ongoing conflicts and helps both you and your child develop important skills. And remember—you never need to agree to a solution that makes you uncomfortable. The goal is to find a resolution that respects both perspectives while maintaining appropriate boundaries.

GUIDING THOUGHTS

- "Without calm, there is no learning"—use proactive Plan B.
- Seek first to understand by listening carefully and asking questions with curiosity before offering solutions.
- Focus on fostering conversations, not confrontations, by inviting your child to be part of the solution rather than positioning them as the focus of the problem.
- Prioritize building skills over simply seeking compliance.
- Strive for progress, not perfection, by acknowledging their effort and small steps forward.
- Avoid shame, blame, and criticism—they shut down communication and connection.
- Change takes energy, patience, and time. Trust the process and give yourself grace to try again if you slip back into old patterns.
- "Kids do well if they can." If they could, they would.

HOMEWORK

1. Continue your one-on-one time with your children.
2. Prepare for a Plan B collaborative conversation with your child:
   a. Review the Guide to Clarifying Your Core Concern to reflect on the specific behavior or challenge you want to address and identify your core concern.
   b. Use the Guide to Listening to Their Concern, Brainstorming a Solution, and Writing the Agreement to plan the conversation, including how to introduce the topic, listen to your child's perspective, and work toward a shared solution.
   c. Consider writing down a few key points you want to share, including your concern, questions to ask, and how you will guide the conversation toward collaboration.
3. Reflect on how the conversation went:
   a. What worked well?

    b. What could you adjust for next time?

    c. Did your child feel heard, and did the discussion lead to a clearer understanding of both perspectives?

4. Schedule a regular time to practice Creating Shared Solutions as a family.

5. Use these moments to introduce the process, practice the skills together, and build trust in its effectiveness.

KEY 6

ACHIEVE CLARITY AND CONSISTENCY
The Power of Predictability

Decide what you want, decide what you are willing to exchange for it.
Establish your priorities and go to work.

—H. L. HUNT, OIL TYCOON

TAILORING PREDICTABILITY TO YOUR CHILD

Some people who have children with ADHD believe that clarity and consistency is the most important place to start working with them. After all, a structured, predictable environment helps children know what is expected of them, and they can simply follow the rules or face the consequences. Many parents who are strict and authoritative tend to excel at being consistent, with clear rules and predictable consequences for breaking them. This parenting style may work well for children who are naturally compliant: those motivated by pleasing their parents and equipped with the skills to meet expectations. In truth, *most parenting styles* work for these children because their inherent compliance makes it easier for them to adapt, regardless of the approach.

However, it's the more strong-willed and challenging children who require us to pay closer attention to how we parent. From a young age, children with ADHD often feel a strong need to control their own lives. Strict parenting can sometimes backfire, triggering more oppositional or obstinate behavior. As we've seen, the way we talk with our children and our willingness to involve them in decision making can significantly influence their behavior and compliance.

The advice to simply be strict and consistent may not always work for these children, especially given the inherently unpredictable environment created by ADHD. Maintaining consistency can be particularly challenging in these circumstances. For these children, the parenting style we choose plays a critical role in shaping their development.

That's why my personal mantra is always *parent the child you have*! Even within the same family, siblings can be vastly different—displaying unique interests, talents, passions, and behaviors, despite being raised by the same parents. Each child is born with a unique temperament and neurological makeup, which greatly impacts how they respond to their world. As I mentioned previously, I've found that children often fall into two camps: those who are generally compliant and able to solve differences relatively easily, and those who are more strong-willed and challenging to parent. Even within the same family, you may need to approach each child differently, recognizing their unique temperament and needs.

Recognizing the importance of flexibility and adaptability in our parenting does not absolve us from the need for clarity and consistency. In fact, it is through being clear and consistent that we help children build the skills they are lacking and develop the emotional self-regulation they need to succeed in life. However, clarity and consistency should be paired with an understanding that every child is unique. For one child, a verbal reminder might be enough, while another might need a visual schedule to stay on track. Tailoring your expectations and approaches ensures that each child gets what they need to thrive. Remember, fair does not always mean equal; it means providing the support and structure that works best for each child. By balancing clarity and consistency with flexibility, we not only teach critical skills but also foster the emotional security children need to grow and thrive.

With this, we can add another part of the roof to our home (Figure 6.1).

I've often found that rules and expectations are discussed only after something has gone wrong. By then, negative habits have already formed, and making adjustments becomes much harder. For children to be held accountable for their actions and responsibilities, they first need to know what's expected of them. It sounds simple, right? Yet,

FIGURE 6.1:

House: Clarity and Consistency

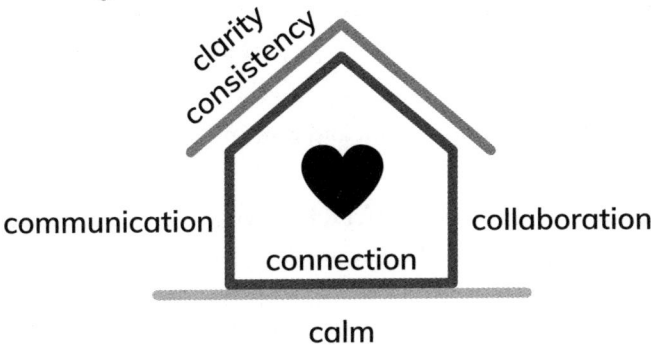

Building our home

clarity
consistency

communication   collaboration

connection

calm

© Cindy Goldrich

so often, parents don't give much thought to what they want their children to do—or not do—until a specific problem arises.

But here's the catch: You can't be clear and consistent if you're not clear with yourself about your bottom line—your nonnegotiable rules.

There's a cartoon I love that perfectly captures this dilemma. It shows two people reviewing a contract. One says to the other, "Sign here to indicate you have no idea what you're signing." Unfortunately, that's often what we're saying to our children when we're not upfront about our rules and expectations. And let's face it: We've all been there.

Think for a moment: Do your children actually know the rules and expectations in your home? Consider these areas:

- *Bedtime*: What does "bedtime" mean—being ready, screens off, and lights out?
- *Cleaning up*: When and what exactly needs to be cleaned?
- *Homework*: Is there a set time and place? How much involvement do you expect from yourself?
- *Electronics*: Are there clear rules for phones, computers, and tablets?
- *Privacy*: When can doors stay closed, and when must they stay open?
- *Dinnertime*: How long should they stay at the table?
- *Language*: What's acceptable, and what's a no-go?
- *Chores*: What are they, and when should they be done?
- *Handling disagreements*: What's the family playbook for resolving conflict?
- *Playdates*: Who arranges them, and how often are they allowed?

Children, especially those with ADHD, need to know what to expect. They need to understand the basic rules of their universe. By being proactive and setting clear expectations from the start, you can create a more predictable environment that benefits both you and your child. After all, wouldn't you rather have a plan than find yourself in cartoon-worthy chaos?

However, consistency is not just about the rules parents set for their children; it's also about how co-parents align in presenting those rules. When parents have differing views on priorities or values, children can become confused about what is expected of them—or worse, feel torn between pleasing one parent over the other. Addressing these differences early and presenting a united front helps create the clarity children need to feel secure and supported. Just as alignment between parents creates clarity for children, the boundaries we set and the predictability we maintain provide a framework that children can rely on to feel secure.

THE POWER OF BOUNDARIES AND PREDICTABILITY

Many children love video games. Why? In addition to being visually stimulating, they are, in certain ways, predictable and consistent. Video games provide immediate feedback. If you lose a challenge, you lose—no amount of yelling, negotiating, or crying will earn you another chance or extra life. Unlike real-world situations, video games never judge, criticize, or make you feel bad about your mistakes. Instead, they offer a clear set of rules and consequences, encouraging children to focus their energy on learning the game rather than fighting the rules—because the rules won't, and don't, change.

Boundaries and predictability work in much the same way in real life. For some children, strict and consistent boundaries work beautifully, helping them feel secure and supported. But for strong-willed children, especially those with ADHD, these same approaches can backfire. A rigid style may trigger resistance or power struggles. By balancing structure with flexibility and adapting to each child's needs, parents can create an environment where clarity thrives without creating unnecessary conflict.

Within families, this clarity must often account for individual differences. Siblings, even when raised by the same parents, frequently display unique temperaments that demand tailored approaches. While one child may thrive under verbal reminders and a simple routine, another may require visual cues or consistent prompts to stay on track. Recognizing these differences ensures fairness—not by treating all children identically but by tailoring strategies to meet their unique needs. This is a critical component of clarity and consistency.

Research has shown that infants thrive in environments with clear boundaries and structure. Studies by Catherine Tamis-LeMonda and Marc Bornstein (2002) highlight how infants' abilities to explore and engage deeply in play is significantly influenced by the clarity of boundaries set by caregivers. When provided with predictable and structured environments, infants feel safer and are more likely to explore their surroundings with confidence (Tamis-LeMonda & Bornstein, 2002).

This principle applies to people of all ages. We function better when we operate within known, reasonable boundaries—clear, predictable expectations that guide us.

For children with ADHD, clarity and consistency aren't just helpful; they are essential. This structure addresses specific challenges, including:

- *Time management*: With difficulties anticipating and measuring time, children benefit from knowing when they are expected to do something, complete something, or be somewhere.
- *Working memory*: Clear, visible, and predictable guidelines reduce the need to hold rules and expectations in their head.
- *Emotional regulation*: Clearly defined rules leave less room for disagreements and arguments.
- *Transitions*: Many children with ADHD struggle to stop one activity and switch to another, often due to hyper-focus or reluctance to start something new. As we discussed in Key 1, transitions involve three parts: stopping the current activity, moving toward the next, and starting the new activity. Each step can pose unique challenges for children with ADHD. Providing clear boundaries and predictable

routines helps ease transitions, offering children the external support they need to navigate these changes more successfully.

Remember, "kids do well if they can." Our goal is to help them manage their emotions and develop their EF skills. By providing consistent *external* supports, we can help them build the *internal* regulation needed to respond thoughtfully rather than react impulsively to life's demands.

FACILITATING SMOOTH TRANSITIONS

Just as boundaries help children feel secure, clear routines and preparation can make transitions more manageable. Preparation, guidance, and connection are the keys to easing transitions. Following are a few tips:

UNDERSTANDING TIME AWARENESS

Children with ADHD often struggle to perceive time accurately, making it challenging for them to plan or transition effectively. Time awareness develops gradually and varies significantly by age. Here's a general guide to typical developmental time awareness:

- *2-year-olds*: Time is "now." Future events hold little meaning.
- *3- to 5-year-olds*: Can conceptualize 5–20 minutes, such as waiting for a snack or transitioning to playtime, but "next week" feels abstract.
- *6- to 8-year-olds (1st–3rd grade)*: Can plan for events happening within 8–12 hours, like understanding something will happen "after school" or "tomorrow." Longer time frames remain vague.
- *9- to 12-year-olds (middle school)*: Start to manage 2–3 days with support, like studying for a test or preparing for a weekend activity.
- *13- to 18-year-olds (high school)*: Can anticipate 2–3 weeks for projects or exams but often struggle to break tasks into steps without guidance.

- *Young adults (18–35 years)*: Continue developing the ability to plan for 3–5 weeks or more, depending on their experience and use of external tools.

Remember that children with ADHD may lag behind their peers in these abilities, requiring additional support to manage tasks and transitions effectively.

STRATEGIES TO MAKE TIME REAL

Making time tangible helps children understand and manage it effectively:

1. *Daily overviews*: Let your child know in advance what their schedule is to avoid surprises. This allows them to plan their time efficiently, whether it's making social plans or preparing for a test or project. It also provides time to voice concerns or make adjustments before the pressure of the moment. If you won't be available for rides or homework help, let them know early so they can plan ahead. Encourage the use of an agenda book to keep appointments in one place, and teach them to handle sensitive entries (like doctor's visits) discreetly.

2. *Visual timers and clocks*: Tools like the "Time Timer" visually represent time passing, making it easier for children to grasp how much time remains for a task. Place clocks in key locations, and encourage children to set their own timers for tasks to build responsibility. These timers are particularly effective for younger children or those who have difficulty perceiving time.

3. *Encourage your child to set timers for time-based tasks*: For example, instead of saying, "Come down in 5 minutes," say, "Set your timer for 5 minutes." This approach fosters responsibility and reduces the need for constant reminders. Together, these tools create a structured environment that makes transitions smoother and more predictable.

4. *Visual aids*: Use visual schedules, charts, or checklists to make transitions clearer and more predictable. For example, a morning checklist can outline tasks like brushing teeth, eating breakfast, and packing a bag for school. These tools provide a concrete reference point and reduce the cognitive load of trying to remember everything. Younger children might benefit from pictures alongside text, while older children may prefer written or digital lists.

5. *Break tasks into chunks*: For long-term projects, divide the work into smaller, manageable steps with clear deadlines. Use calendars or checklists to track progress and keep the timeline visible.

6. *Ample warning*: Even with tools like timers, children may need extra time to finish activities, especially if they're deeply engaged. If patterns of resistance emerge, have a Plan B-type collaborative conversation to address the underlying issues and find durable solutions.

7. *Choosing a stopping point*: Help your child identify a natural stopping point before transitioning. For example, suggest they complete two more game turns, finish four more pages of a book, or add 10 more beads to a craft. This gives them a sense of control and makes transitions feel less abrupt.

8. *Acknowledgment*: Before asking your child to switch tasks, acknowledge what they're doing. This small gesture shows respect for their activity and teaches them to reciprocate. For instance: "I see you're engrossed in your book. Can you help me unload the groceries in a few minutes?"

9. *Joining in*: Sometimes, children need a little extra support to transition successfully. For example, if your child is playing a video game, sit with them and take an interest in their progress. Ask where a good stopping point might be and show enthusiasm as they reach it. A brief moment of connection can make transitions smoother and build trust.

10. *Routines that signal it's time to start*: Just as athletes and chefs have routines to prepare for their tasks, help your child create a con-

sistent routine for starting work. Creating consistent routines for starting tasks, like clearing the desk, grabbing a snack, or using a favorite item signal readiness and ease the initiation of work.

Our own upbringing uniquely shapes our parenting style. Some parents consciously or unconsciously mimic their own upbringing, while others intentionally strive to do the opposite of what their parents did. Partners may love and respect each other but don't necessarily share the same set of parenting ideas and values. This can lead to children playing one parent off the other or behaving differently depending on which parent is present.

If you have a parenting partner, it's crucial to explicitly discuss your beliefs about core issues and parenting styles. Work together to reach an agreement on your nonnegotiable rules and expectations, ensuring you parent as a team. Without these conversations, differences in your approaches are more likely to emerge during moments of stress or conflict—precisely when productive problem solving is hardest to achieve.

Parenting a child with special needs often adds additional layers of complexity. The divorce rate among parents of children with special needs is significantly higher than average. This is not just due to the challenges of raising a child with unique needs but also because these challenges often force parents to confront their own differences more frequently. While other couples may spend evenings socializing, parents of children with special needs may find themselves canceling plans or spending their rare moments together discussing how to face the next challenge.

The added stress makes it vital to address and resolve differences with care and attention. Unresolved tensions not only strain the partnership but can also create confusion and stress for the child. Sometimes, having a third person to help guide these conversations can be invaluable. When I work with couples, I remind them that while they may have different beliefs and perspectives, their love for their child is the common thread that unites them. Putting egos aside and working collaboratively is essential.

Keep your disagreements private whenever possible—children generally shouldn't be involved in or witness these conversations. However, if your children happen to observe you disagreeing, take the opportunity to model conflict resolution. Children often see their parents argue, only to watch them retreat and then return as if nothing happened. This can leave children wondering whether their parents truly resolved the issue or simply ignored it.

Whenever appropriate, briefly share that you and your partner worked together to understand each other and find a solution. For example, you might say, "We had different ideas about how to handle this, but we talked about it, listened to each other, and came to an agreement." This transparency teaches children that disagreements can be worked through respectfully and helps them understand what healthy conflict resolution looks like.

Use the Creating Shared Solutions skills we've discussed to resolve your differences, and don't hesitate to seek outside support if needed. A neutral third party can help facilitate clearer communication and mediate differences, making the journey just a little bit easier for everyone.

RIGHTS VERSUS PRIVILEGES

One of our responsibilities as parents is to teach our children how life works in the real world. We need to parent in a way that doesn't "bend the universe" by creating vastly different rules at home than what they'll encounter in society. Instead, our role is to build an environment that gradually prepares them for adult expectations and helps them understand what they can reasonably expect from others.

For the most part, I strongly believe we need to help children develop their own pathways and give them plenty of autonomy in doing so. However, we also need to ensure they are building good habits, morals, and opportunities—even when they are too young to fully appreciate the impact of their behaviors.

As we explored in Key 5, *motivation* thrives when we have a sense of autonomy, mastery, and purpose. However, motivation isn't always present when we want or need it to be. Some children are naturally compliant and will follow directions to please their parents or teachers. Others require more motivation. For instance, a 7-year-old likely won't feel a deep sense of purpose in cleaning their room. In these cases, we may need to use our best communication skills and Plan B conversations to understand and address their concerns.

Sometimes, even after these discussions, providing an incentive may be helpful as they build new habits. Over time, children often come to appreciate the benefits of routines like cleaning their room—even if they don't want to admit it to you!

One critical concept to teach children is the distinction between a *right* and a *privilege*: what they can reasonably expect versus the privileges we provide. If this distinction isn't clear, children may develop a misguided sense of entitlement, both at home and in life. This becomes even more important as children grow older, especially if you decide to restrict certain privileges based on behavior.

I believe children have the right to security, food, shelter, education, and love. Most other things can be considered privileges, such as having playdates, desserts, or getting a small toy for good behavior during errands. Many parents are lenient with certain activities—like screen time, treats, or playdates—because the perceived negative effects seem minimal. However, when these privileges are given freely and without clear boundaries, children may begin to view them as rights. This leniency can create a pattern where privileges lose their value and their connection to behavior becomes unclear.

While this might suggest treating everything besides security, food, shelter, and education as a privilege, it's often more nuanced. When considering restricting a privilege, think about the developmental benefits of the activity. For example, taking guitar lessons might seem like a privilege, but it could also be the one area where your child feels competent and passionate. Canceling a lesson might undermine their confidence or waste resources if payments have already been made. Similarly, skipping a soccer practice could impact teammates and coaches or create long-term consequences for your child's growth and development.

In the next chapter, we explore how to determine when and how to use boundaries and privileges effectively. For now, remember that your child's brain is "under construction." Balancing discipline with opportunities for growth and connection is essential to supporting their development.

Take some time to reflect on what you consider your child's rights versus their privileges. Discuss these with your partner to ensure you're aligned. This clarity will help you establish boundaries that are both consistent and fair.

A NOTE ABOUT GIFTS

When children receive gifts—especially expensive ones like phones or gaming systems—they often assume these items are theirs to use whenever and however they wish. If you anticipate issues regarding the use of a gift, it's better to establish conditions from the beginning. For example, you might explain that while the item belongs to them, its use is contingent on specific guidelines you set. Having this discussion upfront can prevent conflicts later and ensure everyone understands the expectations.

DEVELOPING A LIST OF INCENTIVES

Proactively developing a list of potential incentives can be a powerful tool for motivating your child toward positive behavior. It can also save you from the trap of spontaneously offering something you might regret moments later! Involve your child in creating this list so they feel invested in earning the rewards. You may even be surprised by what truly motivates them—insights you hadn't considered before.

Here are some questions to guide your conversation:

- What are your child's favorite restaurants or dessert places?
- What special games or activities do they enjoy?
- What small toy, book, or other material item might they find exciting to earn? (Avoid items that would take too long to work toward.)
- What task or responsibility would they like to "opt out of" in exchange for completing another?
- What special privilege would motivate them?

Have fun and be creative when brainstorming—think pillow fights, mini golf outings, or a late bedtime. Remember, one of the most valuable rewards (often overlooked or unspoken, especially by older children) is time spent with you. Whenever possible, try to include yourself in the incentive. For example, you could shop for the reward together, watch a movie as a family, or share a special outing. These moments not only reinforce the reward but also strengthen your connection with your child.

TO BE RESPONSIBLE, THEY MUST BE RESPONSE-ABLE!

Just because your child *should* be able to keep track of their time, materials, and obligations doesn't mean they are ready yet. Remember, ADHD is a developmental disorder. Sometimes, it can be helpful to create your own "504 plan" for the home. The goal isn't just compliance—it's about helping your child develop the proper life skills they'll need to thrive. This means making accommodations and modifications that allow them to build success incrementally.

Here are two ways you can help compensate for weak or developing EF skills:

1. *Modify the expectation*: Break tasks into smaller, manageable parts so your child can gradually take responsibility. For example, instead of asking them to make the entire bed before school, start by asking them to pull up the blanket and place the pillow where it belongs. This helps them get used to setting aside time, following directions, and creating order without feeling overwhelmed.

2. *Modify the environment*: Just as we modify environments for younger children (e.g., safety locks on cabinets, cushioning sharp corners), children with ADHD often benefit from adjustments to reduce distractions and challenges. While some parents consider removing all distractions from a child's room, this can feel restrictive for a child who values having their "stuff" around them. Instead, work together to identify helpful changes. For instance, a trifold poster board—like those used for school projects—can be placed on a desk or work area to block out distractions and create a focused space.

By making these adjustments, you're not lowering the bar—you're creating the scaffolding they need to meet expectations successfully. Over time, these supports help them build the skills and confidence to take on more responsibilities independently.

JUST WHAT ARE YOUR CHILD'S RESPONSIBILITIES?

As we discussed earlier in this chapter, being clear and upfront about your expectations makes it much easier to identify areas in need of improvement. Once you've created a list of routine responsibilities for your child, it's important to communicate these clearly. This isn't about imposing an entirely new set of expectations but rather clarifying and articulating their current responsibilities to eliminate misunderstandings.

Start with the basics—perhaps tasks your child is already doing—and add one or two areas where you'd like to see improvement. For any new responsibilities, take time to discuss them in detail and ask your child if they anticipate any challenges in following through. Depending on their age and development, you may also want to break each task into smaller, more manageable steps.

For Younger Children

For younger children, a checklist can help create structure and consistency. For example:

Morning Checklist
- Eat breakfast.
- Brush and floss teeth.
- Wash face.
- Brush hair.
- Get dressed.
- Make bed.

Make this process fun by inviting your child to decorate the list. If they're too young to read, use pictures or photographs of them doing the tasks. Laminating the chart allows for reusable checkmarks, adding an interactive element.

For Older Children and Teens

Older children or teens may need less detail but more responsibility. For instance:

Daily Responsibilities
- Hang up coat in the closet when you get home.
- Clear dishes after meals.

- Put dirty clothes in the hamper before bed.
- Set alarm for the morning.
- Straighten up the bathroom.

Each responsibility should be specific, achievable, and not tied to behavior (e.g., avoid tasks related to language or conflict). If time sensitive, include a clear expectation, such as "Get dressed by 8:15 a.m.," and ensure tools like clocks and timers are available to help them succeed.

BUILDING HABITS WITH SUPPORT

Keep in mind that it may take months to establish a new habit. Continued support and reminders will likely be necessary as your child learns to take responsibility. If your child struggles to comply, involve them in finding solutions. For example, they could set an alarm or agree to one reminder from you. This might also be a time to introduce a small incentive to help them stay motivated as they work on building this new habit.

Remember to use your communication skills and the Creating Shared Solutions approach to foster collaboration and understanding. Above all, focus on helping your child succeed. For now, don't worry about what to do if they don't comply—we'll tackle that issue shortly.

A THOUGHT ABOUT CHORES

One of the best ways to create order and balance at home is by having children contribute to the family through chores. Here, I define chores as tasks or responsibilities that impact not just the child but the entire family. For instance, cleaning their own room primarily benefits them, but taking out the garbage, setting the dinner table, or emptying the dishwasher benefits everyone.

In households where there is a lot of noncompliance or stress, parents sometimes avoid asking children to do family chores. Some even skip asking for basic help, like grabbing an item from the pantry or helping unpack groceries. However, assigning family chores sends an important message: Contributing to the household is a shared responsibility.

It's up to each family to decide what chores should be shared among its members. These decisions will depend on your values, household needs, available time, and other factors. At a minimum, I recommend assigning at least one age-appropriate chore that directly impacts the family. Beyond contributing to the household, these responsibilities help children develop planning, organizational, and cooperation skills.

Family chores can also include larger, occasional tasks, like a seasonal or annual "clean out." This involves each family member going through their personal belongings to decide what to give away, throw away, or keep. As a shared activity, it might include organizing the playroom or cleaning out the garage. This is a great way to help children reflect on their growth—physically and emotionally—as they outgrow certain items. It's also a perfect opportunity to reestablish order and cleanliness in your home. Consider timing these clean outs around birthdays, seasonal changes, or major holidays for a natural rhythm.

AND ABOUT THEIR ROOM . . .

Many parents find themselves in ongoing battles over the cleanliness and orderliness of their child's room. This issue often becomes more pronounced during the tween and teen years. For children with ADHD, who may already struggle with organization and time management, maintaining a tidy room can feel overwhelming. Without clear guidelines, their space can quickly get out of hand, turning into a daunting project to bring back order.

To avoid unnecessary conflict, I recommend creating an explicit agreement about what is required versus what is suggested. For example, if the state of your child's room begins to negatively impact their ability to function—whether it's finding things, completing homework, or socializing—it may be time to set clear expectations. Some families find it helpful to establish a once-a-week cleaning rule, such as "the room must be clean by Sunday night at 7 p.m." Be sure to define what "clean" means to avoid misunderstandings.

You might also want to set specific rules regarding food and beverages in their room, especially if these items aren't being removed in a timely manner. For laundry, consider establishing a rule that if your child wants their clothes washed, they are responsible for getting them to the hamper by a designated time. If they miss the deadline, they'll learn the natural consequence of not having their favorite shirt clean when they want it—an easy life lesson for you to let unfold without intervention.

When it comes to doing laundry, children can learn this skill at a surprisingly young age with your guidance. Even if they aren't responsible for laundry on a regular basis, you might consider making it their responsibility during vacations or summer breaks when they aren't as busy. Not only does this prepare them for the future (think college or living independently) but it also gives you a well-deserved break.

USING INCENTIVES TO MOTIVATE COMPLIANCE WITH RESPONSIBILITIES

As we discussed in Key 5, when a task is clear, manageable, and within your child's capability (response-able), incentives or rewards can help improve compliance by creating a connection between effort and achievement. If your child is struggling with certain responsibilities, consider focusing on just one or two tasks and providing incentives to help them develop a habit.

Many parents have tried sticker charts and similar tools, only to find them ineffective. Often, the problem lies in the complexity of the system—too many tasks or unclear expectations. Keep it simple and focused.

If you decide to use an incentive, discuss with your child how and when they can earn a reward. Make sure they understand the expectations and agree on the terms. Encourage your child to take responsibility for tracking their progress and be consistent and timely in providing the rewards they've earned. Remember, your ongoing praise—Notice, Name, Nourish—remains a vital motivator, regardless of the incentive system.

KEEPING TRACK OF INCENTIVE PROGRAMS

1. *Clarity is key*: Be specific about your expectations and how rewards can be earned. Incentives should focus on task compliance, not behavior.

2. *Start small*: Especially at the beginning, offer support to help your child succeed. Provide reminders as necessary, but gradually reduce these to encourage independence.

3. *Visual tools*: Use stickers, marbles, coins, or even apps to track progress. Visual reminders, such as a dot-to-dot drawing where completing the picture leads to a reward, can keep motivation high.

4. *Rewards are final*: Once a child earns points or rewards, don't take them away. This helps maintain trust and motivation. Consider offering bonus points for tasks done exceptionally well or in a timely manner.

5. *Be discreet*: Avoid exposing your child's incentive program to outsiders. Public attention may feel embarrassing and reduce their willingness to participate.

SHORT, IMMEDIATE REWARDS FOR BEHAVIOR

If shopping or errands are stressful, try implementing a brief, specific incentive program for the event. For example:

- Set a goal for good behavior (e.g., no wandering, whining, or begging).
- Define the reward in advance and specify how it can be earned. For instance, your child could earn 5 points for every 10 minutes of good behavior, needing X points for the reward.

Ensure the reward can be earned during the trip to help them stay focused. If they fall short, allow them to save their points for future use. When rewarding behavior, be specific about what your child did well: "You stayed by my side at the mall today, and I really appreciated your cooperation." This reinforces the desired behavior and helps your child understand exactly what they did right.

BALANCING PERFORMANCE AND BEHAVIOR

Remember, age is just a number—it doesn't define readiness or ability. Your child may need your presence and support to stay on task and feel grounded. Be patient and maintain perspective.

Pushing too hard for performance can create stress, making it harder for your child to regulate their emotions. Sometimes, adjusting expectations in one area can reduce tension and make room for progress in another. For example, if the battle over room cleanliness is straining your relationship, you might scale back expectations there to focus more on fostering cooperation in other areas.

ARE YOU TRYING TO DO TOO MUCH?

In our efforts to be loving, caring, and supportive, some parents unintentionally take on too much—regardless of whether their child has ADHD or other challenges. We strive to be all things to all people, rarely saying no to requests for help and often sacrificing our own wants, needs, and desires for the benefit of others.

If this sounds like you, take a moment to consider the message this may be sending to your family. While your actions may come from a place of love and care, they might unintentionally convey that others are not as capable, that they don't need to be as responsible, or even that their needs are more important than yours. As your children grow, it's essential to ensure they become strong, independent, and capable adults who also respect your independence and worth.

Taking care of yourself isn't selfish—it's essential. When you prioritize your own needs, you model balance and self-respect for your children. This teaches them that caring for oneself is a key part of healthy relationships and life. By creating space for your well-being, you also recharge your capacity to be present and supportive of those you love most.

It's worth pausing to evaluate what you're doing. Is there room to let others in your family do more for themselves—or perhaps even more for you? You might also reflect on whether certain tasks or responsibilities can be modified or eliminated entirely. If you're finding it difficult to make time for yourself or other truly important priorities, it could be a sign that you're trying to do too much.

GUIDING THOUGHTS

- Strive to be consistent—but *parent the child you have.*
- To be responsible, your child must first be response-able.
- Be clear and explicit about rights versus privileges.

- Keep reward programs simple and structured.
- Real change takes time (30–40 times or 2–4 months)—be patient and persevere.
- Don't try to be a "super-parent"—take care of yourself too.

HOMEWORK

1. *Determine your nonnegotiable house rules*: Be clear, concise, and specific.
2. *Discuss chores and responsibilities*: Work with your child to clarify their responsibilities and provide the tools and support they need to succeed.
3. *Define rights, gifts, and privileges*: Clearly distinguish between what your child can expect and what must be earned.
4. *Create a list of potential incentives*: Collaborate with your child to develop motivating rewards and include opportunities to share the payoff together.
5. *Identify possible consequences*: Develop a thoughtful list of items or privileges you might take away if necessary, considering potential unintended consequences.
6. *Spend one-on-one time*: Continue prioritizing moments of connection to strengthen your relationship.

KEY 7

IMPACTFUL CONSEQUENCES
Building Accountability
and Growth

The consequences of an act affect the probability of its occurring again.

—B. F. SKINNER

Many parents who work with me want to start by outlining consequences to ensure their children cooperate and meet expectations. However, our goal is not merely compliance; we seek systemic and sustainable changes. This means helping children internalize behaviors and skills that will serve them in the long term, rather than just reacting to immediate challenges.

Consequences, whether positive or negative, are not a stand-alone solution. They are a complementary tool in the parenting toolbox to guide behavior and foster accountability. As we explore, the process of helping children build compliance and responsibility is far more complex than simply taking things away.

Unfortunately, as you probably understand by now, there is no easy fix, no easy answer. Sometimes, enforcing a consequence for one behavior may unintentionally create larger challenges in other areas. (So, if you have skipped ahead to this chapter, my apologies!)

With a deeper understanding of how a child's neurological makeup and environment influence their behavior, we can now introduce meaningful consequences. Think of consequences as the protective layer that supports the foundation you've already built. Figure 7.1 illustrates how meaningful consequences form part of the roof, protecting and completing the structure of effective parenting.

As you face parenting challenges, pay attention to your own behavior and mindset. Notice when you feel overly anxious or frustrated, as losing your calmness means losing control. Your child may sense this and feel empowered in those moments. Step back, regain your composure, and provide them with the stability they need to feel secure and guided. *Remember*: Your calm is your power. Without calm, there is no learning, no connection, and no opportunity for growth—for you or your child.

FIGURE 7.1:
House: Consequences

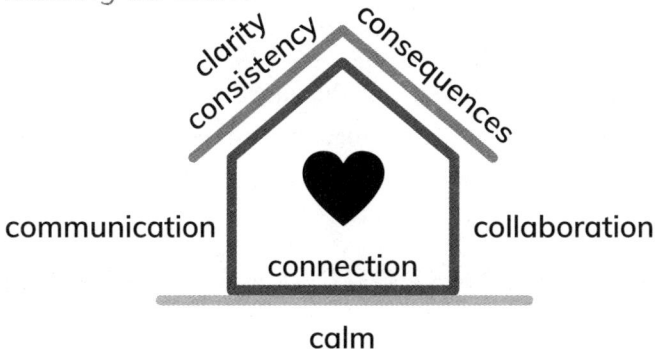

Building our home
clarity
consistency
consequences
communication
connection
collaboration
calm

© Cindy Goldrich

WHY ARE NEGATIVE CONSEQUENCES NECESSARY?

Negative consequences serve important purposes, not just within families but across society as a whole.

1. *To help societies run smoothly and safely*: Consequences create order and structure, ensuring that everyone understands the boundaries of acceptable behavior. For example, speeding, vandalizing, or assaulting others leads to penalties, discouraging harmful actions and promoting safety. Similarly, failing to fulfill obligations, like paying taxes or registering a vehicle, results in legal consequences to maintain societal order.

2. *To ensure the rights of others are not violated*: Consequences help safeguard individual freedoms by holding people accountable for respecting others' rights. Without clear consequences, people may act in ways that disregard the well-being of others, creating chaos or harm. For instance, laws against theft or property damage protect personal ownership and foster trust within communities.

3. *To protect against failure*: This means helping children learn from mistakes and develop the resilience and skills needed to overcome challenges. (We delve into this one later!)

While negative consequences are an essential part of parenting and society, they are just one part of the equation. Building compliance and cooperation requires a broader understanding of why behavior happens and how to guide it effectively.

WHERE DO CONSEQUENCES COME FROM?

There are five key areas of life where individuals experience consequences:

1. *Government*: Rules and laws create consequences, such as fines for speeding or penalties for neglecting civic responsibilities. These consequences maintain order and safety at a societal level.
2. *Society/peers*: Social interactions bring their own consequences. For example, children may face exclusion or ostracism if they struggle with social norms, while positive interactions can build friendships and community.
3. *Biology*: The body imposes its own consequences. Poor hygiene, unhealthy eating habits, or lack of exercise can lead to health problems, no matter how nice and well-meaning you are!
4. *School*: Academic settings have structured consequences, such as detention, suspension, or grade retention. Opportunities for advancement are tied to performance and behavior.
5. *Family*: Within the family, parents hold the greatest control over consequences. This is where expectations, rules, and boundaries are directly shaped and enforced by caregivers.

LEVELS OF PARENTAL CONTROL

Our influence as parents varies across these five areas:
- In *government*, *society/peers*, and *biology*, we have limited control. For younger children, we can guide behavior behind the scenes—such as arranging or avoiding certain playdates, encouraging good hygiene, or making healthy food choices. But as children grow, our influence in these areas naturally diminishes.
- In *school*, we have greater input. While we may not control the school's policies, we can advocate for our children by collaborating with teachers and administrators. In some cases, we may even choose to change schools to better support their needs.
- In *family life*, we hold the most control. Within our homes, we set the tone, create the rules, and establish the consequences for behavior.

Understanding where we have influence—and where we don't—helps us focus our energy on the areas where we can make the most meaningful impact.

WHAT MAKES A CONSEQUENCE EFFECTIVE?

For a consequence to be effective, it must meet several criteria:

1. It Is as Closely Related to the Offense as Possible—a "Natural Consequence"

Natural consequences allow children to experience the real-world impact of their actions. For example:

- If a 5-year-old repeatedly throws their toy truck despite warnings and the wheel breaks off, they can't play with it until it's fixed.
- If a 12-year-old forgets to put their bike in the garage, they wake up to find it wet and rusty.
- If a 17-year-old consistently arrives late to their part-time job, the boss might reduce their hours.

Natural consequences are impactful because they directly connect the behavior to the outcome, helping children internalize the lesson.

2. The Child Cares Enough About the Outcome to Adjust Their Actions

For a consequence to influence behavior, it must matter to the child. For example:

- If taking away a phone doesn't motivate change because the child switches to their computer, the consequence loses its effectiveness.
- Conversely, a child who remembers to return borrowed items might notice their friends trust them more, naturally reinforcing the positive behavior.

3. The Child Is Response-Able and Can Anticipate the Impact of Their Actions

Children with ADHD often struggle with time perception and connecting present actions to future outcomes. For a consequence to work, children must have the tools, skills, and understanding to meet expectations:

- This means tailoring consequences to the child's developmental level and providing clear guidance to help them succeed.

TIMING AND RELEVANCE MATTER

Consequences are most effective when they are timely and relevant. For children with ADHD, the closer the consequence is to the behavior, the greater the impact. For instance, an earlier bedtime tonight is more effective than missing a playdate several days later.

SEVERITY VERSUS CONNECTION

Harsh consequences often lead children to focus on their anger rather than the lesson. Effective consequences should teach expected behavior while maintaining connection and trust. Consequences should generally last no longer than 24 hours. By the next day, many children have reframed what happened, minimizing the severity of their actions and viewing the consequence as unreasonable. This can lead to challenges if the behavior repeats—extended consequences can quickly escalate into unrealistic restrictions.

BE SPECIFIC AND CLEAR

Vague expectations like "behave better" or "act responsibly" can leave your child confused and frustrated. They need to know exactly what is expected of them and what will happen if those expectations aren't met. For instance, if a child behaves well most of the day but struggles in the evening, does this one difficult moment erase all the positive behavior? Ambiguity like this can feel unfair and de-motivating. Specific expectations help children understand what is required of them and connect their actions to outcomes in a fair and meaningful way.

Instead of general statements, be clear and actionable. For example:

- *Time-oriented consequence*: "If you're not ready for school by 7:30 a.m., you'll lose your screen time after school today." This sets a specific time frame and a clear consequence tied to the behavior.
- *Task-oriented consequence*: "You need to clean up your toys before dinner. If you don't, I'll put them away and you won't have them to play with tomorrow." This directly connects the task to the outcome.

Specificity not only helps your child understand what is expected of them but it also makes it easier for you to follow through consistently. When expectations are clear and measurable, children can more effectively connect their actions to outcomes, giving them a sense of fairness and predictability.

CONSIDER ACCIDENTS AND REMORSE

Notice whether the behavior was truly an accident and if the child is genuinely remorseful. For instance, if your child brings a friend into the house to use the bathroom and absentmindedly bounces a ball indoors, immediately realizing their mistake, a typical consequence for playing ball inside might not be necessary. Their self-awareness and remorse may be enough of a lesson.

WHEN ARE WE ABLE TO GIVE EFFECTIVE CONSEQUENCES?

Our metaphorical house has prepared us to give consequences effectively. Each part of the house represents a key element that needs to be in place before consequences can truly work. Here's a quick breakdown:

- When calm is the foundation, we can think clearly and act on predetermined rules, expectations, and consequences.
- When connection strengthens the heart of the home, we can guide with compassion and acceptance of who our children are.
- When communication is the framework, we can deliver our message effectively and respectfully.
- When collaboration supports the walls, we can use tools like shared solutions to understand concerns and perspectives.
- When clarity and consistency build the structure, children know what is expected of them.
- When children are response-able, they have the skills needed to meet expectations.

When all these elements are in place, consequences can teach more than accountability: They can help your child develop important life skills while strengthening your relationship.

WHAT IMPACT DO IMPOSED CONSEQUENCES HAVE ON KIDS?

Traditionally, we have been taught that imposed consequences play a key role in teaching children important life skills. It's a commonly held view that when used thoughtfully, consequences can guide behavior and foster growth. Here's how these beliefs are typically framed:

1. *Learning to delay gratification*: Imposed consequences can help children understand the value of patience and effort. For example, completing homework before playing a favorite game teaches them that working toward a future benefit is worth the wait.

2. *Doing necessary or worthwhile tasks, even when they don't want to*: Life often requires us to do things we don't feel like doing, and consequences are seen as a way to help children practice this skill.

Whether it's tidying their room or helping with family chores, the idea is that they'll learn responsibility and perseverance through repeated experiences.

3. *Considering the thoughts and needs of others*: Consequences can teach empathy and accountability by showing children how their actions affect others. For instance, if a child interrupts a sibling's study time and is asked to make amends, they learn the importance of respecting others' needs.

These ideas form the foundation of traditional approaches to parenting, and they reflect the belief that imposed consequences shape behavior and build character.

A FOUNDATION FOR EXPLORATION

While these points resonate with many parents, the reality of how imposed consequences impact children—especially those with ADHD or EF challenges—is more complex. As we move through this chapter, we explore how and when consequences can be effective, as well as the limitations they may have in fostering long-term growth and accountability.

REMEMBER: KIDS DO WELL IF THEY CAN

If not, it's because of lagging skills resulting in unmet expectations and unsolved problems.

Why?
- Time is now and not now.
- Kids are often "motivationally challenged" and have a harder time being motivated toward future outcomes.
- They have difficulty delaying gratification.

- They have difficulty regulating their emotions and putting on the brakes, leading to inflexibility and poor frustration tolerance.

Sometimes, the "unsolved problem" is that they are not connecting the impact their present actions will have on their potential future opportunities or relationships. Lagging skills are often tied to underdeveloped EF abilities, such as planning, time management, and impulse control, particularly for children with ADHD, who often operate at a developmental level years behind their peers.

LETTING LIFE TEACH LESSONS: THE BALANCE BETWEEN SUPPORT AND ACCOUNTABILITY

Once a child begins to understand the potential impact of their actions, natural consequences can be one of life's greatest teachers. But as parents, we must navigate a delicate balance. On one hand, we want to step back and let them learn from their mistakes. After all, if we shield them from every consequence, we risk *bending the universe* too much—creating a reality that doesn't reflect the world they'll grow up in. Letting them "get away" with things that other children their age wouldn't can leave them unprepared for the expectations they'll face as they become more independent. For example, a child who refuses to clean up after themselves may miss out on learning how their contributions impact the family, a lesson they'll need to carry into school, work, and relationships.

But here's the tricky part: Not every child is fully ready to manage those expectations on their own. Some children, especially those with ADHD or other neurodiverse needs, are not always *response-able*. They may forget responsibilities, act impulsively, or struggle to regulate their emotions—not out of defiance but because they lack the skills. That's where our role as parents becomes both a guide and a cushion. We don't *bend the universe too much* but we also don't let them flounder. Instead, we step in to provide support as they learn and develop. This balance—allowing natural consequences to unfold, while offering the guidance and tools they need—teaches them the lessons life brings, but in a way that builds confidence and skills for the future.

When delivering consequences, remember that the goal is to teach and build skills. Harsh consequences often backfire, shifting your child's focus to their anger at you rather than the lesson they need to learn. Instead, aim for consequences that are relevant and directly tied to the behavior. For instance, if your child refuses to clean up after using art supplies, a natural consequence might be pausing art time until they're ready to take responsibility for cleaning up.

It's also important to keep your own emotions in check. Children may react with anger or defiance, but this doesn't mean you're doing the wrong thing. *Don't take their behavior personally!* Instead, speak little, emote less, and let the consequence do the teaching. A simple statement like "You didn't clean up, so we'll need to wait on the next activity," is often more effective than a long explanation.

Above all, stay calm and confident. The way you deliver the consequence sets the tone for how your child receives it. Speak clearly, enforce consistently, and trust the process. You're teaching skills, building trust, and guiding your child toward greater accountability—all while strengthening your connection with them.

SOME FINAL GUIDELINES WHEN GIVING CONSEQUENCES

When it comes to giving consequences, the goal is to teach and guide rather than punish. Maintaining connection, clarity, and trust throughout the process is essential for making the lesson impactful and meaningful.

Connect Before You Correct

Start with connection—not just for your child but for yourself. If you're feeling frustrated or upset, taking a moment to reconnect with your own calmness can make all the difference. Before addressing what went wrong, ensure your child feels seen and heard. If they're upset, acknowledging their feelings with a simple "I can see you're upset," can set a collaborative tone. If they're not visibly upset or unaware of the issue, approach the conversation calmly, making sure they're open to hearing your concerns. Even a neutral "Can we talk about what happened earlier?" can open the door to a constructive discussion.

Name It to Tame It

Helping your child identify and name their emotions engages the *thinking* part of their brain while calming the *emotional* response. This could mean taking a moment to ask, "How are you feeling right now?" or reflecting back with "It seems like you're frustrated." This pause helps them regulate their emotions and engage in problem solving.

Focus on the Facts, Not the Feelings

While emotions are valid, they don't excuse inappropriate behavior. Remind your child that rules for respectful and proper behavior don't change just because they don't like the situation. For example, you might say, "I understand you're upset, but yelling at your sibling is not okay."

Adjust Your Approach

Avoid insisting that they sit still or make eye contact while discussing consequences. For some children, particularly those with ADHD or sensory sensitivities, these requirements can feel intimidating or overly intense. Instead, focus on confirming that they are listening and understand what you're saying.

Reflect and Plan for the Future

Once emotions have settled, take the opportunity to explore what triggered the behavior and discuss strategies for next time. This helps your child develop self-awareness and learn alternative responses to challenging situations. If needed, this conversation can even happen the next day, especially for older or more mature children.

Stay Strong and Confident

Delivering consequences calmly and confidently ensures the focus remains on learning. Avoid overexplaining or reacting emotionally, as this can shift the focus away from the lesson. Don't take their behavior personally. Just because they are upset doesn't mean you did the wrong thing. Speak clearly, keep your emotions in check, and trust that you are guiding your child toward greater accountability and growth.

PUNISHMENT VERSUS DISCIPLINE

While punishment and discipline are often used interchangeably, they serve very different purposes. Punishment focuses on imposing a penalty for a past action, typically in the hope of changing future behavior. It is often reactive—delivered spontaneously or inconsistently—and emphasizes external control, reinforcing the idea of "who's in charge." Punishment appeals to the emotional part of the brain, often triggering defensiveness or resentment rather than reflection. While it may stop a behavior temporarily, it can erode connection and trust between parent and child, making it less effective as a long-term strategy.

Discipline, on the other hand, is rooted in the idea of teaching and training. It is proactive and grounded in predictability, helping children understand the logical outcomes of their actions. Effective discipline teaches self-control, responsibility, and the ability to reflect on choices. By appealing to the thinking part of the brain, it encourages self-talk, reflection, and self-regulation—essential skills for long-term growth. Unlike punishment, discipline builds trust and integrity, strengthening the parent–child relationship.

Establishing clear boundaries is a cornerstone of effective discipline. When you set and consistently enforce limits, your child feels safe and understands what's expected of them. This consistency helps them connect their actions to outcomes, making it easier to foster responsibility and self-regulation. For example, if you let your child know that screen time is allowed only after homework is completed, sticking to this rule shows them the importance of meeting obligations before enjoying privileges. Your boundaries create the structure they need to thrive while reminding them that you're there to guide and support them every step of the way.

Our goal is to help your child stop, pause, think, and make better choices now for their future.

POSITIVE ACTIONS AND MAKING AMENDS

When relationships are built on trust and connection, it's important to repair the damage when things go wrong. Instead of focusing solely on negative consequences, consider the power of positive actions. These actions not only help mend relationships but also teach meaningful life lessons along the way.

The Power of a Proper Apology

A genuine apology can repair emotional harm and rebuild trust. A full apology has four parts:

1. *Acknowledging the action*: "This is what I did." Taking ownership shows accountability and a willingness to face the consequences of one's behavior.
2. *Expressing regret*: "I'm sorry." This communicates care and understanding of how the action impacted others.
3. *Making amends*: "What can I do to make it right?" Offering to repair the harm caused demonstrates responsibility and empathy.

4. *Committing to change*: "I'll do my best not to make this mistake again." This step focuses on growth and learning from past behavior.

You don't need to ask your child to say each step each time they apologize but they should understand the meaning behind a true apology. And remember, you can model this by apologizing for your mistakes and showing your child that relationships can always be repaired, even after missteps.

The Role of Positive Actions

Positive actions can often teach more meaningful lessons than traditional consequences. These actions provide an opportunity to make amends and restore balance. Ideally, they should relate to the original offense to create a sense of justice. For example:

- If your child disrupts their sibling's project, you might ask them to do their sibling's chore. This gives their sibling extra time to rebuild or enjoy another activity.
- If your child breaks a family rule, you might have them choose a household task, like folding laundry or organizing a shared space, to make amends—giving back some of the time you had to spend managing the situation.

If no directly related action is appropriate, a general task can still serve as a meaningful consequence. Some families even keep a "Making Amends" jar filled with tasks, allowing the child to choose an action to repair their mistake.

PRACTICAL EXAMPLE

Imagine this scenario: Charlie and Sally are building independently with blocks when Charlie grabs a piece from Sally's structure, causing it to collapse. While many parents might suggest that Charlie help

Sally rebuild, this might not be an ideal solution. Charlie may enjoy building and not see this as a real consequence, while Sally might prefer to work alone. Instead, Charlie could do one of Sally's chores, giving her extra time to rebuild her structure on her terms.

AVOID LECTURES AND SHAME

When guiding your child through positive actions, avoid adding lectures, shame, or unnecessary drama. Let the action itself convey the lesson. A thoughtful conversation afterward can help them understand why their behavior was problematic and how they can approach similar situations differently in the future.

Positive actions encourage accountability while maintaining the connection and trust that form the foundation of healthy relationships. They remind children that mistakes are opportunities to learn and grow, both in their behavior and in their relationships.

AREA 1: DISRESPECTING FAMILY MEMBERS OR FAMILY VALUE RULES

Respectful communication is the foundation of healthy relationships and a harmonious household. Rules for respectful behavior do not change based on mood or circumstance. Disrespect, whether through words, body language, or actions, must be addressed in a way that reinforces the importance of treating others with kindness and consideration.

Teach Your Children the Four Rs

When more significant rude words or acts occur, the Four Rs—reflect, review, redo, respond—can help address the behavior constructively:

1. *Reflect*: Acknowledge what your child did or said. Focus on the behavior—what you saw and heard.
2. *Review*: Explore the emotion or concern behind their behavior.

For example: "It seems like you're frustrated," or "Do you feel upset because of what happened earlier?" Avoid answering their demand or offering solutions yet.

3. *Redo*: Give your child an opportunity to try again. Model how they could express their concerns respectfully. If necessary, allow them time to calm down before revisiting the situation.

4. *Respond*: Discuss their concern, answer their question, and offer options where appropriate.

For example, if your child pushes their plate away at dinner and says, "I'm not eating this!" pause before reacting. Reflect on their tone, review their possible frustration or hunger, guide them to redo their response respectfully, and finally, respond to their concern. Perhaps they just had the same dish as a snack or feel it's not enough after a long soccer practice. By calmly exploring the issue together, you teach them how to communicate their needs effectively without resorting to disrespect.

Handling Simple Acts of Misbehavior or Noncompliance

The Four Rs—Reflect, Review, Redo, Respond—are invaluable tools for addressing significant moments of rudeness or disrespect. They help your child process emotions and learn better ways to communicate. But not every misstep requires such a structured approach. For simpler acts of misbehavior or noncompliance—like forgetting to clean up or refusing to follow a basic rule—a lighter, more flexible response is often enough.

These everyday challenges are opportunities to reinforce expectations without escalating the situation. By tailoring your response to the severity of the behavior, you can address the issue calmly and effectively while maintaining your connection and focus on teaching.

Children aren't perfect—and neither are adults! Sometimes, a moment of noncompliance or misbehavior doesn't require a major consequence but rather an opportunity to pause and recalibrate. When these situations arise, taking a measured, step-by-step approach can help guide your child toward better behavior while maintaining connection and respect. Some suggestions:

1. *Acknowledge what happened*: Start by calmly naming the behavior without judgment. This helps your child see that you've noticed the issue without escalating emotions.

2. *Remind them of the rule or expectation*: Briefly restate the family rule or boundary they've crossed. For example: "Remember, our rule is to keep the bathroom clean after using it."

3. *Offer one opportunity to change the behavior*: Give them a chance to correct their actions. For example: "You can quickly pick up your clothes, and we'll head to soccer practice right after." This approach emphasizes accountability while allowing them to address the issue independently.

4. *Implement a predetermined consequence if necessary*: If the behavior continues, follow through with a consequence that has been clearly communicated beforehand. For example, you might pause privileges, such as screen time, until they address the issue.

Time Stops: When Boundaries Are Crossed

Sometimes, when boundaries or expectations are repeatedly ignored, a "time stop" is necessary. During a time stop, privileges are paused, and assistance is withheld until your child demonstrates readiness to meet the expectations. This approach isn't about punishment but about creating space for reflection and accountability.

If conditions for a time stop aren't respected, a predetermined consequence should follow. For example, if your child leaves their clothes in the bathroom when it's time to leave for soccer, you might say, "I'll take you as soon as the bathroom is cleaned up." The same principle applies if they are speaking to you inappropriately—you can calmly state, "I'll be happy to help with your homework once you're speaking respectfully."

Remember

- "The arguing, defiance, refusal is a learned behavior—not genetic, not biological."—Russell Barkley
- When parents avoid pursuing their expectations due to fear of emotional outbursts or rely too heavily on strict, authoritative measures, children may inadvertently learn that emotions are tools to manipulate others. They may come to believe that displays of anger or frustration will help them get their way or avoid accountability.

Instead, stand firm in your boundaries while maintaining a calm and compassionate demeanor.

Walking Away From Power Struggles

Sometimes, the best response is to step away. When emotions are running high, your presence can unintentionally escalate the situation. It's important to make it clear that you're not rejecting or abandoning your child but rather giving both of you space to cool down and think more clearly. By stepping away, you model how to manage big emotions and demonstrate that conflicts don't have to be solved in the heat of the moment. *Remember*: Walking away is not giving up—it's a powerful tool for de-escalation and maintaining connection. Returning to the conversation once emotions have settled allows for clearer communication and reinforces the expectation that respectful behavior is nonnegotiable.

To make this approach effective, it's helpful to discuss it during a calm moment. Let your child know ahead of time that sometimes you may step away to give everyone a chance to reset. Set clear expectations for how they should handle this time apart and establish any consequences if those boundaries aren't respected. This proactive communication helps your child feel secure, even in moments of separation, and reinforces your role as a calm and steady guide.

Taking Time to Regroup

Sometimes, you may need a moment to figure out your next move or to calm yourself down—and that's okay! Parenting isn't about having all the answers instantly. Taking time to collect your thoughts can prevent reactive decisions and help you approach the situation with clarity and confidence. Remind yourself:

- Just because they need an answer right now doesn't mean I can't take the time to think about my response.
- Just because they yell doesn't mean I have to comply with their demands.
- I didn't like how they responded when I said "No." I need to let them know how it feels when they speak to me that way.

Start by taking two long, deep breaths and call upon your other calming strategies. Whether it's stepping away for a moment, grounding yourself, or mentally rehearsing your response, these small actions can make all the difference.

AREA 2: NOT FULFILLING FAMILY OBLIGATIONS OR CHORES

Contributing to the household is an essential life skill. It teaches children responsibility, cooperation, and accountability—qualities they'll need as they grow and take on greater independence. However, this can be a stressful area for parents, especially when expectations aren't being met. Let's start by asking some key questions:

- Are you and your child both clear about the expectations? Do they know which tasks are daily obligations versus simple requests or preferences? For example, is cleaning their room a request or a required responsibility?

- Do they understand what will happen if they don't meet expectations? What would you like to happen?
- Are they response-able? Truly capable of handling the task? Or do they still need support, like a chart, a timer, or a gentle reminder?

Being clear and consistent about expectations is a foundational step. It can help to write these expectations down as a simple contract. Collaborate with your child to create an agreement that everyone understands. For example:

"You are responsible for taking out the garbage on Monday and Thursday evenings by 5:30 p.m. If you're not home, it must be done within 30 minutes of your return." Also, keep in mind the following:

- *Privilege*: Each day you remember without a reminder, you earn $1.
- *Consequence*: Until this chore is complete, there's no food, screen time, phone, music, or social time, and your door must remain open.

Keep the contract simple and structured. You can always revisit it if adjustments are needed, but having a clear, written agreement can eliminate misunderstandings and reduce arguments.

This skill—doing something you don't want to do to make someone else happy or to meet a requirement—is an important part of maturity. It's something we all do in relationships, whether it's keeping shared spaces tidy or doing small acts of kindness for a partner. By practicing family chores, children have the opportunity to learn and experience this life skill in a safe, supportive environment.

First Work, Then Play: The Premack Principle

For example, "Eat your dinner, then you can have dessert." The Premack principle states that a person is more willing to complete a less desirable activity to gain access to a more desirable one.

You may not have heard of the Premack principle but you've probably heard of "Grandma's rule": *First, you work; then, you play*—the idea that you must complete a less desirable task before earning the chance to do something enjoyable. For example: "Finish your dinner, then you can have dessert," or "Clean your room, and then you can go outside and play." This concept can be a helpful tool for motivating children to complete tasks they'd otherwise avoid.

But here's the challenge: For children with ADHD, this principle doesn't always work as intended. Why? Because ADHD impacts their ability to anticipate future rewards and connect them to present actions. Their sense of time is often skewed, with their brain perceiving the world in terms of "now" and "not now." When asked to do something undesirable, like homework, they may feel stuck in the frustration or boredom of the moment, unable to envision the relief or satisfaction they'll feel once it's done.

So, what can you do? Help your child bridge the gap by making the future reward feel more real and attainable:

- *Paint a picture of success*: Talk with your child about what they can look forward to after completing the task. For example: "Once you finish your homework, we'll have time to play your favorite game together," can help them visualize the reward.

- *Acknowledge their feelings*: Let them know you understand the task may feel frustrating or boring. A simple "I know this isn't fun right now but I believe you can do it" can go a long way in keeping them motivated.

- *Break it down*: For larger tasks, help your child focus on one small step at a time. Completing smaller chunks can build momentum and make the end goal feel less overwhelming.

Ultimately, the Premack principle works best when paired with empathy and scaffolding. By helping your child connect their efforts to a meaningful outcome, you're not just getting the task done— you're teaching them resilience and perseverance, skills they'll use far beyond the dinner table or homework desk.

Promoting Learning and Accountability

When expectations aren't met, consider consequences that teach accountability while maintaining trust. This could mean completing additional tasks or engaging in positive actions to make up for what wasn't done. For example, some families use "family service cards" where children choose a chore to complete as a way to make amends.

The bottom line is that family expectations provide opportunities for children to practice responsibility and experience the satisfaction of knowing they can succeed. When things don't go as planned, revisit the agreement or try a Plan B conversation to address the underlying challenges. The goal is to create an environment where your child feels supported and empowered to meet reasonable expectations.

AREA 3: POOR PERFORMANCE IN SCHOOL OR MANDATORY ACTIVITIES

The third area of consequences involves poor performance in school or in other required activities that parents expect children to participate in—such as taking music lessons, playing a sport, or attending an extracurricular program.

Earlier in this chapter, we explored the impact that imposed consequences have on children. We said:

- "Consequences help them learn to *delay gratification* for a more valuable future outcome."
- "Consequences help them learn to do necessary or worthwhile tasks *even if they don't want to.*"
- "Consequences help them learn to put the *thoughts and needs of others* ahead of their own."

I'm going to challenge these now and say, "Not necessarily!"

Understanding Your Child's Perspective: The Funnel Metaphor

A seventh-grade student once shared with me a powerful doodle he had drawn during math class. In his drawing, he depicted himself with a funnel on his head, with letters and information spilling out of the funnel, unable to all fit inside. This simple yet profound illustration perfectly captured his experience of feeling overwhelmed in the classroom. Despite being a bright and capable learner, he felt there was just too much information coming in, and his "funnel to the brain" wasn't big enough to process it all.

Now imagine being in that child's shoes. The teacher's voice becomes a constant stream of instructions, assignments, and expectations, while his mind struggles to grasp even half of what is being said. It's as though the information keeps piling up, spilling over, and becoming impossible to manage.

As parents and educators, we may unknowingly add to this stress by offering well-meaning but demanding phrases like:

- "Sit still."
- "Do it my way."
- "Try harder."
- "Focus just here."
- "Work longer."
- "Deal with your boredom."

While our intentions are often to motivate or guide, these words can unintentionally reinforce the feeling that the child is falling short—that no matter how hard they try, they can't meet the expectations placed on them.

What's Happening Inside Their Mind?

For children with ADHD, the challenges they face are not simply about being distracted or "lazy." They grapple with working memory deficits, slower processing speeds, underactive neurotransmitters when they're bored, and difficulties regulating their attention. These challenges make it significantly harder for them to process and respond to information effectively. And yet, these same children often possess incredible strengths, such as:

- An internal motor that drives their energy and enthusiasm.
- Curiosity that inspires them to explore and question the world around them.
- A creative, out-of-the-box way of thinking that leads to innovative ideas.

The cognitive and emotional demands of managing their unique challenges often leave little room for pursuing personal interests or socializing. Over time, this isolation can further exacerbate their struggles.

The Need for a "Disability Perspective"

When I talk about adopting a "disability perspective," it's not about labeling your child or focusing on their limitations. Instead, it's about acknowledging the reality of their challenges and providing them with the understanding and support they need to thrive. Without this perspective, we risk expecting them to function like neurotypical children in a world designed for neurotypical brains—a world where the "funnel to the brain" works as expected.

For children with ADHD, their developmental timeline often doesn't match their chronological age. Remember, research shows that children with ADHD can experience a 30% developmental delay compared to their peers. While your 10-year-old may look and act their age in some ways, they might have the emotional regulation or processing abilities of a 7-year-old. Recognizing this gap allows us to adjust our expectations and meet them where they are, setting the stage for success.

What Impact Do Imposed Consequences Really Have on Kids?

When children struggle with flexibility, frustration tolerance, adaptability, slower processing speed, or other learning challenges, what is the impact of our well-intentioned promises of rewards, threats of punishment, or behavior modification programs?

For many of these children, imposed consequences can backfire. Instead of teaching the intended lesson, they can:

- Shut them down.
- Increase their anxiety and feelings of shame.
- Erode their self-confidence.
- Damage their trust and connection with others.
- Cause them to focus more on resisting or defying than on learning or growing.

As we discussed in Key 2, children under tremendous stress often enter survival mode: fight, flight, freeze, fib, or fawn. They may shut down completely, avoid addressing the issue, or spin stories to avoid discomfort. At times, they may even rely on *magical thinking*, convincing themselves of things that aren't realistic. You may have heard comments like:

- "I don't need to write it down; I'll remember."
- "I still have plenty of time to get the paper done."
- "I don't have to practice; I'll still make the team."
- "It's not important to me."

This kind of thinking is their way of coping. But for parents and caregivers, it can feel maddening.

So, I ask you: *How's that working for you?*

"But They're Just Not Motivated ... "

I hear you. Many parents come to me with this concern, convinced their child lacks motivation. But here's the truth: *They are motivated.*

They are motivated to resist, avoid, and retain some sense of control over their lives. They are not helpless victims or simply irresponsible. What they lack are the tools, skills, and strategies to handle their challenges effectively in the moment.

This is where our mantra comes back into play: *Kids do well if they can.*

Their poor behavior is often a mask—a smoke screen to distract from deeper feelings of anxiety, insecurity, or a need for control. It's their way of saying, "I'm struggling," even if they don't have the words or self-awareness to express it that way.

Yes, their communication might be inappropriate or even infuriating at times. But beneath the surface is a message we need to hear.

Listening Beyond the Behavior

Our job is to look past the smoke screen and truly listen. What is the behavior telling you? What emotions or struggles are driving it?

Instead of reacting with frustration or punishment, we need to use our communication skills to understand and help them handle their emotions differently. A calm, empathetic response can turn a tense moment into a teaching opportunity.

But I know what you're thinking:

"If I back off, won't they just . . . "

"Won't they take advantage?"

"What if they never learn to . . . "

These fears are valid, and I address them as we continue.

MOVING FORWARD

Before diving into the next chapter, take a moment to reflect on what we've discussed. Review the guiding thoughts below and consider how they apply to your child and family dynamic. Remember, this isn't about perfection—it's about progress.

And don't forget to revisit the homework for this session. The insights and strategies we're building are all part of helping you connect with your child, guide them effectively, and foster the skills they need to succeed.

GUIDING THOUGHTS

- We cannot control their behavior but we can give explicit messages as to what we expect and will accept.
- Negative consequences may stop negative behavior, but positive consequences are the best way to encourage positive behavior and teach skills.
- Be willing sometimes to give extra chances and praise to counteract their outside world and internal beliefs.
- Plan ahead and anticipate trouble spots.
- Look for conversations, not confrontations.
- Act, don't yak!—give clear choices and hold the lecture.
- Do not bend the universe—too much!
- Do not always take their behavior personally. Stay strong.
- Requiring a positive action rather than taking something away can teach a more powerful lesson.
- Reflect, Review, Redo, Respond.
- Be willing to walk away for now.
- No lectures when it's over. Reconnect as soon as possible.

HOMEWORK

1. Choose one or two behaviors or responsibilities you want to focus on. Create an incentive plan with your child to encourage their compliance and effort.
2. Develop a list of chores or tasks your child can do to make amends

in case of disrespect or noncompliance. Include a mix of quick tasks and more involved ones.

3. Clearly write down the rules for when "Time Stops." Discuss these proactively with your child to set expectations.

4. Teach your child the Four Rs (Reflect, Review, Redo, Respond) and the four steps to a proper apology.

5. Acknowledge and reinforce positive behaviors and progress with specific observations. For example: "I notice that you put your plate in the sink without being reminded—thank you!"

6. If your child tends to follow you when you try to walk away during a conflict, discuss this concern in advance. Create a plan together, including possible consequences if they cannot separate appropriately.

7. Help your child visualize future rewards or outcomes to make abstract concepts feel more tangible. For example, talk about how good it will feel to finish homework early and have time to relax.

8. Revisit responsibilities or tasks that may require extra support. Ensure your child is response-able by providing scaffolding, such as charts, timers, or reminders, as needed.

9. If needed, set up a written contract for a responsibility or chore. Be clear about the expectation, the privilege earned for following through, and the consequence for noncompliance.

10. Reflect on your own responses during challenging moments. Practice staying calm, stepping away when necessary, and planning your next move thoughtfully.

KEY 8

NAVIGATING CHOICES
Empowering You and Your Child

In the long run, we shape our lives, and we shape ourselves. The process never ends until we die. And the choices we make are ultimately our own responsibility.

—ELEANOR ROOSEVELT

This wisdom resonates deeply when considering the journey of parenting a child with ADHD, where choices shape not only their lives but also ours.

We started this journey with the goal of helping our children grow into confident, respectful, self-aware, self-disciplined, responsible, independent, successful, and resilient individuals. Just as important, we want them to remain emotionally connected to us and those around them.

Now that you've explored how ADHD impacts your child's life and have seen the importance of *Calm, Connection, Communication, Collaboration, Clarity, Consistency,* and *Consequences,* we arrive at perhaps the most pivotal lesson of all: *Choices.* Choices are the capstone of the house we've been building together—the piece that ties everything else together and ensures the structure supports your child's growth (Figure 8.1).

FIGURE 8.1:
House: Choices

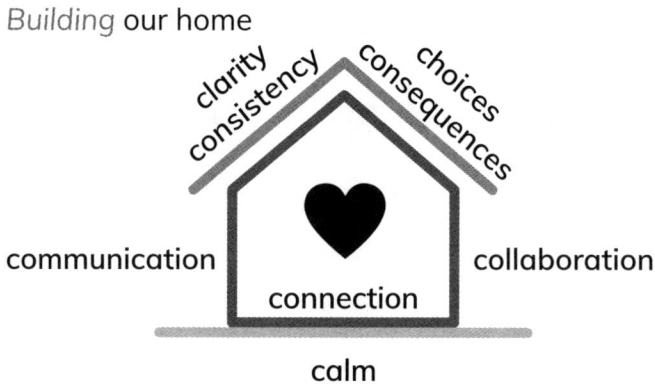

© Cindy Goldrich

CHOICES AS POWER

As parents, it's natural to want to guide our children's paths, but ultimately, the most profound growth happens when they take ownership of their choices. *Choice is power*—a power that teaches responsibility, autonomy, and self-confidence. It's through choices, both big and small, that children learn to navigate life's challenges and opportunities.

Choice means more than deciding between right and wrong. It means having the freedom to influence outcomes, the courage to embrace responsibility, and the willingness to accept the consequences. Empowering your child to understand this connection helps them recognize that with every choice comes a responsibility: to their goals, their well-being, and their future.

As your child begins to take ownership of their choices, you might find yourself grappling with questions:

- Will they be ready to fly when the time comes?
- How much independence is too much too soon?
- How will we know when to step in or step back?

These questions can't always be answered definitively but they reflect the delicate balance of parenting—allowing independence while maintaining connection.

The truth is that parenting isn't about controlling every outcome. *What is our role?* It's to give our children the tools, strategies, and support they need to develop their EF skills, including their ability to reflect and engage in positive self-talk. It's about building their confidence by showing faith in their ability to learn and grow, being clear about expectations and potential consequences, and staying present when they come to us for support. We want to equip them with the skills they need to navigate life independently while remaining connected to us and those around them. These qualities form the foundation of a fulfilling and balanced life, cultivated not just through guidance but through trust in their ability to make choices.

Yet, letting go can feel terrifying.

We concluded the last chapter by noting "But if I back off, they might . . . " I know, letting go is hard, especially when your child resists or struggles to make good choices. This is one of the greatest challenges and concerns many parents face when their child strongly resists their best attempts to guide and support them:

- *Fail at what?* Remember, there are many things children are learning as students. Academics are clearly important—however, even academics must be seen in balance with all the child's challenges.
- *At whose agenda?* Children aren't born signing a contract agreeing to spend 13 years in school, attending classes, and completing assignments. That's our agenda as parents and society. While we believe in the importance of education, it's important to recognize that the child must ultimately choose to engage and learn. Our role

is to guide and support them, helping them connect with their internal motivations rather than relying solely on external expectations.

• *Are they failing?* Or are they just not meeting other people's expectations?

As parents, we often feel the stakes are too big to step back. At every stage of our child's growth, there's a sense of urgency, a fear that if we don't intervene, everything will fall apart.

• In kindergarten, it might sound like "I have to make sure they're prepared each day so they can get ready to learn."

• By third grade, we think, "This is such an important year. It's when they transition from learning how to learn to actually learning."

• By fifth grade, the concern shifts to "I need to prepare them for the transition to middle school."

• And then there's eighth grade: "High school is just around the corner. I can't back off now; this is when everything starts to count."

• By eleventh grade, the pressure feels unbearable: "This is the big year. SATs, ACTs, and college transcripts—I can't let them fail now."

It's not just the big transitions that weigh on us. The day-to-day responsibilities feel equally critical:

• "If I don't help them every morning, they'll forget something important for school."

• "If I don't stay on top of their homework, they'll fall behind in class."

• "I have to stay involved, or they'll never be ready for middle school, high school, or college!"

It's exhausting, isn't it?

But here's the thing: Are these fears about their actual needs, or are they projections of our own anxieties? Are we stepping in because they truly need our help—or because it feels safer for us to hold on?

These fears stem from love and a deep desire to see our children succeed. However, it's important to recognize when these fears are driving our actions, possibly overshadowing the lessons we hope to impart. It's normal to feel this way. We all want the best for our children.

RICOCHET: A STORY OF TRANSFORMATION

During my workshops, I often share a video of Ricochet, a dog trained to assist individuals with disabilities (https://bit.ly/ptssurficedog). Ricochet struggled to meet the program's requirements because of her instinct to chase birds (think—dog with ADHD!). Eventually, her trainer released her from the program. While the trainer was disappointed, she chose to focus on what Ricochet could do instead of what she couldn't. She realized:

> She was a different dog when she surfed . . . totally joyful and 100% committed to her new direction. When I let go of who I wanted her to be and just let her 'be,' she completely flourished, and I reveled in knowing she is perfect just the way she is.

As the Ricochet video plays, we can hear Taylor Hicks's song "Do I Make You Proud?"

Ricochet discovered joy and commitment in surfing, helping children with disabilities ride the waves. By allowing her to follow her natural talents, her trainer witnessed her thrive.

FAILURE AS GROWTH

Failure can be one of life's most powerful teachers—if we allow it to be. For children with ADHD, who often face challenges with EF and emotional regulation, failure may feel overwhelming. Yet, stepping back and allowing them to experience setbacks is a vital part of fostering independence and growth.

When children are given the opportunity to make choices and experience the results—whether successful or not—they begin to understand that their actions matter. This connection between effort and outcomes helps them build pride and self-esteem.

FREEDOM TO FAIL

It is not the challenges you face, but the choices you make in facing those challenges that matter.

—ANONYMOUS

At the heart of this learning process is the concept of *freedom to fail.* When we talk about the freedom to fail, it's not just about trying something new or learning through mistakes—it's about recognizing that effort is a choice. As parents, we can control the external: curating opportunities, setting boundaries, and guiding decisions. Yet, we cannot control their internal choices: the thoughts, attitudes, and motivations behind their actions.

You can wake them up early, arrange extra help, and even hire a tutor, but ultimately, they must decide how much effort to invest. A bumper sticker I once saw captured this perfectly: "They can send me to college, but they can't make me think."

This freedom includes the possibility of choosing not to put in that effort and risking failure. While this can be frustrating for parents, it's an essential learning opportunity. Imagine telling your child, "It's your choice. You know the consequences of not studying for this test."

This is the power of the *freedom to fail*—it connects their internal motivation with the external opportunities you've provided. With this freedom comes an essential lesson: *the responsibility to yourself.* When children begin to connect their decisions with outcomes, they start to see that their efforts—or lack of effort—directly shape their experiences. This awareness fosters accountability and a sense of ownership over their lives.

Freedom to choose builds not only independence but also resilience. Allowing your child to experience the consequences of their choices teaches them to adapt, persist, and grow. As parents, this can be one of the hardest lessons to embrace. The urge to protect them from failure is strong, but failure itself is often a stepping stone to success.

And then, there's the fear of the ultimate "failure": The moment when you realize your child isn't equipped to handle life on their own. Parents often call me, desperate and bewildered:

"I don't understand what happened. They did fine all through high school. They got into the college of their dreams. And now, after one semester of college, they're home on academic probation. Can you help?"

If your child is not being as productive as they "need" to be, allowing that concern to escalate into an emotional battle may create or exacerbate behavioral problems. At their core, children—like all of us—are motivated by an innate desire to be self-directed, to grow, and to feel in control of their lives. Recognizing this can help us reframe conflicts. Instead of reacting with frustration or criticism, consider whether a power struggle is emerging.

NAVIGATING CONCERNS ABOUT
ANXIETY AND DEPRESSION

For many parents, the thought of allowing their child to experience failure raises valid concerns about increasing anxiety or depression. It's very hard to consider stepping back when it feels that you're risking aggravating your child's mental health.

Children with ADHD may already face heightened feelings of frustration, self-doubt, or being misunderstood. Experiencing failure can feel like an additional burden, making it important to assess your child's unique needs and readiness to handle setbacks. Here are some considerations to guide your approach:

- *Evaluate the circumstances*: Is the failure happening within a safe and supportive environment, or is it compounding existing stressors? Consider how factors like school expectations, peer relationships, or family dynamics might impact them.
- *Observe patterns*: If failure consistently leads to prolonged anxiety, withdrawal, or a significant drop in self-esteem, it may signal deeper challenges that need addressing.

WHEN TO SEEK HELP

While it's normal for children to feel upset or discouraged after a setback, there are times when professional intervention may be necessary. Consider seeking support if you observe any of the following:

- Persistent sadness or withdrawal from activities they once enjoyed.
- Excessive worry or difficulty sleeping.
- Expressions of hopelessness or negative self-talk.
- A significant decline in academic or social engagement.

In some cases, these signs may indicate that your child's medication or treatment plan needs to be reassessed. ADHD and its related challenges can impact emotional regulation, and ensuring your child's care is optimized is an essential part of their success. Speak with your child's health care provider to explore whether adjustments are needed or if additional therapeutic support could be beneficial.

Keep open lines of communication. Let your child know you're there to support them without judgment. Ask how they're feeling about challenges and what support they might need.

A SHIFT IN FOCUS: BIG PICTURE GOALS

While the freedom to fail focuses on letting children experience the consequences of their choices, *failure as growth* emphasizes what they learn from those experiences. Failure teaches:

- *Resilience*: Bouncing back builds mental toughness and emotional endurance.
- *Responsibility*: Taking ownership of their actions helps children see how their choices shape outcomes.
- *Adaptability*: Adjusting plans fosters creativity and problem solving.

Very often, parents focus on goals they think are important without regard for the big picture of how the trade-offs involved in reaching these goals may affect their child. Sometimes, we become so invested in what we believe they *should* accomplish that we risk losing sight of the broader goal: fostering independence and resilience.

As the story of Ricochet reminds us, failure often opens the door to new opportunities. By letting go of rigid expectations, we allow our children to discover their strengths and passions.

It's important to ask yourself: "Are the expectations I have for my child in line with their current developmental stage, or am I projecting future worries onto the present?" As we progress through this chapter, we confront those fears directly. We examine how to balance guidance with independence, how to use failure as a tool for growth, and how to empower your child to take responsibility for their choices—all while preserving a strong, loving connection.

You must still be the parent; you must still be present and effective in ensuring that your child is safe, morally appropriate, and setting themselves toward a productive future. However, your primary concern in the present might need to shift focus while you create and maintain an atmosphere of calm and reestablish connection. As we've discussed before, this must be the foundation and core of your home. Without calm and connection, learning—whether academic, social, or emotional—becomes much harder to achieve.

REFRAMING FAILURE

Reframing failure as a step toward growth helps both you and your child shift the focus from setbacks to opportunities. When your child experiences failure, ask thoughtful questions that encourage reflection and learning:

- "What did you learn from this?"
- "What would you do differently next time?"
- "What part of this experience can you feel proud of?"

Parenting isn't about doing everything for your child or ensuring they never fail. Nor is it about controlling their every decision. It's about equipping them with tools, strategies, and support to boost their EF skills, especially their self-awareness and ability to reflect on their decisions.

While freedom is critical, as we explored in Keys 4 and 5, so too are structures, rules, and boundaries. These guardrails create a safe environment for exploration while helping your child understand the responsibilities tied to their decisions.

You are their coach, not their manager. You are there to listen, guide, and provide support, always holding the vision of their potential in mind. Your role is to cheer them on when they succeed, help them navigate challenges, and encourage them to keep going when they stumble. You're there not to control the outcome but to walk alongside them as they develop their own path, reminding them that they are capable and loved, no matter what.

Empowering your child with choices is like helping them develop their "sea legs." They need to test their footing, weather a few storms, and learn what they can handle. Through this process, they discover their strength, resilience, and ability to captain their own ship.

I am the master of my fate., I am the captain of my soul.

—WILLIAM ERNEST HENLEY, "INVICTUS"

NAVIGATING EXPECTATIONS

As parents, it's natural to have expectations for our children. We want them to succeed, to meet their potential, and to have every opportunity in life. Expectations often stem from a combination of love, fear, and societal pressure. We want the best for our children and worry about their future, so we create goals to guide them. We see far into the future and understand the impact their actions and decisions today may have down the road.

However, expectations can become a source of tension—both for parents and children—when they don't align with a child's unique abilities, interests, or challenges. And yet, life is filled with examples of children growing up to chart new courses, surprising their parents in wonderful and unexpected ways. Navigating expectations is about finding a balance: encouraging growth while respecting individuality and pacing.

It's helpful to pause and reflect:

- Are these expectations realistic for my child's current developmental stage?
- Do they reflect my child's strengths and interests, or are they shaped by external pressures?
- Am I leaving enough space for my child to experience freedom while still being close enough to catch them when needed?

Think of this as a baton relay race: You need the right distance between the runner holding the baton and the one reaching to take it. Too far apart, and the exchange may falter; too close, and you might hold them back.

ENABLING VERSUS SUPPORTING

Remember we asked:
- Will they be ready to fly when the time comes?
- How much independence is too much too soon?
- How will we know when to step in or step back?

One of the most common questions parents ask is "How do I know if I'm enabling or supporting my child?" Let's explore this with a real-life example:

Imagine your child forgets their violin for the third time this month, and you're debating whether to bring it to school. Is bringing the violin to school *enabling* or *supporting*? At first glance, it might feel like enabling—you're stepping in again instead of letting them face the consequences. But let's look closer.

Last night, when Joni went to practice her violin, you reminded her it was time to get ready for bed. She dutifully showered and got ready for the next day, but in the process, the violin was left downstairs. This morning, she made it to the bus on time, her shoes matched, and her homework was done. Sure, her room is still a mess, and she had an argument with her sister, but you have those on your ever-growing list of things to work on.

Perhaps bringing the violin to school is not *enabling*—it's *prioritizing*. *Parent the child you have* means recognizing that remembering the violin might not be the most pressing skill to tackle today. By bringing it to school, you're not enabling reliance on you; you're supporting her by preventing unnecessary stress or demerits while focusing on the bigger picture.

Here is my definition of *enabling*: Enabling is doing something for someone *without a plan* to teach them to do it for themselves. Supporting, on the other hand, means helping them in a way that aligns with their developmental needs and prioritizes growth.

ARE THEY DEVELOPING IMPORTANT LIFE SKILLS?

In an ideal world, it would be wonderful to see our children managing the essential aspects of their lives independently. However, we understand that learning to manage oneself, time, possessions, and obligations takes time. During this period, we must ensure that our families continue to thrive. Balance is crucial. Occasionally, it's necessary to step in and help your child with their challenges without overwhelming them. It's important to give yourself grace from time to time. Recognize that those who may judge are not walking in your shoes. Remember, *people do their best if they can*. The goal is to gradually transition responsibilities to foster growth and resilience.

I encourage you to think about some of the things you are doing for your children now that they need to learn by the time they leave your home. Here are a few examples to get you started:

1. Wake up independently.
2. Ask for help or seek guidance when faced with a problem.
3. Basic budgeting.

4. Schedule appointments (doctor, dentist, haircuts).

5. Follow a recipe to prepare a simple meal or dessert.

6. Do laundry (sort, wash, dry, fold, and put away).

7. Plunge a toilet or unclog a sink.

8. Replace batteries in household items like remotes and smoke detectors.

9. Introduce themselves to new people in a polite and confident way.

10. Change a lightbulb.

For each task, ask yourself:

- Am I doing this for my child, or am I teaching them to do it for themselves?
- What small steps can I take to give them more control and responsibility?

Growth often happens in small, uneven steps. Celebrate their successes, no matter how minor, to build their confidence and sense of competence.

ADJUSTING EXPECTATIONS

When expectations are rigid or misaligned, they can inadvertently become a source of frustration or shame for children, leading to resistance, withdrawal, or even defiance. Adjusting expectations doesn't mean lowering your standards; it means meeting your child where they are and supporting them as they grow into who they are meant to be. For example:

- If your child struggles to keep up with an advanced academic program, consider whether the added stress is worth the trade-off. Perhaps focusing on one or two subjects where they excel is a better fit.
- If extracurricular activities are piling up and creating burnout, think

about prioritizing activities that align with their passions and leave room for downtime.

Children are more likely to thrive when they feel ownership over their goals. Helping your child allocate their "time currency" thoughtfully teaches them to value balance and prioritize what matters most to them. Instead of imposing expectations, involve your child in setting goals that feel meaningful to them. Ask questions like:

- "What do you want to work on this semester?"
- "What's something you're excited to try or improve?"

Success doesn't have to mean achieving perfection or meeting every standard. It can be about showing effort, demonstrating growth, or discovering something new about themselves. By reframing success, you give your child permission to define their own achievements.

This approach fosters intrinsic motivation, helping your child feel empowered rather than pressured.

PROVIDING A SAFETY NET: TOOLS FOR GUIDANCE

As parents, we can't always control the outcomes but we can equip our children with the tools they need to navigate life's challenges with confidence and resilience. Allowing failure doesn't mean leaving your child to struggle alone or shielding them from every consequence. You might say, "I'm here to support you if you need help." This approach respects their autonomy while allowing them to feel the weight of their decisions.

Encouraging Self-Reflection

One of the most valuable skills you can help your child develop is self-reflection. By learning to pause and consider their choices, children begin to understand how their actions connect to outcomes. You can guide this process by asking questions like "What do you think went well?" or "What would you do differently next time?"

When you make a mistake, consider sharing your reflections aloud. For example, you might say, "I rushed into that decision and didn't think it through. Next time, I'll take a moment to consider my options." This shows your child that everyone learns through experience and that self-reflection is a skill they will use for life.

Collaborating to Solve Problems

Rather than imposing solutions, engage your child in finding answers collaboratively. This approach empowers them to take ownership of their choices while teaching critical problem-solving skills. For example, if your child struggles with staying organized, you might start by asking, "What do you think might work to help you remember your assignments?"

Together, you can brainstorm options. Maybe they'd like to try using a calendar or setting reminders on their phone. Let them choose what feels most manageable and then evaluate together later: "How did that system work for you? Should we make any changes?"

Teaching Emotional Awareness

Emotional awareness is another powerful tool you can offer your child. When children learn to name and understand their emotions, they are better equipped to manage them. You might use tools like emotion wheels to help them identify what they're feeling or encourage them to "name it to tame it." Simply labeling emotions like anger, frustration, or disappointment can help reduce their intensity.

Teaching mindfulness techniques, like pausing to take a deep breath before responding, can also make a big difference. These small strategies help children approach challenges with a calmer, more thoughtful mindset.

Using Visual and Technological Tools

Many children, especially those with ADHD, benefit from tools that provide structure and clarity. Checklists, calendars, and decision trees can make abstract tasks more concrete and manageable. For example, a checklist might break a big homework project into smaller, more achievable steps, helping your child see their progress and stay on track.

Technology can also be a valuable ally. Apps for task management, goal tracking, or reminders can help your child stay organized and feel in control of their responsibilities. The key is to collaborate with your child to find tools that match their preferences and learning style.

The tools you offer your child—whether they're practical strategies, emotional insights, or opportunities to problem solve collaboratively—are the scaffolding that helps them build independence. By teaching reflection, emotional awareness, and the ability to approach challenges creatively, you're not just solving today's problems—you're helping your child develop the skills they'll need for a lifetime of growth and resilience.

Understanding Your Child's Perspective About School

It's easy to feel frustrated when your child resists going to school, completing assignments, or engaging with teachers. For a child with ADHD, the combination of EF challenges, social pressures, and academic demands can feel insurmountable. But consider this: When a child withdraws, it's not a sign of laziness or defiance; it's a signal that something isn't working.

These days, with the added competition and pressure on children to qualify for admission to colleges and universities and on high schools to show that they are offering top-level classes, more and more children are feeling pressure from their parents, their peers, and their schools to take advanced placement (AP) and/or international baccalaureate (IB) courses. Additionally, many children feel pressure to become very involved in extracurricular activities to develop a stellar resume for college applications.

While these courses and activities are appropriate and reasonable for some children, many (with and without ADHD) are working beyond what they can reasonably manage well. The level of pressure they are under is impacting them developmentally by leaving them little time to exercise, sleep, or spend important time with family or friends, not to mention the impact we know stress has on learning!

It is especially important (and understandably frustrating) for children with ADHD (and their parents) to recognize that while they may be *academically qualified* for certain AP/IB classes, the extra time they need for reading, studying, and projects may prevent them from keeping up—or they may do so at the expense of other courses or obligations. These are still important growing years. I encourage all parents to recognize, and help their children recognize, that there are an abundance of excellent college and post–high school programs available. You want your child not only to get into the next program but also *to thrive there.* The trade-off of taking certain AP/IB classes may be that the child cannot excel in multiple areas of their current life due to spending too much time on these specific classes. I explain this concept to parents and teachers with this analogy:

Let's assume you have $1 to spend on grades in your academic courses. In terms of time and effort, it would cost you the following to get a B+ or higher in each class:

Math: 20¢

AP social studies: 40¢ (you struggle with all the reading)

Science: 10¢ (your passion)

Spanish: 30¢

English: 20¢

Clearly, if the child had more money (extra time), they might be able to succeed at all these subjects. Instead, to keep up with the goal or expectation, time is often taken away from sleep, food, exercise, or other developmentally valuable activities. Be prepared in advance so you can *each* set *reasonable expectations.*

Instead of pushing your child to "just try harder" or "tough it out," partnering with them to figure out how to make school manageable and meaningful is key. This collaborative approach helps rebuild their confidence and trust, creating a foundation for progress. Taking the time to understand their experience can provide invaluable insight. Ask your child open-ended questions like:

- "What feels hardest for you about school right now?"
- "When you think about your classes, what's the part that feels the most frustrating?"
- "If you could change one thing about school, what would it be?"

These conversations may reveal underlying challenges, such as difficulty understanding assignments, feeling unsupported by teachers, or struggling with peer relationships. Validating your child's feelings— "That does sound really hard. I can see why you feel upset about it"—is the first step toward finding solutions.

Once you understand your child's concerns, work together to create a plan. This might include breaking assignments into smaller steps, setting realistic goals, or finding ways to make school feel more rewarding. Involving your child in this process helps them feel heard and reinforces their role in creating positive changes.

For example, you might say:

- "I know you're feeling overwhelmed by math right now. What if we set a goal to focus on just today's assignment? After that, we can take a break and see how you feel."

- "It sounds like your teacher's instructions aren't very clear. Would it help if we emailed her together to ask for clarification?"

By focusing on manageable steps, you help your child regain a sense of control and agency.

Collaborating With Schools

For many parents, navigating the school system can feel overwhelming and stressful. You want to advocate for your child, ensure they receive the support they need, and help them thrive academically and socially. But working with teachers, counselors, and administrators—especially when challenges arise—can feel daunting.

Remember, most teachers choose this profession because they're passionate about education and genuinely want to help children succeed. While it's frustrating when your child's needs aren't fully met, starting from a place of empathy and partnership can open the door to meaningful collaboration.

Take time to connect with your child's teacher. Share your observations and concerns, and invite them to share theirs. Phrases like "I'd like to better understand what you're seeing in the classroom" or "What strategies do you think might help my child engage more?" can set a constructive tone and show that you're on the same team.

DEALING WITH SCHOOL REFUSAL

One of the hardest truths for parents to face is that sometimes, despite your best efforts, children become so stressed out by school that they disengage entirely. If your child is consistently refusing to go to school, experiencing severe anxiety, or showing signs of depression, it's crucial to take these concerns seriously and address them with compassion. Start by acknowledging their feelings. Let them know: "We're in this together. I see how hard this is, and I'm here to help you figure it out."

If your child doesn't care about school right now, take a step back. Instead of pushing them to pretend or focus their energy on avoiding the truth, create a space where they feel safe to be honest. When children feel pressured—whether it's from school, expectations, or their own struggles—their brain can shift into survival mode. This might look like a *Fight, Flight, Freeze, Fib,* or *Fawn* response. Sometimes, children lie or avoid tasks not to be difficult but because it feels like the safest way to cope in the moment.

Stress can overwhelm the part of the brain responsible for big-picture thinking, planning, and problem solving, making it hard for your child to engage fully with learning. Instead of focusing on whether they hate school, help them see that learning how to learn is what really matters—even if the subject isn't their favorite. When you approach them with patience and understanding, you help reduce their stress, allowing them to reconnect with their ability to think, explore, and grow. That's when real learning happens.

FLEXIBLE OPTIONS TO CONSIDER

Collaborate with your child and their school to explore flexible solutions that reduce pressure while maintaining engagement:

- *Adjust expectations*: Focus on turning in assignments, attending class, and completing the required reading rather than aiming for perfect grades. A pass/fail option may help relieve the anxiety tied to performance.
- *Prioritize passion*: If your child has a strong interest or passion,

use it as an anchor. Let them devote energy to exploring that interest while putting minimal effort into other subjects. For example, they might deeply engage in art or science while meeting basic requirements in other areas.

• *Create a reduced schedule*: Work with the school to lighten their load, whether by reducing the number of classes or allowing "reset days" to recharge.

• *Alternative learning environments*: Consider options like virtual school, hybrid programs, or other alternative environments where your child can feel less overwhelmed.

FOCUSING ON SUCCESS, NOT AVOIDANCE

By creating a manageable path forward, you help your child redirect their energy from avoidance to small successes. For example, you might say:

• "Let's focus on just completing today's assignment and turning it in on time. We'll take it one day at a time."

• "What's one subject you feel you can give your energy to right now? Let's work on building momentum there."

As Mark Twain wisely said, "I have never let my schooling interfere with my education." This perspective reminds us that helping children see the value of learning—even outside traditional systems—is more important than perfect grades.

Through this process, your child can begin to feel less trapped by school's demands and more empowered to learn and grow on their own terms.

ADVOCATING FOR YOUR CHILD

Working with schools often requires taking on an advocacy role. This can seem intimidating, but remember—you are your child's strongest ally. Here are essential strategies to prepare yourself for success:

1. *Build a team mentality*: One of the most effective ways to collaborate with schools is to approach the relationship as a partnership. Instead of viewing teachers or administrators as adversaries, position yourself as part of the same team with a shared goal: supporting your child. Phrases like "What can we do together to help my child succeed?" or "How can we best support my child during this tough time?" can set a collaborative tone. Early on, establish open communication with your child's teachers and school staff and share information about your child's strengths, challenges, and needs.

2. *Be clear and specific*: Focus on specific challenges and actionable solutions. For example, instead of saying, "They're struggling," you might say, "They have difficulty following multistep directions. Could we explore ways to simplify instructions?"

3. *Know your rights*: Familiarize yourself with education laws— Individuals With Disabilities Education Act (IDEA) and Section 504. Understanding your child's rights and entitlements will help you advocate more effectively. The "Dear Colleague Letter and Resource Guide on Students With ADHD" by the U.S. Department of Education Office for Civil Rights emphasizes that public schools must ensure equal access to education for students with ADHD under Section 504 of the Rehabilitation Act (https://sites.ed.gov/idea/files/ocr-letter-07-26 -2016.pdf). This guide clarifies that students with ADHD are entitled to appropriate evaluations and accommodations, even if they are performing well academically. It reminds parents that academic success does not eliminate the need for support, as ADHD can significantly impact other areas, such as behavior, focus, and EF, which are essential to a child's overall learning experience.

4. *Submit a formal request when necessary*: If you feel that your child's needs are not being adequately addressed, submitting a formal "Letter of Request" for evaluation or services can be an impor-

tant step. Appendix J provides guidance on when and why to submit a formal letter, along with a sample letter to assist you in getting started.

5. *Bring a trusted ally to your meetings*: Even in the best circumstances, these meetings can feel stressful. Remember, you are discussing your child—the person you love most—and the challenges they face. It's natural to feel overwhelmed or to forget what you wanted to say in the moment. Consider bringing a trusted friend or family member to the meeting. They can help you stay focused, take notes, and remind you of key points you wanted to address. Having an ally by your side ensures you leave the meeting with a clear understanding of what was discussed and agreed upon.

6. *Consider hiring an advocate if necessary*: When collaboration with your child's teacher doesn't lead to progress, the next step is to approach school administration. Be clear and specific about your concerns, while remaining open to understanding the broader constraints the school may face, such as class size or limited resources.

7. If these steps still don't resolve the issue, it may be time to involve an advocate. Appendix J offers detailed guidance on when and how to involve an advocate, as well as questions to ask when selecting the right professional.

LIFE AFTER HIGH SCHOOL

For some of you reading this, you might be thinking, "I just have to get them through high school!" But remember, our goal as parents isn't just to get them launched—it's to guide them toward a future that reflects their potential, expressing their greatest gifts, talents, and passions. For many children, those gifts may take a while to reveal themselves. Henry Winkler's words, mentioned earlier, are worth repeating: "A child knows they are not doing well, you don't need to remind them. All you need to do is keep that child buoyed. Because when you are not doing well, your self-image plummets to your ankles."

There are two things to consider while they are developing, discussed next.

1. Education Path

Some children may need a break before going to college or may prefer a path other than full-time participation in a 4-year college. I often joke that although my practice, *PTS Coaching*, stands for *Pathways to Success* (because I believe these children have multiple, sometimes rocky roads to get there), PTS could also stand for *Post-Traumatic School!* These are kids who may need time to choose whether and how they want to re-engage in the intensive academic work required for college.

Here are a few alternatives to consider:

- A *gap year*, where they explore a job or internship that helps them discover their interests.
- Taking a few courses at a *community college*. It's often more affordable and can be a less intense way to handle required courses.
- *Lighter course loads* during their first semester of college to give them space to adjust to the new expectations and experiences.

When is the best time to have these discussions with your child? Start early—perhaps in eighth or ninth grade. You don't want them to feel that you doubt their ability to handle 4 years of college. Instead, frame it as believing in their ability to find their best path forward.

2. Career Awareness

I'm a big proponent of career development awareness starting at an early age. It's not about pushing children to choose a career young; after all, many of us have had several careers. Rather, it's about helping them become aware of the wide range of opportunities out there and encouraging them to think about how their interests, talents, and passions might be expressed in different ways.

Help your child become curious about the vast world of careers and how their present self can relate to future possibilities. Encourage them to casually interview you and other adults in their lives, or those in careers they find interesting:

- How did you get into this career?
- What do you enjoy about your work?
- What does a typical day or week look like?
- What best prepared you for this work?

Start early and revisit these conversations every year.

FAMOUS FAILURES AND LATE BLOOMERS

If you or your child needs some comfort or inspiration from seeing other people experience tremendous success after significant failure, here are a few wonderful examples from history:

- *The Beatles* were turned away by Decca Records because it felt that guitar groups were on the way out and that the Beatles had no future in show business. However, the band went on to become one of the most iconic bands in music history.
- *Michael Jordan* was cut from his high school basketball team, yet he went on to win the NBA championship title with the Chicago Bulls six times and is widely regarded as one of the greatest basketball players of all time.
- *Thomas Edison* was considered a poor student and was pulled out early on. His mother eventually homeschooled him. He persevered to become one of the greatest inventors in history, holding over 1,000 patents.
- *Colonel Harland Sanders* launched Kentucky Fried Chicken (KFC) at the age of 65 using his first Social Security check. After numerous rejections, his fried chicken recipe turned into a worldwide phenomenon.
- *Oprah Winfrey* was fired from her first job as a television news anchor

because she was deemed "unfit for TV." She later became a ground-breaking talk show host and media mogul.

- *Vera Wang* didn't enter the fashion industry until she was 40 years old, having previously worked as a figure skater and journalist. Today, she is one of the most renowned designers in the world.
- *Grandma Moses* started her painting career at 78 after arthritis compelled her to stop embroidery. She became one of the most renowned American folk artists, with her artwork exhibited in museums around the globe.
- *Samuel L. Jackson* didn't achieve fame as an actor until he was 43, despite working in the industry for years. He is now one of Hollywood's most celebrated actors.

These examples remind us that failure and setbacks are not the end of the road but are often a stepping stone to greatness. They also show that success can come at any time in life, reinforcing the value of perseverance and believing in oneself.

In the 1998 Apple computer ad "Think Different," several illustrious, successful people, many known or assumed to have ADHD (such as Ted Turner, Sir Richard Branson, Jim Henson, and Albert Einstein) were shown on screen as the following words played:

Here's to the crazy ones.

The misfits.

The rebels.

The troublemakers.

The round pegs in the square holes.

The ones who see things differently.

They're not fond of rules.

And they have no respect for the status quo.

You can quote them, disagree with them, glorify or vilify them. About the only thing you can't do is ignore them.

Because they change things.

They push the human race forward.

While some see them as the crazy ones, we see genius.

Because the people who are crazy enough to think they can change the world, are the ones who do.

CHOICES: YOURS AND THEIRS

When things go wrong—and they will—it's important to pause and take a breath. How you respond in these moments sets the tone for how your child learns to handle their own mistakes and challenges. Here are some guiding principles to keep in mind:

- *Stay calm*: Pause before reacting. Give yourself space to stop and think. Your calm is your power.
- *Get curious*: Remember the guiding principle: *Kids do well if they can*. Is there something you might be missing? What's behind their behavior?
- *No negotiating or problem solving until they're calm*: If your child is upset, wait until they've calmed down and can speak appropriately before attempting to work things out.
- *Less talking, less emotion*: Restate the rules and the consequences clearly and calmly. Avoid lecturing or overexplaining in the heat of the moment.
- *Offer a chance to "chill"*: Sometimes a brief break can help everyone reset before moving forward.
- *Avoid shame, blame, or criticism*: Model the behavior you want to see. Your response teaches them how to handle tough situations.

- *Remind them of their power*: Say, "The choice is yours. The ball is in your court," to help them take ownership of their actions.
- *Be ready to follow through*: This might mean "turning the car around," even if it means sacrificing your own plans. Consistency reinforces your child's understanding of choices and consequences.
- *Stay calm*: Yes, this is worth repeating. Your calm presence helps de-escalate the situation and shows your child how to regulate their emotions.

Ultimately, how you handle these moments teaches your child more than words ever could. By staying calm, curious, and consistent, you help them learn that their choices matter—and that mistakes are opportunities to grow.

LIVE IT TO LEARN IT

Parenting a child with ADHD often requires letting go of the instinct to control every aspect of their journey. A powerful mantra I learned from a friend is that our children must "live it to learn it." This philosophy reminds us that while we can guide and support our children, true growth comes from experiencing life's challenges and opportunities firsthand.

Remember I mentioned earlier that some children are like cactus flowers, blooming only on their own terms and timelines. These strong-willed and independent children can resist being rushed or pushed, and even simple, well-meaning requests—like starting homework or cleaning up—might feel like an unwelcome challenge. By keeping this perspective in mind, we can step back and trust their process, even when it doesn't match with our expectations.

Each child is born with innate gifts, talents, and passions. Sometimes your child's interests are not what you might expect—or even what you would prefer. And sometimes it may feel like they drift from one interest to the next so often that it's hard to tell what truly matters to them. Be patient. These years are a time for exploration, and very rarely does someone follow the exact career path they imagined as a child. For now, the most important thing is helping your child feel good about who they are and knowing that you believe in them. That foundation will support them as they navigate their journey.

One mother shared how difficult it was to let her son, who has ADHD, make his own decisions—even when they felt risky. Yet in giving him the space to explore his own dreams, she saw him learn responsibility, develop resilience, and discover his passion and purpose. By stepping back, she gave him the freedom to take ownership of his life and build the skills he needed to succeed.

HOW ARE YOU DOING?

Sometimes, as parents, it's easy to become so focused on our children's needs and future that we overlook our own well-being. Many parents I work with have shared that their anxiety—or even their own dreams for their children—has occasionally gotten in the way of truly "parenting the child they have." If this resonates with you, know that you are not alone.

Take a moment to reflect on your own life. Are you finding fulfillment and balance outside your role as a parent? Perhaps using tools like the "Wheel of Life" in Appendix K can help you identify areas that might need more attention. There you will also see samples of the "Wheel of Life" for children. Engaging with hobbies, work, or other passions can bring joy and perspective back into your life.

Self-care is not a luxury—it's essential. Ensuring you get enough sleep, exercise regularly, and nourish your body with healthy foods helps you show up as your best self for your child. Likewise, nurturing your relationship with your partner and maintaining meaningful friendships can prevent feelings of isolation and burnout.

It can also help to seek out support from others who understand your journey. Connecting with parents facing similar challenges can provide comfort, ideas, and perspective. And sometimes, it's okay to be open with your child about the growth you're experiencing as a parent. Framing it positively can build their confidence while showing them the value of adaptability. For instance, you might say, "It's not easy for me to pull back; I've been 'Mom' all these years. But I see you are growing, and I have to get used to the changes that are happening. Promise, I'm working on it."

Parenting is a journey of learning for all of us, and tending to your own needs helps you meet the challenges with strength and grace.

CONCLUDING THOUGHTS: PARENT THE CHILD YOU HAVE

As you reflect on this chapter, remember that parenting a child with ADHD is not about striving for perfection. It's about progress, connection, and learning and growing alongside your child. The choices you make, along with the choices you empower your child to make, shape not only their present but also their future as independent, capable individuals.

Parenting children with ADHD and EF challenges is a delicate balancing act. It means knowing when to step back so your child can experience the consequences of their decisions, while staying close enough to guide and support them. It means encouraging independence without abandoning the structure they still need. It means reminding yourself—and them—that progress matters far more than perfection.

At the heart of this journey is one essential truth: *Parent the child you have.* Every child is unique, with their own strengths, challenges, and pace of growth. Your role is not to compare them to others but to meet them where they are and help them move toward who they are meant to be. While it's easy to get caught up in daily struggles, don't lose sight of the bigger picture. The ultimate goal is to raise a child who is confident, resilient, and ready to navigate the world on their own terms. By focusing on lifelong skills—self-reflection, emotional regulation, problem solving—you are giving them the tools to create a future filled with possibility.

Progress often comes in small, uneven steps, and that's okay. Celebrate every success, no matter how minor it may seem. Whether it's remembering their backpack for a week straight, taking ownership of an assignment, or showing up for class with a positive attitude, these moments are worth recognizing. Just as importantly, give yourself credit for your own efforts. Parenting is hard, meaningful work, and your commitment to understanding and supporting your child makes a tremendous difference. You don't have to be a perfect parent to be a great parent. Listening and caring matter far more than getting everything right.

Growing up happens, even if it takes longer for the pieces to fall into place. Embrace the traffic, find your joy in the journey, and always give your child a sense of hope. Help them discover their own unique pathway to success, knowing that your love and support will guide them every step of the way.

To mark your progress and resilience, I've included a Black Belt Certificate in Appendix L. Think of it as a reflection of the skills and strength you've developed as you've embraced building your new house.

GUIDING THOUGHTS

- Choice is power.
- You cannot control their choices.
- Ask before offering help.
- Stay focused on the big picture.
- Give extra chances and positives to counteract their outside world.
- Try to slow down life—rushing creates stress.
- Pay attention to their strengths—those are the building blocks.
- Remind them: "School may be hard, but in life, you will rock!"

- Growth is not always linear or noticeable but it happens. Help them find their pathway to success!

WHAT'S NEXT?

Parenting a child with ADHD is an ongoing journey. Building the skills, routines, and mindset discussed in this chapter takes time, commitment, and consistency—like developing a muscle. This is just the beginning. Change happens gradually and takes root the more you stay engaged and focused on your goals.

ACTION STEPS

- *Revisit and reflect*: Mark a date in your calendar to reread the Guiding Thoughts at least once a month for 5 months.
- *Check your house*: If you're struggling, take out the "House" model from this chapter and identify which part needs repair or reinforcement.
- *Collaborate with schools*: Work with your child's school to create a united front in supporting your child's growth.
- *Build a portfolio*: Develop an annual portfolio with your child to help them reflect on their progress and goals. Include works they are proud of, pictures that highlight their joy, and any other items that reflect the year.
- *Explore homework strategies*: If managing homework is a challenge, consider enrolling in Managing Homework: Parent Edition ADHD/EF Tips, Tools, & Strategies for Helping Students (https://ptscoaching.com/parents/managing-homework-parents).

WHEN IS IT TIME TO SEEK ADDITIONAL HELP?

There may be times when you need additional support to move forward effectively. Consider reaching out for professional help if:

- You've tried to engage your child in collaborative conversations, including offering incentives rather than punishments, but they remain resistant.
- You fear violence or destructive behavior.
- You suspect anxiety, depression, substance use, or screen addiction are playing a role in their struggles.
- You believe an outside perspective might help open the flow of conversation or address specific disagreements.

You don't have to go through this alone. Support is available to help you and your child navigate these challenges with warmth, guidance, and hope. You may want to consider working with an *ADHD Parent Coach* or seeing if your child is ready for an *ADHD Student Coach*. I have trained therapists and other professionals to support parents, students, and professionals worldwide. Visit my website: www .ptscoaching.com.

And if no one has told you this yet today: You're doing a terrific job!

With warmth and love,
Cindy Goldrich

Resources

With all the websites and books available on ADHD, it can be over-whelming to find helpful and accurate information. Here is a curated list of resources I find most helpful for understanding, supporting, and treating ADHD.

This section is divided into several areas to make it easy for you to find what you need:

Resources for Parents: This section includes books, websites, and tools designed to help parents support their children with ADHD.

Resources for Students: Features books and materials to help children understand ADHD and thrive.

Resources for Professionals: Offers tools and references for professionals working with individuals with ADHD, as well as opportunities for those interested in training to become professionals in the field.

The first part highlights general resources for understanding ADHD and providing support, followed by specialized sections tailored to specific audiences. Whether you're a parent, educator, or a professional seeking to enhance your expertise, this section has something for you.

For an extensive list of tools, books, and other helpful materials, visit the Resources section of my website at https://ptscoaching.com /tools-resources.

WEBSITES

PTS Coaching (www.ptscoaching.com): This is my website, where you'll find articles and resources for parents, students, and educators. Feel free to print and share anything you find helpful. Follow the PTS Coaching Facebook page for current research and updates (https://www.facebook.com/ptscoaching).

ADHD Awareness Month (www.adhdawareness.org): Each year during October, several prominent organizations coordinate efforts to promote ADHD education and awareness. The website offers excellent resources that can be printed and distributed year-round.

CHADD (www.chadd.org): The premier national nonprofit organization providing education, advocacy, and support for individuals with ADHD. CHADD has local chapters and hosts an annual conference featuring top researchers and experts.

Learning Disabilities Association of America (http://ldaamerica .org): An excellent resource for parents and educators on a wide range of learning disabilities.

Lives in the Balance (www.livesinthebalance.org): Created by Ross Greene, this website provides resources and training in Collaborative and Proactive Solutions (CPS) to support children with challenging behaviors.

National Center for Learning Disabilities (http://www.ncld .org): Offers valuable resources for parents and educators about learning disabilities.

National Resource Center on ADHD (https://chadd.org/
about/about-nrc/): A division of CHADD providing scientific
information, resources, and support about ADHD.

International Dyslexia Association https://dyslexiaida.org):
Provides extensive resources for individuals with dyslexia as well as
parents and educators.

Think:Kids (http://thinkkids.org): Provides training and support
for children with behavioral challenges based on the evidence-
based Collaborative Problem-Solving approach.

Wright's Law (http://wrightslaw.com): A valuable site about
education law and advocacy, ideal for parents, educators,
and attorneys.

MAGAZINES

ADDitude magazine (www.additudemag.com): A trusted resource
for practical tips, expert advice, and personal stories about ADHD
and related conditions.

Attention magazine: Provided as a membership benefit for joining
CHADD (www.chadd.org).

BOOKS FOR PARENTS AND
ADULTS WHO HAVE ADHD

*ADHD, Executive Function & Behavioral Challenges in the
Classroom: Managing the Impact on Learning, Motivation, and Stress*
by Cindy Goldrich and Carly Wolf

*The Adult ADHD & Anxiety Workbook: Cognitive Behavioral
Therapy Skills to Manage Stress, Find Focus and Reclaim Your Life* by
J. Russell Ramsay

Between Parent and Child by Haim G. Ginott

Between Parent & Teenager by Haim G. Ginott

Change Your Questions Change Your Life: 12 Powerful Tools for Leadership, Coaching, and Life by Marilee Adams

Driven to Distraction by Edward M. Hallowell

Empowering Youth with ADHD: Your Guide to Coaching Adolescents and Young Adults for Coaches, Parents, and Professionals by Jodi Sleeper-Triplett

The Explosive Child: A New Approach for Understanding and Parenting Easily Frustrated, Chronically Inflexible Children by Ross W. Greene

Helping Your Anxious Child: A Step-by-Step Guide for Parents by Ronald Rapee, Ann Wignall, Susan Spence, Vanessa Cobham, and Heidi Lyneham

How to Win Friends and Influence People: The Only Book You Need to Lead You to Success by Dale Carnegie

Life After High School: A Guide for Students With Disabilities and Their Families by Susan Yellin and Christina Cacioppo Bertsch

The Mindful Child: How to Help Your Kid Manage Stress and Become Happier, Kinder, and More Compassionate by Susan Kaiser Greenland

More Attention, Less Deficit: Success Strategies for Adults with ADHD by Ari Tuckman

The Motivation Breakthrough: 6 Secrets to Turning On the Tuned-Out Child by Richard Lavoie

Ready or Not, Here Life Comes by Mel Levine

The 7 Habits of Highly Effective People by Stephen R. Covey

Smart but Scattered by Peg Dawson and Richard Guare

Socially ADDept: Teaching Social Skills to Children with ADHD, LD, and Asperger's by Janet Z. Giler

Worry: Hope and Help for a Common Condition by Edward M. Hallowell

Your Brain's Not Broken: Strategies for Navigating Your Emotions and Life with ADHD by Tamara Rosier

BOOKS FOR CHILDREN EXPLAINING ADHD

All Dogs Have ADHD by Kathy Hoopmann

Focused by Alyson Gerber

Jimmy Racecar by James B. Snyder

My Brain Needs Glasses: Living With Hyperactivity by Annick Vincent

My Friend the Troublemaker: Learning to Focus and Thriving with ADHD by Rifka Schonfeld

Putting on the Brakes: Understanding and Taking Control of Your ADD or ADHD by Patricia O. Quinn and Judith M. Stern

Smart Girl's Guide to Knowing What to Say: Finding the Words to Fit Any Situation by Patti Kelley Holyoke

A Walk in the Rain With a Brain by Edward M. Hallowell

EXCELLENT CHILDREN'S BOOKS AND SERIES FEATURING LEAD CHARACTERS WHO HAVE ADHD OR DYSLEXIA

The Amazing Ninja Brothers: Entering the Deep Unknown by Robert Martin

The Boy With the Butterfly Mind by Victoria Williamson

Check Mates by Stewart Foster

Each Tiny Spark by Pablo Cartaya

Eliza Bing Is (Not) a Big Fat Quitter by Carmella Van Vleet

Focused by Alyson Gerber

Hank Zipzer series by Henry Winkler

Joey Pigza series by Jack Gantos

Lights, Camera, Disaster by Erin Dionne

My Friend the Troublemaker: Learning to Focus and Thriving with ADHD by Rifka Schonfeld

Percy Jackson and the Olympians series by Rick Riordan

Superhero School series by Gracie Dix

RESOURCES FOR PROFESSIONALS

ADHD, Executive Function & Behavioral Challenges in the Classroom: Managing the Impact on Learning, Motivation and Stress by Cindy Goldrich and Carly Wolf: This book offers practical strategies and tools for educators, parents, and professionals to understand and address the unique needs of students with ADHD and executive function challenges. It emphasizes creating supportive environments to enhance learning, motivation, and emotional regulation.

In-School Training Services: PTS Coaching provides experienced professionals who work directly with school districts to train staff in creating effective environments for children with ADHD and executive function challenges.

PTS Coaching's *ADHD Parent Coach Academy*: A training program designed for professionals who want to specialize in coaching parents of children with ADHD and executive function challenges. Learn how to guide families toward success with tools, strategies, and proven methodologies.

PTS Coaching's *ADHD Teacher Trainer Academy*: A program tailored for professionals who want to train school staff and districts in best practices for supporting students with ADHD and executive function challenges. Graduates are equipped to deliver in-service workshops and professional development sessions.

COACHING SERVICES

Adult Coaching: Coaching for adults with ADHD to improve organization, time management, and overall quality of life.

Parent Coaching: PTS Coaching offers personalized coaching to parents, helping them understand and support their children with ADHD.

Student Coaching: Coaching tailored to children and teens to help them develop executive function skills, manage ADHD symptoms, and thrive academically.

Appendix A

UNDERSTANDING ADHD COACHING

ADHD Coaching is a transformative, collaborative process designed to empower individuals and families navigating the challenges of ADHD and Executive Function (EF) deficits. By fostering accountability and enhancing the ability to set and achieve meaningful goals, it equips clients to build essential skills and strategies for success.

ADHD Coaching is life coaching specifically designed to address the unique concerns of individuals managing the complexities of ADHD. A certified ADHD Coach is specially educated in the science, research, and effective practices for supporting individuals with ADHD, EF disorders, and related challenges. Widely respected organizations and individuals, including the National Institute of Mental Health, Children and Adults with Attention Deficit Disorder (CHADD), Russell Barkley (*ADHD: A Handbook for Diagnosis and Treatment*), and Edward Hallowell (*Driven to Distraction*), have endorsed ADHD Coaching as a vital tool for success.

When seeking an ADHD Coach, it is essential to choose someone with professional training and certification. While personal experience with ADHD can provide insight, it does not replace the specialized knowledge and expertise required to address the neurodiversity of ADHD effectively.

This appendix explores the three key branches of ADHD Coaching: ADHD Parent Coaching, ADHD Student Coaching, and ADHD Adult Coaching. Each branch offers unique benefits and complements the others, with ADHD Parent Coaching providing the foundational tools to guide and empower children effectively. Together, these approaches create a framework for long-term success.

ADHD PARENT COACHING

ADHD Parent Coaching focuses on helping parents develop the knowledge, skills, and strategies needed to guide their children effectively. Parenting neurodiverse children often requires a nuanced approach that goes beyond intuition and traditional methods. Without the right tools and insights, even well-intentioned strategies can inadvertently exacerbate a child's challenges.

Why ADHD Parent Coaching Is Essential

ADHD Parent Coaching equips parents to:
- Understand how ADHD and EF challenges impact their child's learning, behavior, and emotional responses.
- Improve communication with their child, fostering trust and collaboration.
- Set boundaries and consequences that build skills and are constructive rather than punitive.
- Reduce stress within the family, including marital stress from differing parenting approaches.
- Adapt their parenting style to create a calmer, more connected relationship.

A key goal of ADHD Parent Coaching is to help parents foster a relationship that prepares their child to become more "coachable." By building trust and understanding, parents can support their child's readiness for future coaching or professional guidance. Additionally, ADHD Parent Coaches often collaborate with therapists to align parenting strategies with therapeutic goals, creating a unified support system for the child.

ADHD Parent Coaching remains valuable throughout all stages of a child's development. For younger children, it helps parents address immediate challenges and foster growth. For older children transitioning to independence, it provides crucial guidance and adaptability, ensuring parents can continue to offer effective support.

ADHD STUDENT COACHING

ADHD Student Coaching helps older high school and college students develop the EF skills and self-awareness needed to succeed academically and personally. This type of coaching is most effective when the student is ready to engage willingly and independently.

When Is a Student Ready for Coaching?

Indicators of readiness include:
- Recognizing struggles with time management, organization, or goal setting.
- Expressing a desire to improve performance or achieve specific goals.
- Willingness to reflect, take ownership, and engage in the coaching process.

For students who are not yet ready, pushing them into coaching can lead to resistance or negative associations. In these cases, ADHD Parent Coaching can serve as an interim solution, helping parents build the foundation for their child's future coachability.

How ADHD Student Coaching Helps

- Enhances skills like planning, prioritizing, and self-monitoring.
- Builds confidence and resilience through goal setting and celebrating successes.
- Strengthens problem-solving and communication abilities.
- Reduces stress by teaching time and resource management.

ADHD ADULT COACHING

Many adults first become aware of their own ADHD after their children are diagnosed or identified with ADHD. Receiving a diagnosis later in life can be both overwhelming and liberating. ADHD Adult Coaching addresses the unique challenges faced by adults, including time management, organization, career development, and relationships. The good news is that recognizing your own ADHD can open the doors to a deeper understanding of yourself, allowing you to address lifelong challenges and seize opportunities that may have eluded you until now. This form of coaching focuses on the individual's goals and provides tailored support to help them navigate their personal and professional life with confidence. Readers can explore additional insights and strategies in Appendix H, Parenting When You Have ADHD, which complements the tools provided by ADHD Adult Coaching.

Key Benefits of ADHD Adult Coaching

- Provides tools for managing daily responsibilities and long-term objectives.
- Improves workplace performance and career satisfaction.
- Strengthens relationships through better communication and emotional regulation.
- Builds self-confidence by focusing on strengths and achievements.

While ADHD Parent and Student Coaching lay the foundation

during earlier stages of life, ADHD adult coaching demonstrates the lifelong value of tailored support for individuals navigating the complexities of ADHD.

If you are interested in becoming a trained ADHD Parent Coach, refer to the resources section at the end of this book for more information about my ADHD Parent Coach Academy. The program is open to parents, educators, counselors, coaches, and mental health professionals who are passionate about supporting families navigating the complexities of ADHD. By becoming a trained ADHD Parent Coach, you can provide vital guidance to parents and caregivers in your community, helping them foster greater calm, connection, and confidence.

Appendix B

EMPOWERING EDUCATORS AND PARENTS

The Transformative Value of Professional Training

Children with ADHD face a myriad of challenges every day—struggling with focus, behavior, and social interactions both at home and in school. The parents who love and support these children and the educators who genuinely want to help them succeed often find themselves navigating a labyrinth of conflicting advice, limited resources, and emotional hurdles as they strive to help these complex children thrive. When educators and parents are not fully prepared or supported, missteps and misunderstandings about ADHD can multiply, leaving both classrooms and homes less nurturing than they could be.

A full circle of support is essential. By providing targeted training for educators and nurturing coaching for parents, we create a collaborative network that bridges the gap between school and home. This appendix highlights two distinct yet complementary approaches: one to support educators through the *ADHD Teacher Trainer Academy* and one to support parents via the *ADHD Parent Coach Academy*.

SUPPORTING EDUCATORS–ADHD TEACHER TRAINER ACADEMY

Teachers play a vital role in shaping both the academic and social experiences of children with ADHD. Unfortunately, most teachers receive little to no formal training on ADHD during their undergraduate or graduate studies. This gap in knowledge often leaves educators unprepared to manage challenging behaviors, support diverse learning needs, or recognize the subtle signs of ADHD. As a result, students may be misunderstood or inadvertently penalized for traits beyond their control.

When professionals participate in programs like the *ADHD Teacher Trainer Academy*, they gain access to evidence-based strategies—clear instructions, structured routines, and positive reinforcement—that they can use to train teachers and transform classroom dynamics. Once educators are equipped with these skills, they not only improve engagement and reduce disruptions but also foster an inclusive environment where every student can thrive. Moreover, when teachers understand the realities of ADHD, they can better connect with parents, building a bridge that supports consistent, effective strategies both at school and at home.

In public schools, the Individuals With Disabilities Education Act (IDEA) mandates that children with ADHD receive appropriate services and accommodations to support their learning. However, this requirement does not extend to private or nontraditional schools, where teacher training in ADHD may be even more limited. Ensuring that all educators, regardless of school type, have access to quality training is an ethical imperative. Such training empowers teachers to create equitable opportunities for students with ADHD and uphold their right to a meaningful education.

SUPPORTING PARENTS–ADHD PARENT COACH ACADEMY

Parenting a child with ADHD often feels like navigating uncharted territory: balancing emotional challenges with the practicalities of daily life. Many parents struggle with conflicting advice and limited resources, which can lead to feelings of isolation and overwhelm. Parent coaching, however, offers a powerful prescription that transforms these challenges into opportunities for growth.

Through the *ADHD Parent Coach Academy*, professionals are trained to become Parent Coaches who then provide personalized guidance and practical strategies to parents. These coaches help families create effective routines, manage behavior, and advocate successfully for their children. Research shows that when parents receive support through this coaching model, they experience increased confidence, reduced stress, and improved outcomes for their children. These benefits extend beyond the home: Empowered parents can more effectively collaborate with educators, ensuring that strategies are reinforced in both environments.

By engaging in parent coaching, families build resilience and form a supportive community that not only addresses daily challenges but also nurtures long-term success. This approach strengthens the entire network of support around the child, creating a full circle where informed, empowered parents and well-prepared educators work together to foster a brighter future.

ABOUT PTS COACHING

I've dedicated myself to empowering educators, mental health professionals, and others passionate about making a difference for children with ADHD and EF challenges. My programs—the *ADHD Teacher Trainer Academy* and the *ADHD Parent Coach Academy*—are designed not only to provide comprehensive training but also to create a nurturing, collaborative community where every child's potential is recognized. I've seen firsthand how tailored, compassionate support can transform both classrooms and homes.

In addition, I offer on-site, in-service professional development for schools seeking customized support for their staff. For more information about these services and to explore the many resources available, visit my website at ptscoaching.com.

Appendix C

DIAGNOSING ADHD

Who Can Help, What's Involved, and How to Access Testing

WHO CAN DIAGNOSE ADHD?

One of the most common questions I hear from parents is "Who can diagnose ADHD?" Professionals such as psychiatrists, pediatricians, psychologists, social workers, and nurse practitioners are all qualified, but not all specialize in ADHD. It's important to seek someone with specific training and experience in ADHD and the latest research. Since ADHD manifests differently in every child, having an experienced professional conduct the evaluation can make all the difference.

DIAGNOSTIC CRITERIA AND PREVALENCE

ADHD can often be reliably diagnosed as early as age 4, but most children are identified during the school years when academic and social demands start to increase. Children may "hit the wall" at different ages, depending on their challenges:

- *Early elementary school*: The transition to more structured classrooms and expectations in third grade can reveal difficulties with focus or behavior.

- *Middle school*: Managing multiple teachers, assignments, and schedules can become overwhelming.
- *High school*: The intensity of coursework and the need for self-management may uncover hidden struggles that natural talent or earlier interventions could mask.

Recognizing these moments as opportunities to seek help is crucial to setting your child on a positive path.

To be diagnosed with ADHD, at least six of nine inattentive and/or hyperactive–impulsive symptoms listed in the fifth edition of *Diagnostic and Statistical Manual of Mental Disorders* (*DSM-5*) must be present in two or more settings and have been evident before the age of 12. These symptoms must persist for at least 6 months. For adolescents age 17 or older and adults, only five symptoms are required for a diagnosis.

According to the Centers for Disease Control and Prevention, the rate of ADHD is 11% for kids between 4 and 17. Boys are diagnosed at about twice the rate of girls. However, as noted earlier, girls' symptoms are often less disruptive and more internalized, leading to delayed or missed diagnoses. While some people outgrow or learn to manage their ADHD, studies suggest that 30%–50% of adults continue to experience symptoms.

WHAT DOES A COMPREHENSIVE DIAGNOSIS INCLUDE?

A proper ADHD diagnosis should be thorough and comprehensive. It typically involves several key components:

- *Detailed clinical history*: Reviewing your child's developmental, medical, and family history to identify patterns and rule out other causes for symptoms.
- *Physical exam*: Identifying any medical conditions, such as sleep apnea or thyroid issues, that could mimic ADHD symptoms.
- *Behavioral rating scales*: Tools like the Conners Rating Scale or the

Vanderbilt Assessment Scale gather input from parents, teachers, and sometimes the child to assess behaviors across settings.

- *Screening for coexisting conditions*: Many children with ADHD also have learning disabilities, anxiety, or other challenges that must be addressed alongside ADHD.

A neuropsychological evaluation can be particularly valuable. It provides a comprehensive understanding of your child's learning profile, which can uncover hidden challenges, such as learning disabilities masked by high intelligence, that might otherwise go undetected.

ACCESSING TESTING

For many families, the cost of testing can be a barrier. Here are some practical options:

- *School-based evaluations*: Public schools can conduct evaluations if there are concerns about academic difficulties. Although these evaluations focus on educational needs rather than providing a full ADHD diagnosis, they can still offer valuable insights.
- *University clinics*: Psychology or psychiatry programs at universities often offer lower-cost evaluations through their training clinics.
- *Community resources*: Local mental health centers, nonprofits, and community health programs may provide affordable diagnostic services.

For more insights on ADHD diagnosis and treatment, visit ptscoaching.com.

MANAGING SCREEN TIME TOGETHER

Screen time is a significant part of children's lives today, with children ages 8–12 averaging 4–6 hours daily and teens up to 9 hours. While technology can provide entertainment and learning opportunities, excessive screen use can affect development, behavior, and sleep. As a parent, you play a vital role in guiding your child toward healthy technology habits. The key to success? Create *shared solutions* that involve your child in the process, fostering collaboration and reducing resistance.

WHY SHARED SOLUTIONS MATTER

Rather than enforcing rigid screen time rules, involving your child in the decision-making process helps them understand the "why" behind boundaries and builds their problem-solving and accountability skills. Collaborating ensures your child feels heard and respected, increasing their willingness to follow the agreements you create together.

PRACTICAL TOOLS AND TIPS

Here are five actionable strategies to manage screen time effectively while emphasizing collaboration and shared decision making:

1. *Set clear time limits together*: Work with your child to decide on daily or weekly screen time limits. Listen to their insights and needs, share your expectations, and reach an agreement that feels fair to both of you. Use tools like built-in screen monitors, screen time apps, or visual timers to help your child stay accountable to the plan.

2. *Create screen-free spaces*: Establish areas where screens are not allowed, such as bedrooms, bathrooms, and the dinner table. These boundaries encourage family interaction and ensure quality, distraction-free time together. Mealtime, in particular, offers a chance for meaningful conversations and connections that strengthen family bonds.

3. *Watch what they watch*: Spend time viewing shows, games, or other content with your child. This not only allows you to monitor what they're engaging with but also creates opportunities for discussions and teaching moments. Sharing this time helps your child feel connected to you and eases their transition out of screen use when it's time to stop.

4. *Encourage physical play*: Replace some screen time with outdoor or physical activities, even during colder months. A walk, playing in the snow, or engaging in a fun indoor activity can be energizing and beneficial for both physical and mental health.

5. *Limit screens before bed*: Create a screen-free routine at least an hour before bedtime to promote better sleep. This rule applies to everyone in the household, modeling healthy habits and reinforcing the importance of rest for overall well-being.

PROGRESS OVER PERFECTION

Changing screen habits doesn't have to happen overnight. Small, consistent steps make a big difference. Celebrate even minor improvements, like reducing screen time by 30 minutes or introducing one screen-free zone.

Appendix E

UNDERSTANDING IEPs AND 504 PLANS

If your child is struggling in school due to ADHD, it is essential to explore what formal supports and services may be available to help them succeed. While some accommodations can be provided informally by teachers, others require a formal agreement with the school. Two key legal avenues for obtaining these supports are the *Individualized Education Plan* (IEP) and the *504 plan*.

WHAT IS AN IEP?

An IEP is a comprehensive, legally binding document established under the IDEA. To qualify for an IEP, a child must meet the criteria for one of IDEA's specific disability categories. ADHD typically falls under the classification of *Other Health Impairment* (OHI).

An IEP is designed to address your child's unique learning needs and includes:

- *Specific educational goals* tailored to your child's strengths and challenges.
- *Services and supports*, such as specialized instruction or therapy.
- *Accommodations and modifications* to ensure your child can access and succeed in their education.

The IEP process is highly structured and includes regular progress monitoring to ensure that goals are being met and adjustments are made as needed.

WHAT IS A 504 PLAN?

A 504 plan is a legal document established under *Section 504 of the Rehabilitation Act of 1973*, which prohibits discrimination based on disability. A 504 plan is less comprehensive than an IEP and does not include *educational goals*. Instead, it focuses on accommodations and modifications to provide students with equal access to education.

A child qualifies for a 504 plan if they have a physical or mental impairment, such as ADHD, that "substantially limits one or more major life activities," including learning, concentrating, or listening. Examples of accommodations in a 504 plan may include extended time on tests, preferential seating, or access to assistive technology.

IMPORTANT CONSIDERATIONS

It is important to note that IEPs and 504 plans are federally mandated services available only to students attending public schools under IDEA and Section 504. Private or nontraditional schools are not required to provide these supports.

For guidance on how to approach your school about these services, as well as when to involve an advocate, see Appendix J. These sections provide detailed steps and advice to help you navigate the process.

To learn more about advocating for your child and navigating the process, visit these trusted organizations:

- CHADD (www.chadd.org)
- Wrightslaw (www.wrightslaw.com)
- *ADDitude* magazine (www.additudemag.com)

PRACTICAL ACCOMMODATIONS AND MODIFICATIONS FOR STUDENTS WITH ADHD AND EF CHALLENGES

If your child struggles with ADHD or EF challenges, accommodations and modifications can be essential in supporting their learning and success. While some supports may be provided through an IEP or 504 plan, others might be implemented informally through discussions with teachers. However, it's important to remember that informal accommodations provided by a teacher one year may not carry over to the next. As your child transitions to middle school, it becomes even more crucial to formalize accommodations and modifications that were effective in elementary school to ensure continuity of support.

Always involve your child in these conversations, as their insights provide a unique and valuable perspective. Understanding what it feels like for them to be in the classroom and what changes could truly make learning easier is key to creating effective solutions. By including your child, you empower them and ensure that their voice is heard in decisions that directly impact their education. The following are examples of accommodations and modifications you can discuss with your child's teachers and request as part of a 504 plan, IEP, or informal support plan.

TOOLS AND TECHNIQUES FOR LEARNING AND PERFORMANCE

- *Keyboarding skills*: Ensure your child develops efficient keyboarding skills for faster and more accurate written output.
- *Assistive technology*: Utilize tools such as graphic organizer programs and dictation software to support writing and organization.
- *Homework tracking systems*: Implement effective systems for tracking assignments, including planners or apps.
- *Project planning*: Break down long-term assignments into smaller, manageable tasks with individual deadlines.
- *Distraction reduction*: Use tools like blank cards or highlighters to track written material and minimize distractions.
- *Study strategies*: Teach various note-taking, studying, and test-taking methods to help your child discover what works best for them.

SUPPORTING ACTIVE LEARNING

- Provide *class notes* or allow note taking with assistive technology to enhance focus during lessons.
- Assign a *study partner* to encourage collaboration and learning through discussion.
- Reinforce positive behaviors with *specific praise* to boost motivation.
- Provide reading materials suited to both *fluency* and *comprehension* levels; consider audio books as an alternative.
- Highlight key information in reading material to direct attention to essential concepts.

WORKING MEMORY AIDS

- Offer *written instructions* for assignments and classroom activities.
- Allow the use of *calculators, formula sheets*, or *rule guides* when appropriate.
- Use *visual aids* and step-by-step instructions for complex projects or activities.

ORGANIZATIONAL SUPPORTS

- *Color-code materials* by subject to simplify organization.
- *Provide direct support for organizing* multisubject materials and creating systems to manage items for school and home.
- *Incorporate regular check-ins* to assess and improve organizational skills.

ATTENTION AND BEHAVIOR MANAGEMENT

- *Assign seating* to minimize distractions and optimize teacher support.
- *Post classroom rules and schedules* visibly to assist with transitions and expectations.
- *Develop a discreet signal system* to help the student self-monitor or request breaks.
- *Prepare for transitions* with advance warnings and detailed plans.

ENHANCING STUDENT OUTPUT

- Administer quizzes and tests in *small groups* or *one-on-one* settings.
- Provide *extra time* for tests, assignments, and activities.
- Allow *breaks* during extended testing periods or assignments.
- Use *study carrels* or headphones to reduce auditory and visual distractions during independent work.
- Permit the use of *word processors* or *dictation software* to aid in written output.
- *Modify assignments* to reduce length or eliminate repetitive tasks.

- *Provide alternative methods* for demonstrating knowledge, such as oral presentations or creative projects.

ADDITIONAL SUPPORTS

- Adjust schedules so that more demanding classes occur during your child's *peak learning times.*
- Encourage *parent–teacher collaboration*: Establish a communication log for tracking goals, progress, and strategies.
- Conduct *quarterly goal-setting meetings* to focus on behavior, homework completion, and performance improvements.
- Break down grades to *provide feedback* on specific skills, such as content mastery and organization.
- Hold *age-appropriate discussions* about how learning challenges impact your child's experience and strategies for overcoming them.
- Provide *professional development* for teachers to increase understanding of ADHD and EF challenges.

ADDITIONAL ACCOMMODATIONS TO CONSIDER

- Offer *flexible deadlines* for assignments when needed.
- Create opportunities for *movement breaks* during lessons or testing.
- Use *visual timers* to help students manage time and stay on task.
- Provide opportunities for *peer mentoring* to build social skills and academic confidence.
- Introduce *mindfulness* or *self-regulation strategies*, such as deep breathing exercises or sensory tools.

By working collaboratively with your child and their educators, you can create a supportive learning environment tailored to their unique needs. These accommodations and modifications can foster confidence, improve performance, and set your child up for long-term success. If you need additional support, my ADHD Coaches are available to work with you to develop effective strategies and collaborate with your child and their teacher to create the best possible supports.

SUPPORTING YOUR CHILD'S ADHD MEDICATION JOURNEY

If you are currently using or considering medication to help your child manage their ADHD, it's important to work with a provider who is up to date on the range of available options. A knowledgeable provider can help you understand how the medication works and how it can support your child's needs. Below are key considerations, including choosing the right professional, understanding the trial-and-error process, and fostering your child's role in their own treatment.

CHOOSING THE RIGHT PROFESSIONAL

Finding the right professional to guide your child's ADHD treatment is critical. While any medical doctor can prescribe ADHD medication, you want someone who is experienced in ADHD treatment and up to date with the latest research. A pediatrician is often the most accessible starting point, as they know your child well and can initiate treatment. However, if the medication isn't working effectively or side effects arise, a specialist like a psychiatrist or neurologist with expertise in ADHD may be a better fit.

Once the right medication and dosage are established, your pediatrician can typically manage refills and regular check-ins, which is often more cost-effective and convenient. However, stimulant prescriptions require in-person visits every 3 months by law, so finding a provider who understands your child's needs and offers ongoing support is key.

UNDERSTANDING THE TRIAL-AND-ERROR PROCESS

Medication is not a one-size-fits-all solution, and finding the right type and dosage can take time. Be prepared for a trial-and-error process, and keep a detailed log of your child's reactions, including appetite, sleep, mood, and attentiveness. These notes will be invaluable when collaborating with your medical professional to fine-tune your child's treatment plan.

Encouraging your child to track and communicate how they feel on medication fosters self-advocacy, an important life skill as they transition into adolescence and adulthood. The Student Medication Log included at the end of this appendix can serve as a tool to help them take an active role in their treatment.

WHEN TO START AND UTILIZE MEDICATION

Many parents wrestle with the decision of when to start ADHD medication, particularly for younger children. While waiting can feel like the safer option, there are situations where early intervention can be beneficial. If your child's struggles with attention or hyperactivity are interfering with foundational learning experiences, addressing these issues sooner can prevent long-term academic challenges. Similarly, medication can make a difference in safety and social interactions, helping your child pause before impulsive actions and fostering stronger peer connections.

Some parents feel that medication should be taken only on school days. However, it's important to remember that ADHD affects all aspects of life—not just academics but also home routines, social interactions, and extracurricular activities. Many children find that medication helps them engage more successfully in sports, hobbies, and family life, allowing them to better regulate their emotions and focus on activities they enjoy. You and your child may find that a consistent daily medication regimen is best, regardless of the school calendar. Collaboration with your health care provider is essential to ensure the medication plan aligns with your child's daily needs and long-term well-being.

UNDERSTANDING HOW ADHD MEDICATION WORKS

Research shows that ADHD stems from lower activity in the neurotransmission of dopamine and norepinephrine in the brain's prefrontal cortex. This area of the brain is responsible for emotional regulation, working memory, attention, decision making, organization, and impulse control.

ADHD medications, particularly stimulants like amphetamines and methylphenidate, help activate underactive areas of the brain and increase dopamine and norepinephrine levels. These medications can help children with ADHD function more effectively, improving focus, emotional regulation, and impulse control.

For families with concerns about stimulants, non-stimulant medications may be an option. While these may have a slightly lower efficacy on average, they can still provide meaningful benefits, particularly for children who experience significant side effects from stimulants or have other considerations. A knowledgeable provider can help you explore the best options for your child.

TIPS FOR MANAGING ADHD MEDICATION

Keeping accurate records during each provider visit is critical. It may take several months to find the right medication and dosage, and your child's needs may change over time. You may also need to switch medications occasionally, so having a detailed history of how different medications have affected your child can be invaluable. The medication logs included in this appendix can help track each visit and medication adjustment.

Your child's feedback is also essential to managing their treatment effectively. As they grow, it's important to encourage them to be aware of how medication impacts them, both positively and negatively. This will help them develop the life skill of communicating their experiences with their prescribing doctor. The Student Medication Log can serve as a tool or guide for discussions and allow your child to take an active role in their treatment.

QUESTIONS TO ASK YOUR CHILD'S PROVIDER ABOUT ADHD MEDICATION

- What are the intended benefits of this medication?
- What type of medication is this—a stimulant or non-stimulant?
- What are the potential side effects, and are there any specific effects I should pay close attention to?
- How long will it take for the medication to begin working?
- How will I know if this medication is working? What should I notice?
- How long should the effects of the medication last?
- When should the medication be taken? Does it matter if it's in the morning or at night?
- Must the medication be taken every day?
- Does it matter if the medication is taken with or without food?
- When should I follow up with you?
- What information would be helpful for me to keep track of?

ADDRESSING PRIVACY, SECURITY, AND ADVOCACY FOR OLDER CHILDREN

As children grow older, discussions about medication should evolve. Teach them the importance of keeping their medication private and secure, particularly in environments like middle school, high school, and college. Explain the legal and safety risks of sharing prescriptions and help them develop strategies to confidently decline requests from peers.

Advocacy is a learned skill: Don't assume your child knows how to handle these situations. Role-playing scenarios or providing clear examples can help build their confidence in managing medication responsibly.

It's also essential to discuss the potential for misuse or diversion of stimulant medications. By reinforcing the importance of proper storage and emphasizing that sharing prescriptions is both unsafe and illegal, you can help your child understand the serious responsibilities that come with taking medication.

PARENT MEDICATION LOG

Date of visit	Doctor's name	Medication and dose	Time(s) to take

How long does medication generally last?

_____

Rate or describe the following changes since last visit (1 = *bad/less*, 10 = *great/more*)

Category	Before medication (1–10)	After medication (1–10)
Mood		
Irritability/agitation		
Feels restless/fidgets		
Level of energy		

Interrupts/talks out of turn		
Easily distracted		
Ability to concentrate		
Memory		
Motivation		
Appetite		
Difficulty sleeping		
Headache		
Stomach		
Other (specify)		

Side effects and additional observations (if any):

_____

_____

Questions to ask during next visit:

Question	Response

Changes to medication regimen?

Medication	Dose	Take at	Notes

Next appointment:

STUDENT MEDICATION LOG

Week of: _____   Medication: _____

Dosage: _____

	Monday	Tuesday	Wednesday	Thursday	Friday	Saturday	Sunday
At what time(s) did you take your medication?							
About how long after taking the medication did you feel its effects?							
How long did the effects of the medication last?							

Compared to when not taking medication, how would you describe each of the following? (Circle: Greater / The Same / Less)

	Monday	Tuesday	Wednesday	Thursday	Friday	Saturday	Sunday
Appetite while on medication							
I was able to focus and pay attention							
I completed my assignments and chores							
I was able to stay neat and organized							
I was able to sit still when I had to							
I waited for my turn without interrupting							
I didn't lose or misplace things							
It was hard for me to work/play quietly							
I felt like my mind was "sped up"							
I moved/fidgeted my hands or feet a lot							
I felt nervous							

Additional notes: _____

_____

Appendix H

PARENTING WHEN YOU HAVE ADHD

Living with ADHD as a parent comes with unique challenges that can often feel overwhelming. Parenting is demanding for anyone, but when ADHD adds its layer of complexity, the need for self-compassion becomes even greater. Remember, just as we remind ourselves that "kids do well if they can," the same compassion applies to you as a parent. Giving yourself grace means forgiving your mistakes, allowing space for imperfection, and celebrating the small victories that come from simply showing up—even on tough days.

Practical strategies for practicing grace can include mindfulness exercises, journaling to reflect on successes (even the small ones), or reframing challenges as learning opportunities. By shifting your perspective, you can begin to see yourself not as a flawed parent but as someone navigating a unique set of challenges with resilience and care.

COLLABORATING WITH YOUR PARENTING PARTNER

ADHD can influence family dynamics, often placing strain on relationships. Sharing your challenges with your parenting partner in an open and honest way can lead to a deeper understanding and a stronger connection. Consider framing conversations around collaboration rather than burden—discussing ways to support each other and share responsibilities.

It's also essential to recognize that your partner may feel overwhelmed or unsure of how to help. Encouraging mutual vulnerability and expressing gratitude for each other's efforts can create an environment of teamwork rather than tension. Together, you can find practical solutions that work for your unique family dynamic.

THE HEALING POWER OF ADULT DIAGNOSIS

For many parents, an adult ADHD diagnosis can feel like a turning point—a moment of clarity that brings validation and a deeper understanding of themselves. Beyond simply putting a name to lifelong struggles, diagnosis can open the door to healing, offering opportunities for self-compassion and empowerment. Treatment options, which go far beyond medication, can include therapy, coaching, and support groups, each of which plays a vital role in creating a more balanced and fulfilling life.

THE ROLE OF ADHD COACHING

As explored in Appendix A, ADHD coaching can be a transformative resource for both parents and adults. Coaches help individuals develop practical strategies for managing ADHD symptoms, foster self-compassion, and build systems that align with their unique needs. Coaching not only addresses daily challenges but also empowers individuals to approach life with greater confidence and clarity.

Appendix I

FIVE-FINGER STRATEGY

Sometimes, children have difficulty expressing their thoughts and feelings, especially when asked directly about a problem or challenge. The five-finger strategy offers a playful and low-pressure way to help your child share their perspective during the first step of a Creating Shared Solutions (CSS) conversation.

HOW IT WORKS

The five-finger strategy uses a simple, fun scale to encourage your child to share what's on their mind—even if they're hesitant, unsure, or feeling shy. You'll ask your child to rate how true something is by holding up between one and five fingers:

- Five fingers = very true
- One finger = not true at all
- Anything in between = somewhat true

PRACTICE WITH SILLY STATEMENTS

Before beginning a tough conversation, help your child learn how the strategy works with light, silly examples. This keeps the mood playful and builds trust. For instance:

- "You love pizza!"
- "You don't like ice cream!"
- "Your favorite color is green!"

Your child will hold up fingers to rate how true each statement is. This will help them become comfortable with the process.

USE IT TO EXPLORE CONCERNS

Once your child understands the game, you can gently transition to the problem at hand. The goal is to make educated guesses about what might be bothering them, especially if they're having difficulty expressing it outright. For example:

- "You feel like math homework takes too long?"
- "You don't think your teacher explains things clearly?"
- "It's hard to stay focused when the room is noisy?"

Your child can hold up fingers to indicate how true each statement feels. This helps you get closer to uncovering their true concern in a nonconfrontational way.

WHY IT WORKS

The five-finger strategy takes the pressure off your child to immediately put their feelings into words. Instead, it makes the process collaborative, playful, and less intimidating. By guessing and checking with your child, you show them that:

- Their voice matters.
- You're committed to understanding their perspective.
- You're willing to meet them where they are.

NAVIGATING SCHOOL ADVOCACY

When and How to Seek Support for Your Child

Navigating the educational system to secure the right support for your child can feel emotional and overwhelming. If you've ever felt unsure about whether to seek outside help, you're not alone. Most parents try to work collaboratively with schools to meet their child's needs, but there are times when bringing in an advocate might be the right next step. This guidance applies to public schools, where special education services are legally mandated; private schools and homeschooling, however, are not obligated to provide special education support or services. Let's talk about what this means, how to prepare, and when it might be time to call an advocate.

START WITH PREPARATION

Before involving an advocate, there are steps you can take to advocate effectively on your own. These steps not only help you feel more confident but also strengthen your case if additional support is needed.

Keep Detailed Records

Begin by keeping a notebook or journal of specific observations and events. Write down things like:

- How long homework takes and the challenges your child faces.
- Instances where assignments are forgotten or misunderstood.
- What your child shares about their struggles in the classroom. This documentation will help you clarify concerns and provide essential information if you decide to involve an advocate.

Understand Your Rights

Laws like the IDEA and Section 504 of the Rehabilitation Act ensure your child's right to access education. These laws apply specifically to public schools; private schools and homeschooling do not come with any guarantees for special education, support, or services. While these laws can be complex, understanding the basics of your child's entitlements will empower you to advocate effectively. Free resources, such as Wrightslaw or your local Parent Training and Information Center (PTI), can help clarify these rights. You can find your local PTI through the U.S. Department of Education's website or by searching online for state-specific centers.

Clarify Your Goals

Before taking any formal steps, ask yourself what you hope to achieve. Keep in mind that public schools are bound by law to provide support, whereas private schools and homeschooling may not offer the same guarantees. Are you looking for better accommodations, clearer communication with the school, or improved implementation of an IEP or 504 plan? Defining your goals will help you stay focused and aligned.

WHEN TO SUBMIT A FORMAL LETTER OF REQUEST FOR SERVICES

If you feel your child's needs are not being met, a formal letter of request can be a critical first step in ensuring appropriate evaluations and accommodations. (*Note*: A sample letter of request is included at the end of this appendix.) Here are key instances when submitting a letter is essential:

- *Concerns about academic or functional performance*: If you notice your child is struggling with academic tasks, social interactions, or functional skills, and you believe they need additional support, it's time to request an evaluation.

- *Suspected learning or behavioral challenges*: If you suspect your child has a learning disability, ADHD, or other challenges that impact their ability to access education, submitting a formal letter ensures the school addresses these concerns.

- *Requesting evaluations for an IEP or 504 plan*: When you want your child evaluated for special education services (IEP) or accommodations under Section 504, a formal written request is the first step.

- *Lack of progress despite informal efforts*: If you've attempted to address concerns through informal discussions with teachers or staff but haven't seen progress, submitting a formal letter escalates the process to ensure it's documented and taken seriously.

WHY SUBMITTING A LETTER IS IMPORTANT

- *Creates a paper trail*: A written request documents your concerns and starts a formal timeline for the school to respond.

- *Triggers legal obligations*: Under IDEA or Section 504, schools are required to evaluate students within a specific time frame after receiving a written request.

- *Ensures accountability*: A formal request demonstrates your commitment to advocating for your child and holds the school accountable for next steps.

WHAT TO EXPECT AFTER SUBMITTING A LETTER

- *Acknowledgment of the request*: Schools typically acknowledge receipt of the letter within a few days. They may request clarification or additional information.
- *Evaluation timeline*: Under IDEA, the school must conduct the evaluation within 60 calendar days (or a shorter time frame depending on state laws). For Section 504, timelines may vary by district but should still be reasonable.
- *Meeting to discuss results*: Once evaluations are complete, the school holds a meeting to review the findings and determine eligibility for services.
- *Development of an IEP or 504 plan (if eligible)*: If your child qualifies, the school will work with you to develop a plan outlining goals, services, and accommodations.
- *Next steps if services are denied*: If the school determines your child is not eligible, you have the right to appeal the decision, request an independent evaluation, or involve an advocate.

WHEN TO CONSIDER HIRING AN ADVOCATE

There may come a point when you realize that your child's needs aren't being fully met despite your best efforts. Advocates are professionals who specialize in ensuring that children receive the support and services they're entitled to under the law. Here are some signs that it might be time to call in an advocate:

- *Your child's needs are still unmet*: Despite collaboration and clear communication, the school is not providing the accommodations or services your child requires.

- *You feel overwhelmed by the process*: If IEP or 504 meetings feel confusing or you're struggling to navigate the system, an advocate can help guide you.
- *The school isn't fulfilling its legal obligations*: If the accommodations or supports outlined in your child's IEP or 504 plan aren't being implemented, an advocate can ensure these issues are addressed.
- *Communication has become adversarial*: When meetings feel tense or unproductive, an advocate can serve as a neutral third party to refocus discussions on what's best for your child.

WHAT TO EXPECT WHEN HIRING AN ADVOCATE

An advocate can help you by attending meetings, reviewing your child's educational records, and clarifying misunderstandings between you and the school. Their role is to build bridges, not create conflict, and to ensure that the focus stays on your child's success. It's important to stay involved in the process and view the advocate as part of a collaborative team.

QUESTIONS TO ASK POTENTIAL ADVOCATES

Choosing the right advocate is important. Here are a few questions to help you find someone who fits your needs:
- What is your experience working with ADHD and EF challenges?
- How do you approach working with parents and schools?
- Can you share examples of successful outcomes from similar cases?
- How do you typically communicate with families throughout the process?

TRUSTED RESOURCES

If you're ready to look for an advocate, these resources can help:
- Council of Parent Attorneys and Advocates (COPAA): copaa.org
- Wrightslaw: wrightslaw.com
- Parent Training and Information Centers (PTIs): Search for local PTIs funded by the U.S. Department of Education

A FINAL THOUGHT

Remember, your goal isn't to "win" a dispute with the school but to create a collaborative team that supports your child's learning and growth. Keep in mind that your child will be in that classroom all year and likely in that school for several years, so building a positive relationship with teachers and staff is essential. By taking thoughtful steps, you can advocate for your child with confidence, knowing you're doing everything possible to help them thrive.

A SAMPLE LETTER OF REQUEST FOR SERVICES

Dear [principal's name],

I am writing to formally request an evaluation for my child, [child's full name], who is in [grade level] at [school name]. I believe that [child's first name] may benefit from additional support and services to address challenges with [specific challenges; e.g., attention, learning difficulties, or behavior].

I have observed that [describe specific observations; e.g., "homework takes hours to complete," "they struggle with multistep directions," "they have difficulty maintaining focus in class"]. These challenges are affecting their ability to [specific impacts; e.g., "keep up academically," "build positive peer relationships," "stay organized"].

I would appreciate it if the school could conduct a comprehensive evaluation to determine [child's first name]'s eligibility for services under the Individuals With Disabilities Education Act (IDEA) or Section 504 of the Rehabilitation Act.

Please let me know when we can schedule a meeting to discuss this request further. I look forward to collaborating with you to ensure that [child's first name] receives the support they need to succeed.

Thank you for your attention to this matter. Please confirm receipt of this letter at your earliest convenience.

Sincerely,
[Your name and contact information]

Appendix K

THE WHEEL OF LIFE FOR PARENTS AND STUDENTS

Taking time to reflect and evaluate how satisfied we are with our lives is an intentional exercise that can be incredibly beneficial. While it might seem like something meant only for adults, I've found that helping children of all ages examine key areas of their lives can engage them in actively addressing and improving the parts of their lives that create the most stress or dissatisfaction.

Positive change is most likely to occur when we first assess our current situation. The "Wheel of Life" assessment is a safe, nonjudgmental, and nonevaluative tool that fosters reflection and provides a structure and starting point for goal setting.

Think of the wheel of a bicycle divided into sections by several spokes. Each section represents an area of life. For parents, I suggest creating one wheel to reflect your personal life and another to reflect your role as a parent. For your children, you might guide them in creating one wheel for their life as a student and another for their personal life. Performing well in school is not just about knowing the facts; it's also about demonstrating what you've learned. Success often comes from improving EF skills, which help with planning, organization, and achieving goals. Beyond school, life is about more than academics. To feel confident and well-rounded, it's essential to explore and address all the areas of life that bring joy, opportunity, frustration, and challenge.

CREATING YOUR WHEEL OF LIFE

1. *Draw a circle*: Divide it into sections that represent areas relevant to your journey. Use the suggested categories provided in this appendix or create your own to reflect what matters most to you.

2. *Evaluate each section*: Shade in each section to reflect your current level of satisfaction, with the center of the circle representing "not satisfied" and the outer edge representing "very satisfied." This gives you a visual snapshot of your satisfaction and balance across different life areas.

3. *Choose areas to focus on*: Select one or two areas to focus on. It may not necessarily be the area where you feel least satisfied but rather the one where improvement would bring the most overall satisfaction or reduce stress.

4. *Set actionable steps*: Identify one or two specific steps that can help you bring about positive change in that area. This step might be as simple as asking someone for support or guidance.

Below are some suggested categories you can use, but feel free to create whatever feels most important to you.

PARENT WHEEL OF LIFE 1: PARENTING LIFE

1. ADHD/EF knowledge
2. Calm home
3. Connected relationships
4. Good communication
5. Collaborative problem solving
6. Clear and consistent rules
7. Effective consequences
8. Choices (theirs and yours)

PARENT WHEEL OF LIFE 2: PERSONAL LIFE

1. Family relationships
2. Work–life balance
3. Self-care and stress management
4. Hobbies and recreation
5. Parenting confidence
6. Social life and friendships
7. Personal growth
8. Spiritual connections

STUDENT WHEEL 1: SCHOOL LIFE

1. Self-advocacy skills
2. Note-taking skills
3. Study skills
4. Time management skills
5. Organization skills
6. Stress management skills
7. Test-/quiz-taking skills
8. Paper writing skills

STUDENT WHEEL 2: PERSONAL LIFE

1. Family relationships
2. Social life
3. Leisure activities
4. Friendships
5. Exercise and fitness
6. Hobbies and recreation
7. Thoughts about the future
8. Schoolwork balance

I recommend periodically revisiting your wheel to evaluate your progress and adjust your goals. This helps you stay on track and ensure you're addressing what matters most as your needs evolve.

Appendix L

THE BLACK BELT CERTIFICATE

Black Belt Certification

Upon completion of the Calm and Connected workshop, the following skills have been mastered:

- I have the tools to stay calm and return to calm when necessary
- I can set forth realistic expectations & boundaries for my children that I adhere to with rare expectations
- I can distinguish for myself and my child the difference between right and privilege
- I can ignore minor comments, insults, and jabs that are intended to trigger me
- I can objectively assess whether my children are ready to take responsibility on their own before jumping in to aid them
- I can calmly state: "It's your choice," without the need to justify, explain, or go back on my word

_____   _____
            Parent   Date

Parenting a child with ADHD is a journey that demands resilience, patience, and a commitment to growth. At the start of this book, I expressed my belief that raising a child with ADHD takes earning a black belt in parenting. I hope you've acquired valuable insights, tools, and strategies, and that you feel more confident along this journey.

Throughout this process, you've built a foundation of skills that allow you to remain calm, set meaningful boundaries, and foster independence while maintaining a connected and supportive relationship with your child.

This Black Belt Certificate is a reminder of the incredible progress you can achieve by practicing the principles outlined in this book. It's a tool to help you celebrate your accomplishments and identify areas where you may still want to grow.

Take time to review the steps outlined in the certificate. When you feel confident that you've mastered these skills, proudly sign your certificate as a testament to your commitment and growth. If you find yourself struggling along the way, revisit the image of the house to assess which areas need more attention.

Congratulations on the time, love, and dedication you have shown in taking each positive step along the way.

References

ADDitude Magazine. (n.d.). *Social skills and peer acceptance: The role of ADHD medication.* https://www.additudemag.com

ADHD Awareness Month. (n.d.). *ADHD treatment and family dynamics.* https://www.adhdawarenessmonth.org

American Academy of Pediatrics. (2019). *Clinical practice guidelines for the diagnosis, evaluation, and treatment of ADHD in children and adolescents.*

American Psychiatric Association. (1968). *Diagnostic and statistical manual of mental disorders* (2nd ed.). Washington, DC.

American Psychiatric Association. (2013). *Diagnostic and statistical manual of mental disorders* (5th ed.; pp. 59–66).

Angelou, M. (1993). "On the pulse of morning." Random House.

Barkley, R. A. (1997). Behavioral inhibition, sustained attention, and executive functions: Constructing a unifying theory of ADHD. *Journal of the International Neuropsychological Society, 3*(4), 359–369.

Barkley, R. A. (2010). Deficient emotional self-regulation is a core component of ADHD: Evidence and treatment implications. *Journal of ADHD and Related Disorders, 1*(2), 5–37.

Barkley, R. A. (2012, October). Understanding defiance and noncompliance in children with ADHD [Conference presentation]. CHADD Annual International Conference, San Francisco, CA.

Barkley, R. A. (2013). *Attention-deficit hyperactivity disorder: A handbook for diagnosis and treatment* (4th ed.). Guilford Press.

Burke, J. D., Pardini, A., & Lobber, R. (2008). Reciprocal relationships between parenting behavior and disruptive psychopathology from childhood through adolescence. *Journal of Abnormal Child Psychology, 36*(5), 679–692.

Centers for Disease Control and Prevention. (2020). *Data and statistics about ADHD.* https://www.cdc.gov/ncbddd/adhd/data.html

Centers for Disease Control and Prevention. (2022). *Data and statistics about ADHD.* https://www.cdc.gov/adhd/data/index.html

Centers for Disease Control and Prevention. (2023). What is ADHD? https://www.cdc.gov/ncbddd/adhd/facts.html

Cleveland Clinic. (n.d.). *Benefits of ADHD medications on cognitive and emotional functions.* https://my.clevelandclinic.org

Crawford, D. (2021). *Stop asking "How was your day?": 365 better conversation starters for work, life, and love.* Independently published.

DuPaul, G. J., Gormley, M. J., & Laracy, S. D. (2013). Comorbidity of LD and ADHD: Implications of DSM-5 for assessment and treatment. *Journal of Learning Disabilities, 46*(1), 43–51. https://doi.org/10.1177/0022219412464351

Dweck, C. S. (2006). *Mindset: The new psychology of success.* Random House.

Galinsky, E. (n.d.). *Inside the teenage brain* [Interview transcript]. http://www.pbs.org/wgbh/pages/frontline/shows/teenbrain/interviews/galinsky.html

Genomewide Association Studies. (2009). History, rationale, and prospects for psychiatric disorders. *American Journal of Psychiatry, 166*(5), 540–556. https://doi.org/10.1176/appi.ajp.2008.08091354

Goldstein, S. (2013). *Executive function and academic success: Why students struggle and strategies to help. [Conference presentation].* Learning and the Brain Conference, Boston, MA.

Greene, R. W. (1998). *The explosive child: A new approach for understanding and parenting easily frustrated, "chronically inflexible" children.* HarperCollins.

Greenland, S. K. (2010). *The mindful child: How to help your kid manage stress and become happier, kinder, and more compassionate.* Free Press.

Hallowell, E. M., & Ratey, J. J. (1995). *Driven to distraction: Recognizing and coping with attention deficit disorder from childhood through adulthood.* Simon & Schuster.

Keller, J. (1929). "I am blind—yet I see; I am deaf—yet I hear. *The American Magazine.*

Mischke-Reeds, M. (2015). *8 keys to practicing mindfulness: Practical strategies for emotional health and well-being.* W. W. Norton & Company.

National Institute of Mental Health. (n.d.). *ADHD medication: A comprehensive overview.* https://www.nimh.nih.gov

National Institute of Mental Health. (n.d.). Attention-Deficit/Hyperactivity Disorder (ADHD). https://www.nimh.nih.gov/health/topics/attention-deficit-hyperactivity-disorder-adhd

National Institutes of Health. (n.d.). *Functional improvements with ADHD medication.* https://www.nih.gov

Neuroscience News. (n.d.). *Emotional stability and ADHD treatment.* https://neurosciencenews.com

NYU Langone Health. (n.d.). *Managing behavioral challenges with ADHD medication.* https://nyulangone.org

Reuters. (2009). *Sleep problems common in children with ADHD.* https://www.reuters.com/article/2009/03/26/us-sleep-adhd-idUSTRE52P7ED20090326

Shaywitz, S. E., & Shaywitz, B. A. (2008). Paying attention to reading: The neurobiology of reading and dyslexia. *Development and Psychopathology, 20*(4), 1329–1349. https://doi.org/10.1017/S0954579408000631

Tamis-LeMonda, C. S., & Bornstein, M. H. (2002). Infant play and exploration: Advances in competence and mutuality. *Infancy, 3*(3), 287–297.

Thapar, A., Cooper, M., Eyre, O., & Langley, K. (2013). What have we learnt about the causes of ADHD? *Journal of Child Psychology and Psychiatry, 54*(1), 3–16. https://doi.org/10.1111/j.1469-7610.2012.02611.x

Tudisco, R. M. (n.d.). *The wonderfulness of me!* Robert M. Tudisco, used with permission. [Robert M. Tudisco is a disability attorney, author, and an adult diagnosed with ADHD.]

Wilens, T. E., & Morrison, N. R. (2011). The intersection of attention-deficit/hyperactivity disorder and substance abuse. *Current Opinion in Psychiatry, 24*(4), 280–285. https://doi .org/10.1097/YCO.0b013e328345c956

Ziegler Dendy, C. A., & Zeigler, A. (2003). A bird's-eye view of life with ADD and ADHD: Advice from young survivors (p. 144). Ziegler Dendy Consulting.

Index

About the Author

Cindy Goldrich, EdM, ADHD-CCSP, is a mental health counselor, certified ADHD Clinical Services Provider, and internationally recognized expert in ADHD and executive function support. She is the founder of PTS Coaching, LLC, where she helps parents through her Calm and Connected® workshop series and one-on-one coaching, and trains professionals worldwide through her ADHD Parent Coach Academy and ADHD Teacher Training Academy.

Cindy is the author of *8 Keys to Parenting Kids & Teens with ADHD* and coauthor of *ADHD, Executive Function, and Behavioral Challenges in the Classroom.* Her work combines research-based strategies with deep compassion, helping families and professionals foster calm, connection, and resilience.

Cindy holds a master's degree in counseling psychology from Columbia University, Teachers College, and serves on the board of directors for CHADD, the national organization on ADHD. Learn more at ptscoaching.com.